VOL II ONLY

VOL 1 & 2
O.P.
94

VOL III IN PRINT
AT $20.00
94

VOLUME 2
FLYING
COMBAT AIRCRAFT
OF THE
USAAF-USAF

VOLUME 2
FLYING COMBAT

AIRCRAFT
OF THE
USAAF-USAF

edited by

Robin Higham/Carol Williams

USAF

USAF

THE IOWA STATE UNIVERSITY PRESS / AMES, IOWA
1978

AEROSPACE HISTORIAN, sponsor of this book, is an international journal for aerospace history and the official journal of the Air Force Historical Foundation. Established in 1954, it has been published since June 1970 at the Department of History, Kansas State University, Manhattan, Kansas 66506.

This book, the second of a series on American aircraft, is designed to help readers of all ages appreciate the role USAAF-USAF combat aircraft have played in our country's history and respect the gallant men who have flown them in times of war and peace.

By obtaining such personal recollections now, our knowledge of these memorable times can be preserved for the future.

C-141 Starlifter

Library of Congress Cataloging in Publication Data

Main entry under title:

Flying combat aircraft of the USAAF-USAF.

    Vol. 2 edited by R. Higham and C. Williams.
    1. Airplanes, Military—History. 2. Aeronautics, Military—United States—History.
I. Higham, Robin D. S. II. Siddall, Abigail T., 1930–
III. Williams, Carol, 1942–
UG1243.F55   358.41'8'3   75-8932
ISBN 0–8138–0325–X
ISBN 0–8138–0375–6 (v. 2)

Composed and printed by
The Iowa State University Press
Ames, Iowa 50010

First edition, 1978

USAF

McDONNELL DOUGLAS

CONTENTS

An A-1E nicknamed "Balls A'Fire" taxis down the ramp at Nakhon Phanom Air Base, Thailand, on a search and rescue mission in 1970.

A-1 Skyraider

DONALD E. JONES

I remember my feelings in August 1964 when notification came that I had been selected to fly A-1s in South Vietnam. As an F-100 pilot with more than 1,000 hours in the "Hun," I was mildly surprised that the Air Force should want to retrain me and send me into combat in an unfamiliar weapons system. The idea of going into combat wasn't bad, but the thought of not going in the F-100, with which I felt very confident, was disturbing.

In January 1965 I reported to Eglin Auxiliary Field #9 (better known as Hurlburt Field), Florida. There I was to receive approximately 100 hours training in the machine that would see me through my war experiences in Southeast Asia. What an airplane! A "tail dragger," of all things, in this modern day; I had never flown an aircraft with a conventional landing gear. Its reciprocating engine was so high off the ground that I had to chin myself on the cowling to inspect it, and each of its four huge prop blades was longer than my six-foot frame. And bomb racks: all across the bottom were the racks that would carry as much ordnance as a B-17—15 stations in all. With full fuel, oil, and pilot, the aircraft grossed out at approximately 16,000 pounds. Maximum gross weight for takeoff was 25,000 pounds. Climbing up the wing was like scaling a small mountain, and one misstep off the antiskid area during rainy weather could send a guy embarrassingly to the ground.

Preflight inspection of the Skyraider was simple and straightforward. Beginning in the cockpit to ensure that all switches were off (especially the magnetos), the pilot proceeded to the left side-engine upper exhaust pipes, left wing, lower engine, right wing, right side upper engine for oil quantity and exhaust pipes, and finally, around the tail section. We used a locally fabricated, external rudder lock that prevented the rudder from being slammed about by prop wash or wind gusts. One novice had the misfortune to attempt a scramble takeoff from Qui Nhon with the rudder lock in place, and engine torque pulled him off the left side of the runway into soft sand where the gear collapsed and a fire ensued. Luckily, he got out of it with his life, but the accident board nailed him with pilot error.

Preflight became a graceful ballet of putting on and taking off gloves. You could always identify the A-1 pilots by the oil on their flight suits and gloves. You could always pick out the *new* A-1 pilots by the oil on their faces. If you've ever been around a Wright radial engine, you know that oil leaks are normal and extensive. Mission endurance at times became a function of how much *oil* you had on board instead of how much *fuel* you had. Naturally, the entire underside of the fuselage, wing roots, and entire engine section were covered with oil. Flight suits and gloves quickly picked up a share of the mess during preflights. Wipe the sweat from your brow just once with your gloves on and you were marked; forget to have your gloves on during preflight and you were marked.

Preflight of the cockpit began at the left rear, proceeded up the left side across the front instrument panel, across the armament panel beneath the instruments and between your legs, and down the right side. The fuel selector handle on the left console allowed manual selection of internal or external fuel. Special note had to be taken of the manifold pressure gauge before start to determine barometric pressure to be used later during engine run-up.

Starting the A-1 was a real task, especially for those of us who had all-jet experience. No more automatic starting—just push the button, throttle to idle at 12% rpm.

The A-1 engine start was normally accomplished using an external source of D.C. power, although aircraft battery power could be used in an emergency. With external power connected, all caution and warning lights were checked—especially the all-important chip-detector light. The chip detector was the device that informed the pilot that metal pieces were present in the oil sump. Metal chips in the sump were normally the only warning of impending internal engine failure. The fuel-boost pump was turned on and pressure checked on the gauge (normally 21–25 psi). With a "prop clear" call to crew chief, the starter was engaged to rotate the engine through four complete revolutions—16 blades. This initial rotation was a check for fluids (oil, gas, or hydraulic) that may have seeped into any of the cylinders. If the engine failed to rotate normally (hydraulic lock), the start would be aborted, and the lower cylinder ignitor plugs would be removed to drain those cylinders. After 16 blades, the ignition switch was turned to "both," and the primer was used intermittently to pump fuel into the engine.

USAF

These Air Force armament technicians are preparing 250-pound bombs prior to loading them on to the wing pylons of an A-1E in the background.

With a cloud of blue smoke and a burst of noise, the huge engine would hesitatingly come to life, shaking and vibrating the entire airframe. Once all 18 cylinders were going, it felt like you were sitting on the biggest Farmall tractor ever built. The engine was stabilized at about 1,000 rpm on the primer before slowly advancing the mixture lever to transfer to carburetor fuel. With the engine running smoothly, the ground crew was signaled to disconnect external power. Battery, inverters, and radios were turned on, and the aircraft was ready to taxi out. Just prior to taxiing, the fuel selector was placed to the external fuel position to ensure that external tanks would feed properly. Throttle closed, "thumbs out" for chock removal, and the bird was ready to lumber out for run-up.

The A-1 had a couple of unique taxiing aspects. First, the tailwheel had to be unlocked in order to make turns. As in the T-33, the pilot steered by using differential braking. Most of the time the engine produced enough prop blast at idle rpm to make the rudder effective for small corrections.

A-1H aircraft of the 8th Special Operations Squadron in flight over Eglin Auxiliary Air Field, Florida, 1970.

Idle rpm was normally enough power to keep the aircraft moving, depending on the ordnance load; however, the generator would come off the line (not produce electrical power) at idle, with the result that the radios would become weak or inoperative. At about 1,000 rpm, the generator worked fine, but the aircraft would taxi at excess speed. And so it was a game of riding the brakes and jockeying the throttle to keep everything working and at a safe speed. The brakes were very easy to become accustomed to but a "hamhanded" jab on the brakes at almost any speed could bring the tail wheel up off the ground and risk getting a piece of the pavement with the prop. Taxiing could be accomplished with the wings in the folded or extended position, again depending on external loads. Normally, taxi out was with the wings extended and locked, and taxi in was with the wings folded. This ensured that the wing-folding hydraulic system was exercised regularly to keep the seals lubricated.

The aircraft was made with folding wings for the U.S. Navy, to facilitate aircraft carrier operations, and we received our aircraft from the Navy. Because the wing-folding system was connected to the main hydraulic system, the Air Force had a choice of modifying the aircraft or maintaining the existing system, and it was less expensive to maintain the system and practice regular cycling to keep the seals flexible.

Engine run-up was quick and simple. To keep the tail from bouncing or flying up, the control stick had to be held firmly in the full aft position whenever engine power was above idle. With cylinder-head temperature somewhere above 100° C and oil temperature above 40° C, the pilot proceeded to exercise the propeller pitch-changing mechanism from full increase to full decrease. An improperly operating prop control could cause an overboost or overspeed condition, either of which might cause engine failure. Engine power was checked by increasing manifold pressure with the throttle to that manifold pressure noted during cockpit preflight. A check of each magneto for engine roughness or excessive loss of rpm and switching in and out of high blower (the supercharger) completed the engine checks.

The final checks included cycling the oil-cooler door open and closed and visually checking over the left side in front of the wing root to ensure that the door was halfway open. An oil-cooler door stuck in the closed position would cause the oil to overheat. Overheated oil loses its viscosity and can be ingested by the engine, resulting in engine failure. A last check was made of the flight controls (free and clear), wings were checked down and locked (a red, one-inch pipe protruded from the leading edge of each wing when the wings were unlocked), and flaps were set to the takeoff position. The run-up check was then complete.

Takeoff could be made with the cockpit canopy either fully open or fully closed. Carbon monoxide tended to build up in the cockpit if a partially open canopy position was selected. In Vietnam, our squadron was required to take off with canopies closed, and we were required to turn off the cockpit fresh-air nozzles. This procedure resulted from an unfortunate accident when one aircraft on a maintenance test flight developed an engine fuel leak and fire. The fire burned through the cockpit ventilating pipes which are routed from the front cowling to the cockpit. Burning fuel entered the pipes and spewed into the cockpit through the air nozzles, much like a blow torch. The pilot managed to bail out, but his parachute harness had been burned through, and the chute failure caused his death. Takeoff on a hot day was a sweaty experience.

For takeoff, the aircraft was lined up on the runway, tail wheel locked, and a final engine check completed. At brake release, the throttle was smoothly advanced to maximum manifold pressure as 61.5 inches right rudder was applied to control torque. The R-3350 engine, rated at 3,000 hp for the Air Force, produced enough torque to pull the aircraft quickly off the left side of the runway if corrective rudder was not applied. As soon as the aircraft was rolling and everything (engine instruments) looked good, the control stick was pushed firmly forward to fly the tail off the ground. With the tail raised, you felt the aircraft was flying slightly nose down. This attitude insured maximum acceleration and was maintained until reaching takeoff speed (which varied widely from about 80 to more than 100 knots, depending on ordnance load). With a little back pressure, the aircraft would fly smoothly off the ground.

Flying the Skyraider was like living in an earlier era. The noise level in the cockpit was considerable, especially with the canopy open. The cockpit was not air-conditioned, which made for sweating palms and brows on those tropical missions. For a time in Vietnam, we were allowed to cut off the sleeves of our flight suits to be cooler. But then some ''safety types'' decided that short sleeves would be hazardous in the event of cockpit fires, so cut-offs were banned. I remember the sheer pleasure of climbing back to altitude after a strike, opening the canopy, and inching a sweat-soaked, gloved hand above the canopy bow into the cooling slipstream. The canteens of ice water the crew chiefs faithfully passed to us before engine start always helped after working a target.

The A-1 had such an aerodynamically dirty profile that its climbing, accelerating, and high-speed performances were poor. I remember taking a

An A-1 Skyraider drops a 100-pound general purpose bomb on a Viet Cong position in the jungles of South Vietnam in 1965. The targets are located and marked by forward air control crews in low flying observation aircraft.

clean airplane (except for pylons) and applying maximum power in level flight at about 1,000 feet. Slowly, the airspeed increased and stabilized at about 250 knots. With firm back pressure, I zoomed the aircraft to about 30–40° pitch and held it until the airframe gave warning of a stall. I had succeeded in climbing less than 2,000 feet. The same maneuver in an F-100 had netted me over 25,000 feet.

But what the A-1 could not provide in acceleration, climbing, and speed, it more than made up for in turning and lifting ability. The slower speeds allowed us to complete 60–70° high-angle strafing passes and nearly vertical dive-bombing passes from 3,000 feet above ground level. Weapons delivery accuracy from that level was phenomenal in comparison to that of the F-100s and F-4s.

In setting up for a dive-bomb pass, the A-1 was positioned so that the target was just visible over the side of the cockpit. The throttle was closed as the pilot completed a rolling dive toward the target. It was amazing how that huge prop suddenly became a speed brake as the throttle was closed and the prop blades became aligned flat against the wind. The pilot would feel himself partially hanging forward in the seat as he dived toward the target. From that point, it was a simple matter to track the "pipper" or aiming reticle up to the target (we had an adjustable optical sight), hold it there momentarily for airspeed/altitude parameters, and then release the weapons. The "hold it there" part of the maneuver gave me a thrill on more than one occasion. "Bunting" or pushing forward on the stick was sometimes required to prevent the "pipper" from going above the target on a bombing run. The forward stick pressure was often enough to create a zero G or negative G condition in the aircraft. In a negative G condition, all of the dirt and loose items in the cockpit would be thrown from the floor to the ceiling. Likewise, in the fuel tank, the gasoline would move so that the end of the fuel line would become uncovered, causing the engine to quit. I remember occasions when I pulled up from a dive-bomb pass and pushed the throttle forward only to find that the engine would not respond. Fortunately, the propeller would windmill until more gasoline could be sucked up from the tank, and then the engine would start with no effort from the pilot. Believe me, it gives you a "weak in the knees" feeling to think that the engine has failed over unfriendly territory.

Night missions in the A-1 were especially interesting. For ordnance delivery, engine power would be set near maximum, which would cause "torching" from the exhaust stacks. Because this made the aircraft more visible to enemy antiaircraft gunners, the standard procedure was to turn off all lights, reduce throttle, and pull the mixture control to lean before each pass. A night operation with four A-1s and a flare ship was always a bit tense—trying to keep track of everyone and work the target.

Approaches and landings in the A-1 were "no sweat" as long as you were mindful of a few basic precautions. First, the tail wheel had to be in the locked position for landing. Most touchdowns were either three-point or, in some cases, tail wheel first. I took a certain amount of pride in trying to roll the tail wheel on first whenever crosswinds were not a factor. If the tail wheel was free to swivel unlocked, the aircraft could perform some very strange ground maneuvers. Second, you had to respect the throttle when the airspeed was low—like on final approach. Just before I arrived at Bien Hoa in 1965, a pilot was killed when he bounced an aircraft on landing and then throttle-burst the engine (jammed the throttle full open) to make a go-around maneuver. He was unable to counteract engine torque and wound up inverted on the runway.

During my tour of duty in Vietnam, I felt that the A-1 was the best aircraft available for the job. It had the range, endurance, accuracy, and weapons capacity to enable it to go almost any place in-country in support of friendly forces. The UHF-VHF-FM communications radios it carried allowed the pilot to talk with ground forces, the forward air controller, and other fighters. The armor plating on the fuselage and that huge engine up front provided excellent protection for the pilot. And its slower speeds and high maneuverability enabled the pilot to work targets effectively in poor weather conditions.

The motto of the A-1 Skyraider Association is "We flew. We fought." I'm proud to have been one of the men selected to pilot that flying machine.

MAJ. DONALD E. JONES was commissioned into the Air Force at Memphis State University in May 1959 and went on active duty the following month. He took pilot training at Spence Air Base, Georgia, and Greenville AFB, Mississippi. In January 1965 he began transition training into the A-1E Skyraider at Hurlburt Field, Florida. In March he was assigned to the 602nd Fighter Squadron, Bien Hoa Air Base, Vietnam, where he upgraded to instructor pilot and flight leader. Major Jones flew 269 missions over Vietnam and accumulated just under 500 hours in the Skyraider. When he wrote this he was Associate Professor of Aerospace Studies, Kansas State University.

A-7D in flight.

A-7D Crusader

JOHN C. MORRISSEY

LATE on a Friday afternoon in July 1969 six of us finished a one-week A-7D systems and aircraft engineering course at the Ling-Temco-Vought (LTV) facility in Dallas. My boss and I were to stay on for an additional week and receive five hours of flying in the Corsair II before returning to Luke Air Force base to begin the A-7D operational test program. I was scheduled for an early hop on Monday in what was to be my first experience with a "civilian" checkout program. I distinctly remember being asked to show up around 8:00 for a 9:00 takeoff. At this point there were two definite factors working against me: I had never even seen the cockpit of an A-7 and there were no A-7D Dash Ones (pilot handbooks) available.

Not wishing to dent the image of the USAF fighter pilot, I casually accepted the appointment with what was to be my "office" for the next four years. In 1969, LTV was primarily a Navy firm and in retrospect I surmise that they were trying to see what those Air Force types could do.

Facing the A-7 that Monday morning, I had varied feelings. Having come to the A-7 from the F-105, I considered its airframe a step in the wrong direction. A typical F-105 final approach speed was 185 knots, whereas the A-7D was in the 120-knot category. The Thud had taken me through many tough situations over a period of six years; in fact, as I thought about it, I had developed a sort of special affection for my previous steed, an affection that lingers to this day. My F-105 relationship had been forged in and tempered with combat; little did I realize, standing by that A-7D in 1969, that I would finish in it what we had started in the Thud.

Luck was with me that morning in the form of two excellent assistants—a civilian crew chief who had been with Thuds at Takhli, and Jim Marquis from LTV flight operations, also ex-USAF. When we were about 30 feet from the bird, I stopped and took in the view. It was the first time I had seen one up close, and I remember thinking that aesthetically Navy designs left a bit to be desired. Compared to F-100s, F-104s, and F-105s, this was definitely "Cinderella's older sister."

Jim walked around the bird with me and pointed out the high spots of the preflight inspection. There was very little to check, but two items stood out—the hydraulics tended to seep a bit at quite a few connectors, and absolutely no ground support equipment was required for starting. Regarding the former, I was tempted to buy stock in a "hydraulic mine" until the Air Force corrected most of the inherent seepage problems; as to the latter, the on-board starting capability was a tremendous operational advantage in that no ground power units were required for either electric power or external air. The basic electric power was provided by a NICAD battery, and the engine was started by an on-board, turbine-powered starting unit.

Access to the wheelhouse was gained by a self-contained ladder and two "kick in" steps on the left side of the fuselage. Several distinct impressions remain from that first cockpit entry. I enjoyed its compactness, which reminded me in a way of the F-100C. The instruments were laid out in usable fashion, but they were the old "round" type as opposed to the vertical tapes in the F-105. Almost all the switches were comfortably forward of the elbow line. The stick was small and had full travel in pitch only; in roll it was hinged just below the stick grip to allow lateral deflection without leg interference. The seat, with its internal parachute, was very firm, and its geometry made the pilot feel as though he was being pushed forward from the waist up. Comfort was not the plane's strong suit. The seat was raised or lowered electrically, but the canopy operation was entirely manual.

The starting procedure on my checkout was very straightforward. I asked the crew chief if he knew how to start it. He allowed that he did, so I watched as he turned on the battery, moved the throttle inboard to energize the self-contained starting turbine, placed it outboard to provide magneto-supplied ignition, and then at 15% rpm slid it forward to idle. Engine light-off was quick; when rpm stabilized at 52%, he moved the throttle back inboard and that was that. The noise level, even with my helmet off, was much lower than I expected.

Jim then filled me in on a few of the remaining essentials, such as takeoff and landing speeds, the air-start technique, emergency gear- and flap-lowering methods, and finally the ejection (heaven forbid) procedure. As there were no sedan (two-chair) versions of the A-7, I was supposed to be chased by a certain Joe Engle of LTV. But we incorrectly estimated the time required for me to get my jet in motion, and consequently, he was still strolling out to his machine as I began to taxi (AF 1, Navy 0, bottom of the first).

Because of the very narrow gear, there was a softer lateral feel to the aircraft while taxiing than other "bent wings" I had flown. Directional control was straightforward and was accomplished with nosewheel steering. Visibility was excellent in the forward quadrants and straight ahead. In fact, I was struck by the feeling of sitting on the edge of a cliff; the cockpit is so far forward that no part of the aircraft forward of the cockpit is visible to the pilot—quite a switch from the long snouts of the "Hun" and the "Thud."

Because of the absence of published procedures for the "D," my pretakeoff drill was homespun and very straightforward: canopy down and flaps set for takeoff, seat armed, warning light out, controls checked, fuel feeding, trim set, power 90% rpm, engine instruments checked, brakes off, and full power. I had been cautioned not to exceed 90% rpm with the brakes on lest I slide down the runway. It was pointed out that this would cause a flat spot to appear on the tires, which would rapidly deteriorate to a hole, causing all the air to leak out.

A-7D with empty MER racks on stations 2 and 7. Note the 57th FWW emblem near the cockpit and the checkered tail.

Three of the original six TAC pilots who flew the A-7D in the USAF A-7D Cat III test program. This A-7D carried four MK-84 2,000-pound bombs and 1,032 rounds of 20 mm ammunition for a gross takeoff weight of 37,300 pounds. This was the configuration on the Luke-to-Wendover mission.

Squadron emblem on an A-7D of the 357th TFS at Davis Monthan AFB, Arizona.

Acceleration during takeoff was brisk, but not as quick as that of afterburning aircraft. At Luke Air Force Base on a cool morning, the A-7D at 28,000 pounds would accelerate from brake release to approximately 280 knots by the time it reached the far end of a 10,000-foot departure runway. Rotation occurred at 130 knots, with takeoff at 136. Current A-7 drivers may doubt these figures but the empty weight of the early A-7Ds was under 18,000 pounds, and takeoff weights were in the 27,500-pound categories.

Climb performance was very good. The schedule called for 350 knots to be held until reaching .76 Mach and holding .76 until cruise altitude. Time to climb to 30,000 feet on this initial flight was approximately five minutes.

I found the A-7 to have excellent maneuverability in all areas but one—excess thrust. Control authority in roll, pitch, and yaw was more than adequate. The relatively low wing loading (66 pounds per square foot) provided more usable G at lower indicated airspeeds than previous "century series" fighters. It was the most aerobatically suitable fighter I have flown. For example, it was possible to enter a loop at 5,000 MSL (mean sea level) and 400 knots and complete the maneuver at 7,000 feet. With the fuel weight down a bit, loops at altitudes as high as 19,000 feet were possible. Although technically limited to 10 seconds, inverted flying characteristics were very straightforward down to 340 knots. Below that speed, the stick felt a bit soft in pitch. I made several ground-attack simulations. The energy required for reattack was more than ample in the clean configuration, but as I was eventually to find out, reattack at combat weight in warm weather could be interesting. I should point out that a "clean" A-7D has eight nonjettisonable pylons on board. Removing these pylons reduces parasite drag considerably and the weight by 1,280 pounds. I flew the A-7D for more than a month without pylons, and the performance gain was substantial.

On comparison, the F-100D, F-105D, and A-7D have the same wing area—385 square feet. At equal fuel weights, the A-7D had a slightly lower wing loading and approximately the same thrust-to-weight ratio as an F-100C in afterburner. At this thrust level, the fuel flow in the A-7D was one-sixth that of the F-100. This aspect of the bird was very impressive and made unrefueled combat missions of more than three hours an everyday occurrence. In contrast, F-100s and F-105s were logging slightly over 1½ hours on unrefueled sorties, and the unrefueled F-4 capability was even less.

By the time I returned to the landing pattern, my chase had become airborne and was now available for assistance. Fortunately, none was required. This was the first "no flare" aircraft I had flown. Jim had cautioned me that final approach speeds would be in the neighborhood of 124 knots with 4,500 pounds fuel remaining and that an angle of attack technique was to be used with a 3° approach to a no-flare landing.

There was no problem adapting to this technique, which in my mind was obviously superior to the "century series" flare procedure that was dictated, I believe, by their "stiff" landing gear. The relatively low final approach speed came as a bit of a surprise—it seemed that we were on final approach for a considerable length of time. The A-7D had an antiskid system that was capable of a "brakes on" landing. The requirement for this capability seems to be related to carrier operations and is consistent with the naval origin of the A-7. This was discussed before the flight, and it was agreed that my last landing would be "brakes on."

Carrying 20 Snakeye bombs weighing more than 300 pounds each on four of its six wing pylons, an A-7D goes into a dive on a target at Eglin AFB, Florida. The plane was being tested carrying various types of bombs and other ordnance during Project Seek Eagle. Strips on some of the bombs are for photo assessment purposes during drops. On the plane's underbelly can be seen the 20 mm Gatling gun near the nose, the Doppler radar bulge, and a strike assessment camera ahead of the tail hook.

I approached this unique ground-contact method with apprehension. Only 2,800 feet of concrete were traversed between touchdown and stop, but with no blown tires, no overheated brakes, and 4,000 pounds of fuel remaining. The only drawback the A-7D demonstrated in the landing pattern was its relatively low crosswind tolerance. Twenty knots direct crosswind was the limit, and at that velocity it was an exciting affair to keep that narrow gear going straight down the runway.

Over the next four years, my impressions of the "7" became more defined. Historically, it has been a fine aircraft that provided significant technological and operational breakthroughs like the head-up display (HUD), Doppler-bounded inertial platform, digital nav weapons computer, projected map display system (PMDS), and turbofan fuel specifics. Each of these items is either a first or a near-first in the fighter field. The HUD provided A-7 pilots with every visual item needed to fly and fight without looking in the cockpit. Watching through the front window as the runway materializes out of the murk on an instrument approach has to be done to be appreciated. In the attack mode, dive angle, airspeed, altitude, drift, and aiming reticle/target relationship were all available "in the window." Doppler-damped inertial platform eliminated the requirement for long ground runs to align inertial platforms. The F-4 series aircraft required either a 13-minute ground run in the chocks before taxiing or a similar ground alignment period with external electrical source before starting to complete the alignment of the inertial platform. This was always an operational impediment and used much fuel. The A-7D could taxi with a partial alignment 2½ minutes after start and complete the fine alignment in the air. The digital computer successfully tied all of the A-7D avionic subsystems together and, coupled with the HUD, produced a combat dive-bombing CEP (circle of error probability) of approximately 60 feet regardless of aircrew experience. The PMDS provided a very reliable pictorial display of actual present position on two different map scales.

The low fuel specifics of the TF-41-A-1 engine greatly expanded the unfueled radius of our fighter forces. For example, the plane was capable of carrying 12 MK-82 500-pound bombs at 430 KTAS at 33,000 feet while burning only 3,350 pounds/hour. On one well-documented test mission we flew two A-7Ds configured with 4 MK-84 2,000-pound bombs and 1,032 rounds of 20 mm ammunition 440 N.M. to Wendover Range, Utah, and returned to Luke Air Force Base without external tanks or air-to-air refueling. The last 60 miles to the target and the first 60 miles outbound were "on the deck" at full power. Seven attack passes were made in the target area. Two years later, we made a few more 440 N.M. attack missions; the only change was that Korat substituted for Luke and Hanoi replaced Wendover. These features summarize the strong points of the bird.

This A-7D, on the runway at Luke AFB, was one of the first four CAT III test planes. The checkered tail denotes 57th FTR WPNS Wing.

In all candor, it must be mentioned that the takeoff performance at combat weights and warm temperatures made F-84 drivers look down on us, and that the top speed left something to be desired. In tropical climates, a "clean" bird would do well to indicate 530 knots at low altitude, and any bomb load at all, especially on multiple ejector racks, would make 450 a mighty ambitious goal. Although the redline speed was 645 knots, I don't recall ever coming anywhere near the figure. One fellow was heard to relate, "It's not very fast, but it sure is slow!"

The combat record of the A-7D, by any standard, has to be one of the success stories of the Vietnam era. It entered the theater in October 1972 and was assigned every fighter mission except air-to-air. It was flown in South Vietnam, Cambodia, Laos, and North Vietnam on close air support, search-and-rescue, armed reconnaissance, helicopter escort, and interdiction missions. In late November 1972, a young lieutenant in my flight, Mike Shira, flew a helicopter escort mission on a successful rescue attempt near Than Hoa in North Vietnam. On that particular flight, he was airborne for 10 hours and 40 minutes, air refueled four times, and was in the target area for over 8 hours below 6,500 feet. During operations in the Hanoi area on 28 December 1972, nine of us escorted two helicopters to a survivor 13 miles from the center of the city. We operated over 1½ hours at low altitude without tanker, Mig Cap, or anti-SAM support in a vain attempt to save a downed F-111 pilot. Although we were engaged by SAMs and AAA, we suffered no losses and were only forced to withdraw when the survivor's ground position became untenable due to enemy search parties. As of June 1973, I was not aware of any A-7D loss definitely shown to be the result of hostile fire. During Linebacker II, in December 1972, the A-7D dropped more ordnance in the Hanoi area than any other aircraft except the B-52. In executing these missions, it applied far more ordnance per sortie, required less air refueling support per flying hour, achieved the most accurate jet dive-bombing CEP, and sustained the lowest loss rate of any United States fighter employed in Indo-China. In this, the ultimate test, it served our country well, and for this reason alone it must be judged a success.

I climbed down the left side for the last time on 11 June 1973. In the time I have had since then to reflect on the subject, I have become convinced that the A-7D deserved more recognition than it received—especially for extending the frontiers in the field of technical avionic excellence.

MAJ. JOHN C. MORRISSEY accumulated over 3,300 hours in single-seat fighters from 1962 until 1973. He was reassigned to the Army Command and General Staff College in 1973 where he was Senior Air Force Representative.

During the Korean conflict the AT-6 was used for spotting enemy troop concentrations and gun emplacements and marking their positions with smoke rockets to direct fighter-bombers to the attack.

The AT-6

WAYNE S. COLE

W<small>E</small> called it an AT-6 or a "6"; Navy and Marine pilots called it an "SNJ"; British and Canadian flyers called it the "Harvard"; youngsters and reservists who flew it long after World War II called it a "T-6"; and no one called it a "Texan" except journalists, promotional writers, book authors, and people who never flew it. Whatever the label, most who flew the airplane fell in love with it.

Just how much they loved it depended on what they compared it to—what they flew before and what they flew after. For me (and for many thousands of other Army Air Force pilots) it came at the end of my aviation cadet training after 65 hours in an open cockpit 220 hp Boeing PT-17 Stearman biplane, and after 70 hours in a low-wing Vultee Valiant "Vibrator" BT-13. Compared to those planes, the 6 was supreme. The Stearman was more nimble, more fun, better suited for beginners—and more likely to ground loop. The BT would snap-roll (I never tried that in a 6 except when demonstrating cross-control stalls for students), and it was great for teaching cadets to correct for torque (and giving them enlarged right leg muscles in the process). It was pretty good for cross-country flying—if you had the patience and endurance to sit there all day. And it was all right for teaching basic instruments, formation, and night flying.

The BT had hand-cranked flaps and a two-speed propeller (that was incredibly noisy for those who listened from the ground). But it had too much wing and not enough power (450 hp). Its wide landing gear and tendency to float made it too easy to land and allowed one to get a bit casual about crosswind landings. It did not reward precision flying very much, and generally it did not punish sloppy flying very severely. Young men died in it (one of our classmates spun into the Mojave Desert near Lancaster, California, one sunny day, and two classmates on a buddy ride spread themselves and their BT over the desert when they attempted an unauthorized "English bunt"). But the BT-13 generally was about as uninspiring as a Chevrolet station wagon. Coming after the Stearman and the BT-13, the AT-6 seemed like the closest thing to a fighter there was, short of the "real thing." And it was.

The North American AT-6 was an all-metal, full-cantilever, low-wing, tandem two-seater, single-engine, advance trainer. Despite its 5,300-pound weight, it did not seem underpowered with its 9-cylinder, 600 hp, direct-drive, Pratt & Whitney radial, air-cooled engine. Its 42-foot tapered wing was trimmer and racier than the larger, more cumbersome BT-13 wing. The plane had a cruising speed of 150 mph (at 26 inches manifold pressure and 1,850 rpm). The book said it had a top speed of 205 mph, but I never saw a 6 do that in sustained level flight. Normal climb speed was 110 mph, with 2,000 rpm and 30 inches. It stalled at about 75 mph, with wheels and flaps up, and at about 65 with them down. It was redlined at 240 mph. Its 110-gallon fuel capacity gave it about four hours flying time at normal cruise—less than the BT-13. Its constant speed, two-bladed Hamilton Standard propeller, its split-type flaps (maximum 45°), its conventional retractable landing gear, and its brakes all operated from highly reliable hydraulic systems. Altogether more than 15,000 of the various models of the AT-6 were built in the United States, and thousands more in Canada and other countries. When new during World War II, they cost the U.S. government, on an average, about $25,000 each. In the long (and continuing) life of the airplane there were several models and countless modifications, with consequent variations in performance and procedures (most of my flying was in C and D models).

The early morning quiet at wartime flight-training fields was routinely shattered by the roar of engines as ground crews preflighted the planes on the flight line (it came to be a familiar and even comfortable sound—unless one had been up late the night before). But that did not relieve the individual pilot from responsibility for his own careful preflight checks. When approaching an AT-6 parked on the ground, I thought it looked powerful, husky, and slightly stubby.

Practically every fighter pilot in World War II received training in the AT-6.

A standard walk-around ground inspection was a *must*—including visually checking the fuel supply in both wing tanks (55-gallon capacity on each side), checking landing gear struts (1½ inches normal, 1 inch minimum), pulling the prop through ten blades if the engine had been idle an hour or more, making certain the cover was removed from the pitot tube that protruded spearlike at about eye level near the tip of the right wing, securing the baggage compartment and door, and checking that cowl fairings were fastened and that the control surfaces were clear and free. The walkway at the rear root of the wing on the port side and a small metal step protruding on the left side of the fuselage provided easy entry to the cockpit (though new cadets invariably managed to get their feet tangled on the first try). In the front cockpit the pilot checked the Form #1A on maintenance and servicing, unlocked the controls, zeroed the trim tabs, and made certain all switches were off. If it was to be a solo flight, certain chores had to be done in the unused rear cockpit (remove and stow the stick; secure the safety belt, shoulder straps, headset, and microphone; cage the gyros; and close the rear canopy).

In the cockpit, the bucket seat accommodated the seat-pack parachute the pilot wore (often supplemented by cushions to help him see out better). After adjusting rudder pedals and seat, fastening the safety belt and shoulder harness, and setting the parking brakes, the pilot went through a detailed checklist before starting the engine. The hydraulic, flap, gear, trim, and engine controls were on the left side of the cockpit; the radio was on the right side; and electrical switches were in front below the instrument panel. Starting procedure included setting mixture full rich and prop control for low rpm, cracking throttle ½ inch, turning switches on (battery, generator, and ignition), priming (five strokes for a cold engine), energizing the starter for ten seconds, shouting "clear" (and *looking*), and engaging the starter. If oil pressure did not indicate within 30 seconds after starting, the engine was shut down promptly. Manually operated oil shutters were available for use during warm-up in cold weather (we did not use them much in Arizona and California). The pilot checked the operation of flaps, propeller, fuel lines, hand hydraulic pump, controls, engine gauges, and magnetos (maximum drop of 100 rpm on each mag at 1,900 rpm).

On wartime models, the tail wheel was steerable by means of the rudder pedals but was disengaged to swivel freely beyond 15–30° on each side of neutral (depending on the model). Those I flew as a reservist at Offutt Field in 1947 after the war had been modified to full swivel, requiring use of toe brakes for steering while taxiing and locking for takeoffs and landings. As with most "tail draggers," the engine on the 6 blocked forward visibility on the ground so that it was necessary to "S" with small turns left and right to check that the path was clear of obstructions when taxiing. On an Arizona auxiliary field in 1943, I saw one Stearman whose tail and rear fuselage had been chewed to within inches of the rear cockpit by the propeller of a carelessly taxied AT-6.

We used a standard CIGFTPR check prior to takeoff (controls free, instruments okay, gas selector on proper tank, flaps up, trim tabs set, prop set for high rpm, and run-up). On takeoff, the pilot advanced the throttle smoothly to the sea-level stop, kept the plane aligned with the runway by increasing right rudder pressure to correct for torque, raised the tail slightly, and with light back pressure on the stick let the plane fly off the ground at about 80 mph. When airborne, he toed the brakes to stop wheel rotation, pushed the hydraulic button, and pulled up the lever retracting the landing gear. Then he lowered the nose of the plane slightly to let the airspeed increase, throttled back to 30 inches of manifold pressure, set the prop control for 2,000 rpm, and climbed out at 110 mph.

To me the plane seemed brisk and responsive on the controls in flight, particularly on the ailerons. The AT-6 rewarded precision flying, and it revealed sloppy flying for what it was. But it had no unconventional quirks; it behaved itself properly and did what it was told to do. Its stalls were sharp but manageable. It spun furiously, but in literally hundreds of spins I never had one argue seriously with me about coming out of it if I commanded it firmly with brisk, almost violent, recovery procedures (in the spin the pilot reduced power, held full rudder with the spin, and kept the stick all the way back; for recovery, he jammed full opposite rudder and after another half turn he jammed the stick full forward briskly—that was no time to be gentle on the controls; as the plane stopped rotating, he neutralized the rudders, smoothly eased back on the stick to pull out of the dive, and reapplied power). In nearly 600 hours of flying in a 6 in all sorts of situations (as a cadet, a basic flight instructor, and a reservist), I never had an engine stop, a spin persist unduly, a gear fail to lower or retract properly, or a prop run away.

Chandelles and "lazy 8s" were precision maneuvers, but when properly flown in the 6 they were also real works of art and beauty—constantly changing bank, pitch, speed, and torque correction. The AT-6 was a fun airplane for aerobatics. My own personal favorite was the Immelmann (the secret, I thought, was proper entry speed—190 mph—and crossing controls briefly at the beginning of the roll-out at the top of the maneuver). Entry speeds were 180 mph for loops and 160 mph for slow rolls.

Prior to landing, we entered the traffic pattern on a 45° angle to the downwind leg. We used a standard GUMP prelanding check (gas selector on the fuller tank, undercarriage down and checked, mixture full rich, and propeller set at 2,000 rpm). We flew the "45" and downwind legs at 120 mph, the base leg at 110 mph, made the turn onto the final approach at about 100 mph, and flew the approach at 90 mph. Flaps were lowered on base and on final as needed.

Personally, I enjoyed landing the plane. Its gear was narrow enough and its fuselage short enough to require the pilot's full attention and skill; it was not the sort of plane in which one could go to sleep on landings—either figuratively or literally. Pilots were known to find themselves in the midst of a ground loop on the landing roll-out, just after congratulating themselves on having made a nice landing. Proper correction for crosswinds was essential. Generally, I preferred the slipping or cross-control method of correcting for crosswinds. Using that method the pilot lowered the wing on the windward side to prevent the plane from blowing sideways across the approach path and runway, used opposite rudder to keep the plane lined up straight with the runway, and if necessary held the correction right down to touchdown. In unusually strong crosswinds it was necessary to use a combination of the slip and crab methods (but if the wind was that strong I probably should have stayed on the ground in the first place). With proper correction for crosswinds, with accurate airspeed control (normally 90 mph on the final approach), and with gradual dissipation of airspeed in the flare-out by smoothly coming back on the stick as the plane neared the ground, the AT-6 provided a neat, precise, three-point touchdown that gave a pilot a sense of pride in accomplishment. One learned to keep the stick back and to stay alert on the roll-out. The flight was not over until the plane was parked, the engine shut down, the controls locked, the aircraft forms filled out, and the wheels chocked.

During most of World War II, aviation cadets first experienced the AT-6 in advanced flying school (for me that was at Luke Field, Arizona), after already having successfully graduated from primary flight training in a Stearman and from basic in a BT-13. Near the end of 1944, however, that changed. I was then a flight instructor at Merced Army Air Field in California's San Joaquin Valley, a basic flying training field. But it was later rebuilt to serve Strategic Air Command planes and renamed Castle Air Force Base.

In November 1944, we began giving basic flight instruction in AT-6s rather than in BT-13s. That meant cadets went directly from the open cockpit Stearman biplane to the 6. The Canadians and British had been following that general procedure successfully all along, but it was quite a jump for the cadets (and for their instructors who had the responsibility for keeping them alive until they could master their mighty new mounts). At the time, I thought it was a bit like changing them from a kiddy car to a Buick. But most of them caught on more quickly than I had thought they might. It normally took a bit longer for them to solo in the 6 than in the BT, and the "wash out" rate may have been slightly higher, but the difference was not as

Winging their way in echelon, P-40 fighter and AT-6 trainer ships piloted by upper and lower classmen training to be pursuit pilots rendezvous in the Texas sky during a day's maneuvers.

great as one might have expected. And the clumsy BT-13 was bypassed completely, with few tears shed over its demise. I am told that for a time after the war, the Air Force used the 6 as a primary trainer—the first airplane the cadet flew in his pilot training; I'm glad the Army didn't do that when I was a cadet and a military flight instructor

The AT-6 was flown from the front cockpit solo (under a sliding glass canopy). For instrument training the student flew in the rear cockpit under a canvas "hood" to prevent him from seeing outside. The instructor flew in front when teaching instruments, and in the rear at other times. The forward visibility was reasonably good from the front but poor from the rear. Among the more challenging experiences in the plane was instructing cadets before solo when the main responsibility for assuring survival in landings lay with the instructor in the rear cockpit who got only tiny glimpses of the ground at each corner—with the instrument panel, front cockpit, cadet pilot, wing, flaps, and engine obstructing his view forward. But it was not at all impossible, and the difficulty enhanced the pride one felt in doing it well. Similarly, the forward visibility for the instuctor in the rear cockpit when checking out cadets in night flying left much to be desired—particularly on a dark night when checking out someone else's

The AT-6 was the only single-engine advance trainer procured in quantity during World War II.

students whose skills (or lack of same) were not familiar to the instructor. But the visibility from the rear seat of the 6 was sufficiently similar to that in single-engine, single-seater fighters of the era that it was excellent preparation for the transition to fighters later.

Back-seat landings in a 6 were a part of my preparation for flying P-40s in transition at Luke Field in 1945. The Curtiss P-40, of course, was more powerful, faster, and performed better than the AT-6. Its handling characteristics on takeoffs and landings, however, were enough like the 6 so that those of us with instructor time in the back seat of a 6 had advantages over other pilots in transition. But the P-40's temperamental electrical systems and liquid-cooled in-line engine never seemed so comfortably dependable to me as the AT-6's reliable hydraulic systems and its problem-free, air-cooled radial engine (though that may have been partly because I had more experience with the latter).

The AT-6 was used for every imaginable flying purpose: instruments, aerobatics, formation, cross-country, night flying, aerial photography, gunnery, and even combat. I flew it during gunnery training at Ajo Army Air Field in the deserts of southern Arizona, firing its .30 caliber gun at both aerial and ground targets. (When one of my bullets severed the aerial target tow cable, and the metal rod for the target knocked a six-inch hole in the leading edge of my right wing near the pitot tube, the plane continued to fly normally and permitted a beautiful wheel landing that did not need the services of the fire equipment and ambulance that alert tower people had arranged to have available when I touched down.)

One AT-6 was credited with sinking a German submarine in World War II, and others downed Japanese Zeros. As a "spotter" plane, it saw combat in the Korean war in the early 1950s. In the 1960s, some countries modified the 6 as a counterinsurgency light attack plane, with gun pods under the wings and assorted external weaponry. It served as a training plane in the air forces of more than 40 countries, and as late as 1973 was still in service with more than 30 air forces. In 1974, Dr. Richard P. Hallion of the Smithsonian Institution saw 6s flying in the Netherlands Air Force and also saw the three Harvards still used by the RAF at its Empire Test Pilots' School in Wiltshire, England. They were in "magnificent condition"—more than a generation after the first AT-6s came off production lines.

One still sees weary looking AT-6s tied down at remote corners of airports all over the United States and the world. And many of those planes are still flying. They are still challenging the skills of dedicated airmen. They still inspire the love of those who flew—and fly—them. It was—and is—a great airplane!

WAYNE S. COLE received his Ph.D. in history from the University of Wisconsin in 1951 and has taught at the University of Maryland since 1965. His latest book was on Charles A. Lindbergh's opposition to American entry into World War II. Cole served in the Army Air Forces from February 1943 until October 1945 and received his commission and pilot wings at Luke Field in Arizona in February 1944. He attended the Central Instructors School at Randolph Field, and served as a basic flight instructor at Merced and Minter Fields in California. He took fixed-gunnery training at Ajo in Arizona and fighter transition in P-40s at Luke. He first flew the AT-6 at Luke in December 1943 and last flew it at Truax Field in Wisconsin in May 1950. Between those dates he accumulated a total of nearly 600 hours in an AT-6.

*Alaskan flight
taking off from
Bolling Field,
Washington, D.C.*

The Martin Bomber B-10, B-12, B-10B

EDWARD W. VIRGIN

Even in late 1933 when in training on the advanced stage at Kelly Field (San Antonio), stories were coming through telling of the Martin bomber under development, soon to be delivered to the Air Corps. The reports were exciting—a modern twin-engine all metal airplane with a speed of approximately 225 mph. We were flying B-3s, B-4s, and B-5As— (Keystone) bombers—so our interest in something new and modern is understandable.

On graduating from Kelly Field in February 1934, the bombardment pilots were ordered to March Field, Riverside, California. When we arrived, we found that all normal operations were at a standstill. Most of the pilots and airplanes were being used to fly the airmail. As recent graduates, we were used only to ferry planes to and from the overhaul and repair depot at Rickwell Field, San Diego—thank God.

We began getting deliveries of our Martin B-10s and B-12s in the summer. They were beautiful to behold, and we swarmed all over the first ones. They were mixed in with our Douglas B-7s, and we still had some Keystone B-4s (box kites) and, believe it or not, one Curtiss-Wright B-2 on the field. It is hard to find words to describe the order of magnitude advance in this modern airplane over even the B-7, which was far, far ahead of the Keystones.

I mention the Martin B-12 because a service test quantity of this model was delivered. This airplane had two Pratt & Whitney R1690-11 Hornet engines, whereas the B-10B, which was the principal production model, had the Wright R-1820-33 Cyclone engines. I made my first solo flight in a B-12 on 5 July 1934. I was just four months out of the flying school and was checking out in a B-12—man, I had arrived.

A short description of the airplane can start from the bombardier's station in the nose and work to the rear. The entrance to the compartment was a trapdoor in the floor. Forward was a flat shatter-proof inclined glass window just ahead of the Norden bombsight base for forward visibility. The head of the sight (secret) was brought on board for the mission. Above this was a rotatable Plexiglas turret that mounted a single .30 caliber Browning machine gun. The turret was manually operated to swing and aim the gun.

The bombardier was provided with a detachable chest-mounted parachute which was normally stowed. This gave him freedom of action when kneeling over the bombsight or swinging the gun turret without a cumbersome seat-type chute hanging from his rear end. The chest chute could be snapped on quickly in an emergency. There was no way to get into or out of this compartment (like a meat can) except through the floor trapdoor, hence a nose over or a wheels up landing was memorable for the occupant.

The pilot's seat was reached by climbing up the left side of the fuselage with handholds and foot recesses, over the top rail, and into the cavity uncovered by sliding the canopy back. This was luxury—a cockpit that could be closed and protected from the wind and rain. In the event of rain, which reduced forward visibility through the windshield, the sliding glass windows could be opened or the canopy partially cracked to provide good visibility for a landing. The control wheel was on top of the stick post, which came up between the legs. The seat was adjustable vertically; with seat up visibility was excellent even when the plane was in the three-point position. The instrumentation was the latest 1935 vintage, but by today's standards it was primitive. The PDI (indicator) transmitting direction signals from the bombardier was prominently placed front and center. Besides the normal complement of oil pressure, electrical, and fuel gauges there was the flight group made up of the clock, altimeter, turn-and-bank indicator, rate-of-climb indicator, directional gyro, and artificial horizon. The artificial horizon could not be trusted, as it tumbled on occasion when in a steep bank. The low-frequency radio equipment was good for interplane communications but was a poor crutch when flying the airway beams. By lifting the lever (switch) adjacent to the seat on the right side, the landing gear retracted electrically. This was a real luxury, as the B-7 gear had to be pumped up hydraulically by the pilot.

The bomb bay, which had about a dozen stations or racks, was just behind and below the pilot. The bomb load was 2,260 pounds maximum. The one 2,000-pound bomb was carried externally on a rack located between the fuselage and the right engine nacelle. The bomb-bay doors were operated electrically from the bombardier's station or by a crank from the aft end of the bomb bay at the navigator's station. The pilot had a lever he could pull that would split the nut on the doors actuating the screw jack so that the doors would fly open for an emergency. The crew in the rear of the plane bailed out through this opening.

Just aft of the bomb bay was the navigator's station. This was used by the officer copilot when dead-reckoning or celestial navigation were required for over-water flights. A small table, drift meter, clock, speed indicator, and aperiodic compass were provided. A kit containing all the other necessary implements for navigation was brought aboard for the mission.

The copilot sat on a fold-away seat under the rear sliding canopy. The control wheel was attached to a yoke rising from the floor on the right side of the fuselage so that a clear passageway could be had beneath the wheel when the yoke was uncoupled from the elevator cables and stowed forward. Clearing the passageway in this manner made it possible to fire the .30 caliber Browning machine gun mounted on a ϒ-ring behind the copilot's seat or to operate the floor-mounted camera that could be installed just below.

When in position and acting as copilot, the officer could spell the pilot on a long flight even in loose or extended formation. Landing the plane effectively from the rear cockpit was out of the question due to lack of forward visibility, although I am sure that it could be done in an extreme emergency. The copilot's instrumentation was minimal—altimeter, airspeed indicator, turn-and-bank indicator, rate-of-climb indicator, compass, directional gyro, and clock.

The B-10's specifications and performance were as follows: span 70.5 feet, length 44.73 feet; height 11.42 feet; wing area 678.2 square feet; wing loading 21.30 pounds per square foot; weight empty 9,205 pounds; useful load 5,264 pounds; gross weight 14,469 pounds; fuel 452 gallons; oil 63 gallons; maximum speed 214 mph; cruising speed at 67% power 190 mph; landing speed with flaps 65 mph; service ceiling 22,800 feet; rate of climb 1,465 feet per minute; cruising range 1,110 miles at 190 mph and 10,000 feet (with 2,260-pound bomb load—600 miles).

In the fall of 1934, Hamilton Field, located just outside of San Rafael, California (Marin County), was completed, and the 7th Bombardment group was ordered to man the new station. The 9th, 11th, and 31st bombardment plus the 88th Observation Squadrons comprised the 7th Group. We were gradually provided with B-12, B-10, and finally a full complement of B-10B airplanes; the B-10B was the principal production model. The differences between the B-10 and the B-10B were minor. The first B-10s came out equipped with fixed-pitch Hamilton standard propellers and no landing flaps. The B-10Bs had manually operated (hand pump) landing flaps and controllable-pitch propellers. The engine exhaust outlets were relocated to reduce strain on the pilot's eyes when accompanying others in night formation flying.

The B-10s were real dreamboats. The ground handling characteristics were excellent—good brakes and small differences in throttle settings coupled with excellent forward visibility and no tendency for ground loops made for fast, straight-ahead taxiing and formation takeoffs as well as fast clearing of the runway after landing. The in-flight visibility was even better. The controls were effective and the forces reasonable (you could say well harmonized), making it an excellent close-formation airplane day and night. The plane was an excellent bombing

The B-10 had a wing span of 70.5 feet.

The B-10 saw combat service in the Pacific in the early part of World War II.

A cockpit that could be closed was a real luxury.

platform because of its stability around all three axes. Directional changes, as requested on the PDI from the bombardier, could be made quickly. The airplane was very forgiving in every respect, not having any vicious characteristics even in a power-off stall. It would stall straight ahead with adequate warning (buffet). This resulted in a good, safe airplane during landings.

One point that is not absolutely clear is the airplane's capability with an engine failure. It was customary to practice single-engine flight by closing the throttle on one engine, putting the propeller in full-course pitch, advancing the power on the other side, and maintaining flight. This could be accomplished. Though I never had one, I know of two flights when engine failure occurred, which had different results. On one, the pilot was cruising along above 5,000 feet when the engine threw a piston, knocking off a cylinder head and damaging the engine cowling (causing increased drag); the pilot spiraled down for a landing in a field below. He believed that under the circumstances there was no alternative, although he was only 35 or 40 miles from home base with no difficult terrain between. On the other flight, the left engine threw a piston, knocking off a cylinder head during takeoff. The pilot accomplished the takeoff, gained altitude to about 100 feet, circled around, and came in for a successful landing with the prop in a stopped (frozen) position. In both cases the airplanes were at light gross weights. One must conclude that without feathering propellers, the single-engine flying ability of the airplane was marginal; in the second case, the pilot was lucky and did everything right.

Looking back with a critical eye, I would say that the airplane had drawbacks in configuration and in systems. Perhaps the weakest feature was the tandem arrangement and the small fuselage that made it impossible for crew members to go from one station to another in flight. The second officer (copilot, bombardier, navigator) could not be completely utilized. If the mission involved bombing, he took off in the nose compartment and stayed there. So much more flexibility would have been possible if a tunnel had been provided from the nose to the rear section. But we have to evaluate the airplane as it was and not as it could have been.

The B-10's rotatable Plexiglas turret mounted a single .30 caliber Browning machine gun.

Two systems deficiencies plagued B-10 crews. The lack of a heating system forced us to wear heavy leather winter flying suits and boots because at 10,000 or 12,000 feet for extended periods the cold was penetrating. The lack of a good oxygen system also adversely affected pilot and crew efficiency. Prior to flight liquid oxygen (—360° F) was poured by hand from a receptacle into an inaccessibly located generator—a dangerous operation. Once in the generator, the liquid oxygen could not be contained because it boiled off continuously with the result that when reaching Mt. Whitney (14,401 feet) 1½ hours after takeoff, the supply was exhausted. All of our routine bombing runs for training and for record at 15,000 feet were done without the benefit of oxygen. Oxygen was provided for our runs at 18,000 feet, but the supply was generally exhausted before the mission was completed.

What did this great airplane accomplish to be remembered by? It participated in two pioneer flights and one exercise: the Alaska Flight, the Miami Flight, and the bombing of the battleship *Utah*. I had the privilege of being one of those involved in the deployment of a whole group of bombers from the West to the East Coast in less than 24 hours. Twenty-eight airplanes led by General Tinker left March Field, Riverside, California, around noon on 1 December 1935 landing at dusk at Biggs Field, El Paso, to complete the first leg of the trip. After fueling with hand wobble pumps out of barrels and providing necessary maintenance (engines had to be recowled and the rocker boxes lubricated with Zerk guns), we took off individually late that evening down the runway marked with kerosene flares. We landed at Barksdale Field, Shreveport, Louisiana, around dawn. We refueled (this time out of fuel trucks), provided necessary maintenance, and took off for our destination—Vero Beach, Florida. We arrived around 10:30 in the morning EST, which made the flight about 19½ hours elapsed time coast to coast with 27 planes completing the flight together. The bombing of U.S.S. *Utah* (a remote-controlled target battleship) off of San Francisco in August 1937 was a joint exercise with a reluctant Navy. Each of the above, however, is a story in itself.

I understand that the B-10 saw some service in combat with Allied governments in the early part of World War II in the Pacific, but I am not familiar with the record of effectiveness.

Looking back, I feel that the Air Corps and the Martin Company should be given high marks for the conception and development of this wonderful airplane that advanced the state of the art so greatly.

NORTH AMERICAN AVIATION

EDWARD W. VIRGIN, USAF (Ret.), received his Wings and Military Pilot's rating in 1934 and was sent to active duty as a Flying Cadet. He terminated active duty in 1938 and became an Air Corps inspector and engineering representative with duty at North American Aviation, Inglewood, California. He was an engineering test pilot for North American in 1941, was made chief of the Engineering Flight Test Section, and held that position until 1950 when he became the firm's eastern representative in Washington. He retired in 1963 to become vice-president of the Eastern Region for Bell Aerospace Corp., New York, and retired from that in 1970.

B-17 Flying Fortress

JAMES V. EDMUNDSON

USAF

It is impossible to think of the air battles over Europe during World War II without remembering the B-17.

As any pilot knows, an airplane is much more than an inanimate collection of metal. It represents the end product of an idea that developed through a complex process of conception, design, test, and production, and it can be measured in terms of performance criteria such as top speed, service ceiling, useful load, range, rate-of-climb, or takeoff and landing speeds.

To those who have flown them, particularly in combat, airplanes have a character, a personality, and an animate being distinctly their own. In many cases, a specific aircraft will have been dominant during an important part of a pilot's life and will remind him of the crew members who shared so many hours aloft with him, the mechanics who serviced his airplane between missions, and the squadron mates with whom he

lived at the base and with whom he flew in combat. Some of them never returned, but they are not forgotten.

A very few airplanes are of such a special character, so outstanding in design and performance, and so much a part of a particular era that they have a great impact on human awareness, extending far beyond the pilots who flew them. These aircraft can come to represent to a nation, and sometimes to the world, the very essence of the years during which they were dominant in the sky.

Such an airplane was the B-17, the Flying Fortress. For a generation of Americans, British, and Germans it is impossible to think of the air battles over Europe during World War II without remembering the B-17 as it swarmed aloft by the thousands from English bases, formed up in combat boxes, sometimes escorted by friendly fighters (but more often not), penetrated swarms of hostile fighters and flak "thick enough to walk on," bombed the industrial heartland of the enemy in a succession of daylight missions, and returned to base, often having sustained unbelievable battle damage and bearing wounded and dead crew members.

There were other American bombardment aircraft of that time—

In its day the B-17 was queen of the skies.

B-24s, B-25s, B-26s—I have flown them all and they were all fine birds, but the B-17 was the airplane of that era in a way that no other aircraft can ever be.

There were, of course, many models of the Fortress, starting with the 13 YB-17s ordered by the Army Air Corps in 1936. One of these was eventually equipped with turbosuperchargers and became the YB-17A. Relatively modest numbers of B-17Bs, Cs, and Ds were procured, each a refinement of its predecessors. Progressively more powerful versions of the Wright R-1820 engines were provided and equipped with super-chargers for high-altitude flight. Armament was increased and self-sealing fuel tanks and armor plate were added as the requirements for such improvements were recognized.

In the late summer of 1941 a radically new Flying Fortress appeared, known as the B-17E. It had a more massive vertical fin that housed a tail-gun position with twin .50 caliber machine guns. It also had an upper forward power turret and a "bathtub" belly turret in which the gunner aimed and fired using a mirror in which his target appeared upside down and backwards. In later E models the "bathtub" was replaced by a Sperry ball turret in the ventral position, greatly enhancing protection against low attacks.

The B-17 was eventually improved through the F and G models, acquiring still more powerful engines to handle the increased weight, "Toyko tanks" in the wingtips to increase range, and a Bendix chin turret to cope with head-on attacks. Boeing's wisdom in building this growth potential into the original design was, indeed, a key factor in the success of the Fortress, and the Army Air Force eventually bought 12,725.

My first view of the B-17 came in the early summer of 1937 when I was a Flying Cadet in training at Randolph Field, Texas. A flight of YB-17s from the 3rd Bombardment Group at Langley Field stopped through Randolph and remained overnight. The entire Cadet Corps went down to "A" Stage and swarmed around and under those huge, beautiful machines that literally filled the hangars. Looking at my photographs of the occasion brings back the feeling of awe and wonder that I shared with my classmates. The thought that some day some of us might fly B-17s was almost too overwhelming to contemplate.

Those of us in the Attack Section at Kelly got some time in B-3s, 4s, and 5s. In the ensuing years I flew B-10s, B-12s, and B-18s, but I

(Left) In 1937 the B-17s stopped at Randolph Field and the cadets went to look them over. (Right) The huge machines literally filled the hangars.

didn't get to meet the B-17 again until the summer of 1941. I was stationed at Hickam Field, Hawaii, in the 31st Squadron of the 5th Bombardment Group flying B-18s when we were designated to convert to B-17s. A group of old friends from the 19th Bomb Group delivered our first aircraft in a mass flight direct from the mainland. This was an impressive display of range in those days, when the Pan American Clippers were the only planes in regular use capable of such a flight. The delivery pilots stayed long enough to check some of us out in the new big birds before they caught the boat for home.

As my checkout progressed, I became increasingly impressed by the capabilities of this remarkable machine. It truly represented a quantum jump over any previous bombers.

USAF

The B-17H was easy to take off, cruise, and land. It was a real treat to fly.

To get into the B-17 the pilot climbed through a door on the right-hand rear portion of the waist gunners' compartment and proceeded forward through the radio room and the bomb bay, climbed through the upper power turret, and into the cockpit seats. Navigators and bombardiers could enter this way and then go down the crawlway into the nose, but the normal access to their battle stations was through a hatch to the rear of the nose compartment. They chinned themselves and swung their feet up and into the aircraft, then had their parachutes and gear passed up from the ground.

There was really nothing unusual about start-up procedures. Engines were started in normal sequence, 3, 4, 2, and 1. Normal engine power controls were the prop controls, turbosupercharger controls, mixture controls, and throttles.

Taxiing the B-17 was not easy. As with most tail-wheel aircraft, it was clumsy and lumbering on the ground. Also, with the big, high fin, taxiing in a crosswind was a job because the aircraft tended to weathercock and it was easy to overheat the upwind brake in attempting to hold a course. The experienced pilot learned to use the tailwheel lock extensively in taxiing.

On narrow taxiways we learned to taxi mostly with the inboards because the outboards would hang over the edge of the paved strip and using them would tend to blow up a lot of dust and gravel. On the other hand, when taxiing on wide taxiways we used the outboards, primarily because they were higher off the ground and didn't kick up quite as much debris as the inboards.

Prior to takeoff, the engines were run up one at a time, usually in the order in which they had been started, the mags checked, and the turbosupercharger set. In spite of this, the turbos would invariably require adjusting on the takeoff roll to get full power or to avoid excessive manifold pressures.

The tail-wheel lock was a big help on takeoff, and on crosswind takeoffs the tail wheel would be left on the ground as long as possible and the aircraft pulled off from a three-point position in order to avoid weathercocking. On a normal takeoff, the tail wheel was lifted off the ground as soon as the tail would fly, because in this attitude there was less aerodynamic drag and the airplane would gather speed faster and take off shorter. Flaps were normally not used for takeoffs, but a shorter takeoff run could be achieved by using about ¼ flaps.

Synchronizing the props was always a chore in the B-17. The pilot could look back through the number 1 and number 2 props and synchronize these two by sight. The copilot would do the same for the number 3 and number 4 props. Then the two sides could be brought into sync aurally.

In those days we knew nothing about weight and balance. Later, when I was faced with computing weight and balance for B-29s, B-47s, B-52s, and B-58s, I wondered how we ever avoided serious trouble with the B-17s. The answer, of course, is that it was a very forgiving airplane. The CG (center of gravity) limits could vary widely and the airplane might feel uncomfortably nose- or tail-heavy, but it seemed to fly well with some highly unusual loading configurations.

Our first aircraft were Cs and Ds, but later we received Es, sturdier and more heavily armed than previous models. Changing to Es brought one surprise to all of us. In the older models, the tail was light and on landing tended to float even with plenty of aft trim. The heavier fin and the additional weight of guns in the tail of the Es tended to bring the tail down firmly, and our first few attempts at three-pointers turned into rather dismal tail-first landings. To counteract this tail-heaviness at low speeds, we never took off or landed with ammunition installed in the tail or with the tail gunner in his combat position. We also never took off or landed with the ball gunner in his turret because he would be trapped in the event of gear failure. Moreover, it was most important that the ball turret be properly stowed prior to landing in order not to damage the gun barrels.

The three-point landing was ideal because getting the locked tail wheel on the ground early gave good stability, particularly in a crosswind. Having landed, and if we were at light weight at the end of the mission, we would usually check the mags as soon as we had cleared the runway and then shut down either the inboards or the outboards, depending on the taxiing conditions ahead of us.

The B-17 was easy to fly, as are all aircraft, if by flying you mean to take off, bore a hole in the sky, and land. But military flying is much,

much more. It consists of operating the subsystems, coordinating the crew within the plane and with other aircraft and crews in the sky, and flying the aircraft to the outer limits of its operating envelope so that the aircraft is able to perform efficiently the military mission for which it was designed.

For example, the F-102 is undoubtedly one of the simplest and easiest airplanes to take off, fly straight and level, and land. Its controls are simple; it doesn't even have flaps. The delta wing gives it maximum stability in flight, and it is almost spin-proof. On the other hand, to operate the radar and infrared systems skillfully and to fly the aircraft within the altitude, speed, attitude, and performance envelope so that the internally carried Falcon missiles can be fired accurately to secure a kill is *not* simple. It is most complex and requires constant and continuing practice.

The B-17 was easy to take off, cruise, and land. However, to a pilot who wanted to give his bombardier the best possible bomb run with minimum deviations in airspeed, elevation, and attitude, to give his navigator a stable platform for his celestial shots and accurately flown double drifts, to teach his gunners to call out attacks quickly and accurately without cluttering up the interphone and to position them within a formation to give them maximum freedom of fire—to such a pilot, flying the B-17 was a demanding job.

The B-17 was a real treat to fly. It handled honestly on takeoffs and landings, it gave a good, clear stall warning, it carried a far more substantial bomb load than any previous bombers, and with its turbosuperchargers it became the first airplane I ever took to 30,000 feet. It was a beautiful formation aircraft, and it had a unique throttle arrangement that assisted immeasurably in flying formation. The four throttles terminated in three pairs of handles, one above the other. The top grip controlled the outboard engines, the bottom grip controlled the inboard engines, and the central grip enabled the pilot to palm all four throttles. Most of us eventually learned to set the outboards and fly formation with the inboards alone, adjusting the outboards only when large power adjustments became necessasry.

The normal crew for a B-17 was 10 men. The Air Force traditionally has used two pilots in four-engined bombers such as the B-17 and the B-24 as well as in the far smaller and simpler twin-engined bombers like the B-25 and B-26. This is also true of transport and cargo aircraft such as the C-47, C-46, C-54, and all that followed. I do not know the precise grounds for such policy, but logic leads me to believe there were several reasons:

1. We had sufficient pilots to go first class. We were mounting an Air Force on a much broader manpower base than the British, and we were not forced to crew our aircraft on such an austere basis as the RAF had to.

2. There is no question that one pilot and a sort of flying crew chief in the copilot's seat, who could reach the handles that the pilot couldn't get to, could fly any of these aircraft safely. There is also no question that with a well-coordinated, two-pilot team, the aircraft could be operated with greater military efficiency.

3. There is a built-in training advantage in the pilot/copilot system. The copilot learns from helping the pilot under combat conditions, and when he moves into the left-hand seat he will be a far better pilot than if he just started out by himself in a one-pilot airplane.

(This, of course, is why the loss rate on green fighter pilots is so high, in spite of giving them extended periods of supervised flight on the wing of more senior pilots. The fact that a fighter is a one-pilot airplane forces us to commit fighter pilots to combat when they are still relatively inexperienced and thus the loss rate is high. Only the lucky and the quick learners survive.)

4. Without a pilot, the aircraft will not get home. Bombardiers, navigators, and gunners can be killed or wounded and the lives of their crew mates are not placed in serious jeopardy, but if the pilot is knocked out, the entire crew is lost. Providing two pilots gives the crew a safety factor. I believe enough bombers returned to base with one or the other pilot dead or disabled to have made this a policy that paid off.

There are other, more complex reasons in favor of two pilots in bombers, but I believe these four reasons are the main ones and that the policy was wise.

Besides the pilot and copilot there were two other officers, the navigator and bombardier with battle stations in the nose. The B-17 heating system was capable of heating the cockpit to the point where eggs could be fried on the throttle quadrant, but the heat to the nose compartment was always insufficient. The pilot and copilot would be sweltering in their shirt sleeves while the navigator and bombardier were freezing in their fleece-lined winter flying suits. We used to say the B-17 was like a healthy puppy— it had the coldest nose in town.

Additional crew members included the radio operator, belly gunner, two waist gunners, and a tail gunner. Later we modified our aircraft by adding a twin .50 caliber ring-mount firing out the upper radio compartment hatch, and we added an eleventh man to the crew to spell the radio operator and to man these extra guns. Even later, when some of our aircraft were equipped with rudimentary radar equipment, this man became the radar operator.

For those of us stationed in Hawaii, 7 December 1941 will always be a day of memories. One of mine includes a chapter in the continuing history of the B-17.

On the night of 6 December, an element of the 19th Bomb Group under the leadership of Col. Ted Landon had taken off from the mainland for Hawaii on the way to the Philippines. This flight of B-17s arrived in Hawaii on the morning of 7 December just as the Japanese attack was taking place. Some of the crews landed at Hickam in the midst of the uproar and were pretty well shot up by attacking Zeros. Others landed wherever they could. Col. Dick Carmichael landed in the middle of a golf course, as I recall. In an effort to eliminate unnecessary weight, none of the aircraft carried any ammunition for their guns—a commentary on our awareness of the kind of world we were living in.

Shortly after the war began, I was transferred to the 27th Squadron of the 11th Bomb Group, which was commanded by Col. "Blondie" Saunders, one of the truly great combat commanders of World War II. Our B-17s were dispersed throughout the islands and the 26th moved to Wheeler Field, next to Schofield Barracks, where we participated in flying patrols out to the 1,000-mile arc around the Hawaiian Islands.

Our first real action came in June 1942 when all the B-17s were mysteriously ordered to Midway Island. There we were briefed by the Navy that they had succeeded in breaking the Japanese code and had forewarning of an attack headed for Midway. The timing was not precisely known, and we cooled our heels for a couple of days while PBYs probed the most likely approach sectors for signs of the coming attack. One evening just about dusk a PBY limped in badly shot up. It had made contact with a Japanese task force and the Battle of Midway was underway. Naval aircraft from our carriers and Marine aircraft flying from Midway gave the attacking fleet a warm reception, but I'm sure the biggest surprise for the Nipponese Navy was finding itself under attack by B-17s out in the middle of the Pacific Ocean.

Shortly after we returned to Hawaii from Midway, the 11th Group was alerted for a move into the South Pacific and in about 10 days, with Colonel Saunders leading the way, we were off. Our route took us first to Christmas Island where my flying-school classmate, George MacNicol, had a squadron of P-39s, then to Canton Island with its famous lone palm tree, and on to Nandi, a base on Viti Levu, the main island of the Fiji group.

Our first main base was on Efate in the Central New Hebrides Islands, but we soon moved on to a newly constructed base on Espiritu Santo in the Northern New Hebrides. We bombed in support of the Marine landings on Guadalcanal, and our targets consisted of Japanese naval units, bases on nearby islands such as Tulagi, and Japanese military formations on Guadalcanal itself.

During these days we literally lived in our aircraft. When we returned from a mission we would fuel and bomb up our B-17s, often working late into the night. On Efate we had Quonset huts to sleep in, but at Espiritu Santo during the several weeks before our tent camps were erected we slept with our B-17s as cavalry men slept with their horses. We opened the bomb-bay doors and lowered the flaps to give us some protection against tropical storms and set up our folding cots under the wings, tying our mosquito nets to any convenient part of the airplane.

After the Marines had things more or less under control on Guadalcanal, we used Henderson Field as an advance operating base.

The author's crew of the B-17 on Espiritu Santo in the New Hebrides, 1942.

Boeing B-17 Flying Fortresses drop bombs on enemy installations in Europe.

This forward staging permitted us to search out fleet targets much farther north and to hit bases such as Munda, Gigo, Vella Lavella, Bougainville, and Buin.

The 11th Group was actually attached to the 1st Marine Division (Reinforced) and was included in the Naval Distinguished Unit Citation that went to the 1st Marine Division for its Solomon Islands operation. My citation reached me in 1948 after the Air Force had become a separate entity. The paperwork accompanying the award originated with the Navy, was transmitted to the Marine Corps for the 1st Division, was then endorsed to the Army for award to the Army Air Force units involved, and finally was forwarded to the newly created Air Force for presentation. To my knowledge, this was the only B-17 unit to be so honored by a sister service.

Aircraft operation was much the same in Europe and the Pacific. Differences were brought about by the varying military requirements of the two theaters. The aircraft were flown heavier in Europe than in the Pacific. This could be done because the operating bases were better and runways were generally hard-surfaced and longer. More time was spent on formation flying in Europe. The form-up for a major strike there could take 1–1½ hours. In the Pacific, however, formations were generally smaller, and it was usual for the leader to circle the field once and be on his way, with the others forming up enroute.

Missions were generally flown at higher altitude in Europe. Exposure to intense flak for long periods forced operating altitudes up. In the Pacific, however, targets were smaller, sometimes maneuvering surface vessels were targeted, formations were smaller, bomb patterns were less extensive, and bombing had to be done at lower altitudes to give increased accuracy.

The war followed its course. I was privileged to see the magnificent work being done by the British-based 8th Air Force where the B-17 really won its spurs. My own participation in the European air war, however, was cut short. I was called home to take part in the B-29 program, again under General Saunders. This new airplane was destined to see combat in the India-China theater and later in the Marianas, but this is another story. I would only mention as part of the B-17 saga that the vast majority of the key leaders in the early days of the B-29 program were card-carrying members of the B-17 union.

My last contact with the B-17 provides a nostalgic and, in a way, sad touch, but it, too, belongs in this story.

After B-29 combat duty in World War II and in Korea, as well as peacetime tours in B-29s and B-36s in SAC, I found myself during the late 1950s in command of the 36th Air Division at Davis-Monthan Air Force Base near Tucson, Arizona. The division consisted of two wings, the 43rd and the 303rd, both equipped with B-47s.

In 1957, to my surprise and delight, we had a B-17 assigned to the base. It was a museum piece, stripped of all turrets, guns, armor plate, and other combat gear, but it was still a proud B-17. It was actually assigned to the Air Research and Development Command, now known as the Systems Command, and it had been specially instrumented for use in a project to probe and study thunderstorms in conjunction with some Air Force–sponsored research conducted by the University of Arizona. During June, July, and August, the thunderstorm season, it was a very busy bird, but for much of the rest of the time it was available for administrative support flights.

I had a requirement to go to Hamilton Air Force Base, California, to give a talk, and I really looked forward to making the trip in the B-17. As I climbed up through the radio compartment and the bomb bay into the cockpit, it was like coming home. Everything seemed to fit, somehow, and although it had been nearly 15 years since I had been inside a B-17 it all came back to me with a rush. It was a real thrill to start up the engines and taxi out. From that point on I was due for a rude shock.

My B-17 seemed so underpowered. It labored so hard and so long to build up enough speed to stagger into the air. Even after the airplane was cleaned up, the rate of climb was painfully slow. It seemed heavy and sluggish to handle, not at all like the light, responsive bird I remembered, and it took forever to get anywhere. It was noisy and bumpy and rough. I made a lousy landing when we reached Hamilton.

I suppose a man can never step back into the past and find things the way he remembers them. One thousand hours of flying B-47s had altered my sense of values. The B-17 hadn't changed. It was a product of its age and had remained frozen in time while that state of the art had passed by. It was a World War II relic in the jet age. I felt somehow cheated.

Now that I am retired, after 35 years of service and 11,000 hours of pilot time, I can look back on many airplanes I have flown and loved. Time has broadened my perspective, and each aircraft takes its place in my memories in its proper time frame. From my vantage point, each bird is a classic in its own time. Comparison of airplanes of different time frames is as impossible and as unnecessary as trying to compare the friends of each era. To me, the tremendous differences between the PT-3, the first airplane I ever flew, and the F-4, in which I flew my last combat mission in Vietnam, do not seem in the least incongruous.

When I think now of the B-17, it is not the old clunker I flew from Davis-Monthan to Hamilton that I remember. My B-17 is the beautiful bird that we lived with in the steaming jungle of the South Pacific. It is the B-17 that took us into combat so many times and brought us safely home. The B-17 I remember was in its day truly the Queen of the Skies.

LT. GEN. JAMES V. EDMUNDSON, USAF (Ret.), is a command pilot with over 10,000 flying hours. During World War II he flew 107 combat missions and was credited with sinking one of the first Japanese submarines in the war. During the Korean War he flew 32 combat missions. From 1970 until his retirement, he was Deputy Commander-in-Chief, U.S. Readiness Command, MacDill AFB, Florida. Pilot Edmundson & Copilot Jack Lee in 1942. The submarine on the aircraft represents the one they sank off Hawaii.

B-24 Liberator

CARL H. FRITSCHE

THE four-engined B-24 Liberator of World War II was a "truck." It looked like a truck, it hauled a big load like a truck, and it flew like a truck. But trucks were needed at that time of the war, and over 18,000 of the B-24s were built. I am proud to say that I was a "truck driver" and that I flew the B-24 over the world's highest mountains and crossed some of its seas at 50 feet above the waves. It was a good plane for its time in history, but it was not the shapely, romantic beauty some of its contemporaries were. In the air it was like a fat lady doing a ballet—I was always amazed at how beautiful it looked in spite of its bulk as it turned and circled trying its best to be the star of the show. It was never a star. It was an excellent truck.

At Riverside, California, during the winter of 1943–1944, the newspapers reported a tragic B-24 accident. The plane had crashed into an Army barracks and had caused a heavy loss of life. Not too far from Riverside was March Air Force Base. My new crew remarked about the accident as I was leading them out to the ramp for their first look at a B-24. My flight engineer and I were the only two trained on the B-24. Of my total of 325 flying hours, 105 were accumulated in learning how to fly the B-24 at Tarrant Field, Ft. Worth, Texas. My copilot was just out of flying school and had never flown a multiengined airplane. As we made our ground inspection, he was impressed by the 110-foot long wing spread, the 67-foot long fuselage, and the four R-1830-65 Pratt & Whitney engines. I went to the right side of the plane, pulled the small hydraulic lever, and the bomb-bay doors rolled up so that we could climb to the flight deck. My navigator and bombardier crawled under the flight deck up to the nose of the craft for an inspection of their stations and then returned to the flight deck about the same time I had completed my 21 items on the preflight list. Because my engineer was well trained, we had few problems with our checklist, but I knew that my new copilot was

B-24 Liberator in flight.

overwhelmed with all the instruments and levers. After the four gunners, radioman, bombardier, and navigator had crowded on the flight deck, my engineer started the small gasoline auxiliary power "put-put" unit located under the flight deck. He left the unit running and took his position between the pilot's and copilot's seats so that we could begin the starting of the engines.

Because the plane's hydraulic system was operated from a pump located on number 3 engine, we were trained to start that engine first, followed by number 4, number 2, and number 1. The ground crew fire guard moved from engine to engine with a hand-held CO_2 extinguisher during the starting procedure. I told my copilot to turn the ignition switches to "both on," and then turn each electric fuel booster pump on as each engine was started. The fuel pressure gauge would register approximately 8 pounds pressure before each engine was primed with the electric priming switch. I had set all four throttles to ⅓-open position and then energized the number 3 engine. After about 12 seconds of energizing the engine, I flipped the same little switch to the "mesh" position and the engine turned over quickly and started. I moved the mix control to the "auto lean" position and made certain the oil pressure came up to normal within 30 seconds. After I had throttled the engine to about 1,000 rpm, I turned off the booster pump for that particular engine and started the remaining engines. As the engines idled, I checked the flight indicator for rapid erection. Vacuum pumps for these instruments were located on number 1 and number 2 engines, so I switched the selector valve to each engine to make sure that the pressure was 4–4½ lbs at 1,000 rpm. Quickly I scanned the instrument panel checking the oil pressure, oil temperature, engine-head temperature, fuel pressure, carburetor air temperature, free-air pressure, tachometers, manifold pressure, hydraulic pressures, magnetic compass, landing gear warning light, and finally, clock. I called the tower for the altimeter setting and was pleased to find that my altimeter registered the field elevation. I released the hydraulic brakes and started to taxi out for takeoff.

The B-24 was an easy plane to taxi. By using the outboard engines and the hydraulic foot brakes I could turn the plane with ease. The tricycle landing gear supported the plane in a level position, giving me an excellent view of its left side. There was a blind spot where the nose turret blocked the view, but my copilot had good visibility on his side of the plane, so it was his duty to warn me of obstacles. As I grew more experienced with the B-24, I found that I could taxi the plane without excessive use of the brakes. We didn't have to fishtail the plane as we taxied, so on some combat fields where a turnaround was required after the landing roll, we taxied the plane at 40–50 mph.

About 30 planes were ready for takeoff that morning, and my B-24 was the fourth in line. Near the runway we turned our planes 45° to the taxi ramp for engine run-up. I put the mixture control in "auto rich" position. I then ran the props to a full "low" position to check for maximum rpm drop, then back to high rpm for maximum rpm gain, and then returned the turbos to the "off" position. I reduced the throttles to 1,200 rpm and returned the mix to "auto lean." Each engine was then checked in the following order: 4, 3, 2, and 1. I set the mix for the number 4 engine to "auto rich" and opened the throttle to 2,000 rpm. I had my copilot check the mags. He turned to "left mag" and back to "both," then he turned to "right mag" and back to "both" so that we could check the rpm drop and also see the roughness of the engine nacelle

vibration as a visual check of the ignition operation. After checking all the mags, I then advanced the throttle to full "open" position and checked the engine instruments for proper readings. I advanced the turbo and set it carefully to 47 inches and checked the rpm at 2,700. Slowly I reduced the number 4 engine throttle to 1,200 rpm and the mix to "auto lean" and repeated, in sequence, the run-up of the other three engines. My directional gyro was set to correspond to the magnetic compass, the wing flaps were extended to 20° down, and I signaled my engineer to turn on all four generators and turn off the gasoline auxiliary "put-put" power unit. Quickly I moved the gang switch to high rpm for the props and saw that the four green lights came on. I set my trim tabs 3° right rudder, 0° aileron, and 0° elevator. While I checked my surface controls, I told my copilot to place the mix controls into the "auto rich" position and directed my engineer to turn off the electric auxiliary hydraulic pump, close the bomb doors and hatches, and make sure the other crew members were seated on the flight deck in a safe position. All the pilots finished their checklists and lined up ready to roll with the tower's permission.

The first B-24 started down the runway for takeoff, then the second started before the first was in the air. The third B-24 moved out, and then it was my turn. As I pushed the four throttles open to increase speed, I could see the explosions and black clouds of smoke ahead of me where the first two B-24s had crashed on takeoff. The third B-24 was off the ground and in the black smoke. I lifted the nosewheel at about 70

The B-24 looked like a truck, hauled a big load like a truck, and flew like a truck.

mph and at about 130 mph was off the ground and burrowing through the black smoke and fire. Seconds later I was out of the smoke and climbing with the landing gear swinging up into the wheel wells. I reduced the manifold pressure from 49 inches to 45 inches and had my copilot reduce the prop rpm from 2,700 to 2,550 and move the props into synchronization. At 800 feet above the terrain I reduced the flaps to 5° for stability and continued to climb.

With two planes down and 20 men lost, the tower called us and told us the field was closed for investigation and for us to come back and land. I was having problems, too. The main gear would swing up but the nosewheel of the tricycle landing gear was stuck crossways in the wheel well and would not go up or down. My crew was getting initiated to the B-24, and they didn't like what they saw. The other B-24 in the air circled and landed while I tried every trick I knew to get my gear either up or down.

Climbing to 4,000 feet, I snapped my fuel booster pumps off and started to cruise over the field at about 200 mph. I reduced the manifold pressure to 30 inches and the rpm to 2,000. With the flaps up I made a quick check: mixture control in "auto lean" position, oil temperature less than 75° C redline, oil pressure 80 psi, cylinder head temperature well below the 232° C maximum, fuel pressure 15 psi, and cowl flaps closed. The plane was in good shape, with the exception of the nosewheel. I reported my problem to the tower and then told my copilot to fly it straight and level while I went down for a look.

My engineer and I crawled under the flight deck and up to the nosewheel, fighting a tornadolike wind coming in the open wheel-well door. No amount of prying would turn it, as it was wedged at a 90° angle in the door. When I returned to the pilot's seat there was a suggestion from the tower that we might have to go over the Pacific and jump. I asked for another suggestion. After consultation they told me to try a crash landing at San Bernardino repair depot, which had been alerted to my problem. Flying over San Bernardino I could see the fire wagons and "meat" wagons lined up by the runway and a crowd of people out to watch the landing. My crew wasn't too happy about their first B-24 flight. I told them I would make a normal landing but that the main gear touching the runway was their signal to run to the tail of the plane, lie down, and hang on. On the downwind leg I slowed the plane to an airspeed of 155 and put down the main gear. The rpm was raised to 2,550 and the flaps lowered to 20°. We went through the rest of the checklist and on the final approach lowered the flaps to 40° for landing. The plane touched down at about 110 airspeed and all the crew, including the copilot, ran to the rear. As I fought to hold the nose of the plane off the runway, I could hear the fire sirens screeching from the many trucks following me down the landing strip. I had slowed to about 40 mph before the wings of the plane completely lost "lift" and the plane tilted forward allowing the partially retracted nosewheel to strike the runway and skid along sideways. The B-24 then whipped to the right. I slammed left brake, then right, and we slid to a stop with very little damage.

The Air Force's answer to the B-24 accidents came in the form of a tough little captain with a "fruit salad" on his chest. His ramrod straight posture and confidence indicated that he had the world by the tail and wasn't going to let it go. In no uncertain terms he told us that the B-24 was an excellent plane but that the pilot had to fly it. The three accidents, he said, were all caused by pilot error. Investigation had proved that the pilot who had crashed into the army barracks had become confused at night and had thought the main street of the army camp was the runway. He had landed on the street killing the crew and others in the camp. The two planes had crashed on takeoff because the pilots were not used to flying with 91 octane gas. They had trained with 100 octane gas, so instead of ramming the throttles through the instrument panel when they saw they were in trouble the pilots just sat there and took their crews to their death. The number 3 aircraft and I had both gotten off the ground with plenty of runway to spare so we had no cause for alarm. We had trained in Texas where we were instructed on both types of gasoline.

Later the captain complimented me on the way I had landed my damaged plane. He also assigned me to the lead ship in about a 100-plane formation over the city of Los Angeles. Fighter pilots from area fields were to make mock passes at us as we flew over the city. With the captain in the right seat, me in the left, and that long "train" of planes out behind, I felt as safe as though I was in my mother's cradle at home.

As training continued, our confidence in the B-24 increased. The tower called us one day and told us to scatter! A ferry pilot had run out of gas over the field. I was at 8,000 feet when I saw this new B-24, with all four engines feathered, pass me on his way down to the field. My copilot said, "There goes another dead man!" After we were cleared to land I went over to see the "wreckage." The pilot had made a perfect belly landing with no power. I didn't think it was possible to land with so little damage to the belly of the craft. The ground crew jacked the plane up; the wheels were pumped down; and a tow motor pulled it away for repairs.

With our training complete, crews were given brand new B-24Js, and on 7 June 1944, we left California and headed east. I had 513 flying hours—293 of that in B-24s. In addition I had about 53 hours Link trainer or "hood" time. Because none of the pilots of the transit crews had ever been in actual instrument weather, we were required to fly CAVU (clear air, visibility unlimited). We flew under an overcast to the islands of the Azores, over the top, until we found CAVU near the coast of Africa, and from Africa to India, it was CAVU all the way. After assignment delays in Karachi, it was on 29 July 1944 that about 10 new B-24s rolled to a stop on the runway at Dacca, India. We had been assigned to the 492nd Bomb Squadron, 7th Bomb Group, of the 10th AF.

The 7th Bomb Group had temporarily been ordered to aid the 14th AF in China by supplying gasoline carried in bomb-bay tanks of combat B-24s. Single planes flew across 500 miles of enemy territory. It was an emergency measure and the enemy planes, weather, and mountains made it dangerous. The Hump, as it was called, was littered with more than 900 crashed planes—most downed by weather. As newly trained bomber pilots, most of us had never made an actual instrument let down, nor had we ever been in a storm cloud. On 14 August 1944 I made my first trip to China as a copilot so I could learn the route. The Hump was "asleep," and we just had a few fair-weather clouds to pass. On the next flight I took my own crew, and when I approached the Burma foothills I saw a solid line of black thunderheads reaching thousands of feet into the air. My last time in a Link trainer had been in April, so I had to make a couple of circles to build up my courage. I knew I couldn't stay there forever, so I headed straight into the boiling mass. Somehow I got

through and when I came out on the other side, I saw a buddy of mine, on his way back in another 24, circling to get up his courage. He radioed, "If you can make it then I can too!" The Hump made you an instrument pilot or a casualty.

B-24 at Thurleigh, England, December 5, 1942.

The B-24 was an excellent instrument ship. I think this was partly due to its weight of 36,000 pounds empty and 65,000 pounds loaded. Some planes were even loaded up over 70,000 pounds. In fact, it was the heavily loaded takeoff and landing that was the grim reaper rather than the difficult weather on the Hump. Most of the pilots soon learned that the B-24 was just an overgrown Link trainer with a built-in fatality factor if they made a mistake. The controls of the plane were hard to move, reducing the pilot's chance of overcontrolling in the clouds—even if his knees were shaking.

To take off from a hot runway in India with a heavily loaded B-24 was always a challenge. The bamboo trees at the end of the 6,000-foot runway were too close, and many a B-24 had pinched bamboo limbs into the wheel wells and carried them flapping in the breeze all the way to China. If there was an accident with a gasoline-loaded plane on takeoff or landing, there never were any survivors. Once the plane was in the air you could parachute out if you got into trouble. I talked to two crews that did parachute out of their B-24s. One crew walked into Kunming and the other parachuted into the Burma jungle and came back to India by elephant. Both crews agreed that the best way to leave a 24 was to dive out the bomb bays. One pilot told me that the worst ordeal was not bailing out of the plane but eating roast monkey with the natives in Burma. He said, "As hungry as I was, there was just no way that I could eat those little hands and feet!"

Icing was always a serious problem on the Hump. Deicing boots had been removed from all our combat planes because most of the boots had small flak holes in them. Without the boots the pilot's only defense was to get out of the icing layer. You could do this in an overcast but not in the violence of a Hump storm. On one flight I had a two-inch layer of ice all around the pilot's windows and my flight instruments froze and tumbled. The ice must have bridged the pitot tube because the heater did no good. I let the autopilot have it and we bounced around in the terrible up and down drafts for about an hour before we got out. We had unloaded our gas in China so the lighter weight did help the plane carry the great load of ice. When the ice started to melt in the warm air of India, I chipped a hole big enough to look out at the engine nacelles and wings. I was amazed that the B-24 would stay in the air with so much ice welded to it. Once the ice melted, the flight instruments erected and the two vacuum pumps worked normally. After I landed, I crawled out the upper hatch and checked the pitot tube. It was so hot you couldn't touch it. By the time a few of the B-24s with thermal deicers came into the theater we were off the Hump flights and didn't get to test them.

The 492nd and the 493rd Bomb Squadrons each had about 100 flying officers. With four officers to a crew (plus six enlisted men), each squadron usually had 18 to 20 combat-armed B-24s on the Hump gas haul each day. Most of the pilots made 25 to 30 round trips to China with gas before the units were returned to bombardment work.

Several crews from the 492nd and 493rd were sent to China to haul gas and help evacuate the eastern air bases. We not only had to fly on instruments; we also had "hitch-hikers." The Flying Tigers would bring their fighter planes in on us for a free, no-think ride down through the overcast. I would turn on my wing lights and these jockeys would grab hold of my hip pockets—one behind each wing and sometimes one above or below for a "hen and chickens" letdown through several thousand feet of solid overcast. At Suichuan, China, we had to make two 180s on letdown with the fighters because of the high mountains. The B-24 could hold a good rate of descent and make standard turns easily. But it was not a fun way to fly. The fighters were usually very low on gas and had to get down as fast as they could.

I was always concerned with the weight and balance of the plane, especially when we were hauling gas to the eastern China bases. The four big bomb-bay gas tanks were heavy and caused problems getting off the ground. In addition the ground crews would back a truck up to the waist windows and dump in a large quantity of materials.

At Luliang, China, which has an altitude of 6,000 feet, I complained bitterly about this practice. But the situation in the East was critical, so I was given a pat on the shoulder and told to get flying. My plane was already overloaded when I started to taxi out, so when I was flagged down and six fighter pilots climbed aboard I was furious. My gunners had to go to the rear of the plane, causing the plane's tail skid to drag the ground like a ruptured goose. The fighter pilots, a "gung ho" gang with a lot of energy and chatter, were just in from the States to ferry planes back from the eastern China bases. The flight deck was crawling with people.

Luliang's gravel runway was 10,000 feet long and built high in the mountains. The hundreds of Chinese who maintained the runway had a custom of running across as a plane took off so that when it passed close behind them, it would cut off the evil spirits they believed followed them. The closer the plane came to them the more evil spirits were cut off. From a standing start I rammed the throttles forward, released the brakes, and started to roll. The Chinese saw us coming and huge numbers started running. Several men with water buffalo and carts plodded across and made it just as number 4 prop passed over them. The fighter pilots had never seen any thing like this, so they were having the time of their lives.

I wasn't laughing! We were down the field and not near the speed we should have been. The fighter pilots kept laughing and shouted, "Pull'er off into a good chandelle!" As we closed in on the end of the runway I took a quick look over my shoulder. The chatter had stopped and all I could see was a bunch of pale-faced pilots with eyes about twice the size they ought to be. My engineer kicked the gear handle when we ran off the 10,000-foot runway. As the gear started up, I could feel the plane settle off the end of the runway and into a ravine down the mountain. I had dropped below the level of the runway and the tower kept calling to ask if I was in trouble. Ever so carefully I followed the ravine until I felt secure enough to try to climb. When we were finally out of danger, the fighter pilots were no longer jovial. One of them shook my hand and said, "They ought to give you boys the Distinguished Flying Cross every time you take off in one of these SOBs!"

Later in the year when I flew bombing missions, it was the ground engineering officer's duty to figure the weight and balance of the plane. With bombs loaded according to the design of the plane, getting off the ground was much easier. When the plane was used for a "moving van," the ground crews filled it full without regard for the balance.

When the whiskey ration came in the first of the month, I flew from China to Calcutta, India, to pick it up in my B-24. My hometown is Westerville, Ohio, the home of the Anti-Saloon League and the "Dry Capital Of The World." Speakers and literature were sent all over the world from Westerville for the "dry" cause. The 18th Amendment to the U.S. Constitution was engineered from Westerville. I knew the leaders of the dry movement and had taken the dry pledge from Dr. Howard Hyde Russell himself. In China I was told that a lot of whiskey was being lost on the black market so they were giving me—the "Drytowner"—the booze run. Several times my B-24 was piled full of cartons of whiskey and, with all gun turrets manned, I skimmed across 500 miles of enemy territory so that the Flying Tigers could have a "happy hour." I never lost a bottle nor had one explode from too high an altitude.

When those of us who had served with the 14th AF in China returned to India, we found that the 492nd Squadron had moved from Dacca, India, to a base called Madhaiganj near Asansol. Living conditions were good at our new base and the pilots breathed a sigh of relief when they saw that there were no trees hugging the end of the runway.

(Above) The B-24 was considered an "ugly duckling"; the narrow, high-speed Davis wing was the only part critics thought beautiful. (Below) B-24 cockpit with its many "confusing" instruments.

From this new base we flew in a 40-plane formation to bomb from high level the rail yards at Mandalay, Burma. Most of our missions from this base were flown at cruising speeds of about 225 mph, and they lasted from 7 to about 18 hours. By adding the two bomb-bay tanks again and filling the rear bays with bombs, the B-24 had a range of about 3,000 miles. Strikes were made from India against the shipping and the docks at Bangkok, Thailand.

To fly formation for several hours in a B-24 required endurance. The controls took so much strength to move that you didn't have to worry about getting to sleep after a long mission. At the close of my tour of duty I did get to fly on two missions the model of the 24 that had the hydraulic booster controls. It was extremely easy to fly.

Although the B-24 carried ten .50 caliber machine guns and could put up a good fight, it could be shot down if you attended the right social gathering. It didn't take a 24 pilot long to discover that he was riding a ''slow horse'' and that his best insurance was to stay in formation. The J model of the 24 had twin-gun nose, top, and tail hydraulic turrets plus the Sperry ball turret and two waist flexible guns of the same .50 caliber. The flight engineer operated the top turret and the four gunners operated the rest. Most of the gun turrets were equipped with electric flight suits to keep the gunners comfortable at high altitudes. These thin suits worked well in the plane but they were extremely poor protection if you had to bail out onto the high snow-covered mountains. Very few of our flight deck heaters worked satisfactorily, so most of the crews wore heavy clothing and forgot the turret suits.

Enemy fighter planes had been thinned down in Burma by March 1945. Small B-24 formations, in combinations of three, were sent against targets. Ack-ack fire was still extremely heavy over most targets. In a large formation you never really knew who they were shooting at, but in a small formation you got the full concentration of fire in one direction. Over the rail yards of a large city we might have six three-plane formations coming in on the target from different directions and at proper intervals. My navigator would get us to the target I.P. (initial point) and on the proper heading. I would put the plane on autopilot and then my bombardier would guide the plane with the combination autopilot and the Norden bomb sight until ''bombs away.'' At that point I would snap off the autopilot and try evasive action with the plane until we got out of the range of the ack-ack.

My copilot was a Golden Gloves boxing champion—tough and intelligent—with very little use for religion. I had attended a small country community church. My bombardier was a devout Roman Catholic, and my navigator was a cantor in the Syrian Orthodox Church. We had some interesting conversations. When Rangoon was still a very ''hot'' target, I led one of the three-plane formations over that city. The navigator shouted, ''We're picking up heavy ack-ack!'' Just then the sky was black with explosions. In awe I exclaimed, ''Oh my God!'' The bombardier, who was still on the flight deck, dropped to his knees with his rosary in his hand. The blood drained out of my copilot's face as explosions bracketed the plane. In panic he looked around the flight deck and saw the bombardier on his knees with the rosary. In a pleading voice he said, ''Leonard, you better give those beads hell! Things look terrible up here!'' In spite of our great danger, all three of us laughed almost hysterically, for we knew that a reluctant believer had just uttered his first prayer.

Our first effort at low-level bombing of bridges with B-24s ended in disaster. In single file, six planes were flying down a narrow Burma mountain valley toward a large railroad bridge. We were to fly over the bridge at 50–100 feet and let the bombardier "guess" where to toggle out the bombs. I was flying the second plane and I noticed that beyond the bridge the railroad made a sharp bend around a cliff. As low as we were, I didn't think a B-24 could make that turn. We were flying into a box canyon! I grabbed the radio mike and warned everyone to pull up. The first plane kept right on going and crashed into the cliff. All the other planes followed me in a frantic climb to get over the mountains. My navigator, who was looking out the nose window and watching the rocks go by kept shouting, "Pull 'er up! We're going to crash!" I reached to the left side of the pilot's seat and grabbed the bomb salvo lever. The five tons of bombs dropped and the plane went up like an elevator, dusting off the top of the mountain as we flew by.

Back at our home base a practice bridge was built. The abutments were made of 50-gallon oil drums. A single-bomb release button was put on the pilot's control wheel. Bombardiers were not carried on the B-24s for these practice missions. Each pilot was given 12 sand-filled bombs to practice his technique on the bridge. Because the nose of the plane obstructed the view on a low-level flight, we were forced to use a diving approach to the target. We flew in a circle at an altitude of 500–1,000 feet and then dived the plane at a speed of about 300 mph toward the bridge. The pilot pulled out of his gradual dive at 50–100 feet above the bridge and pressed the special bomb release button on the control column. It was all guesswork, for there was no bombsight; the pilot dropped the bomb where he thought it might be effective. I noticed a row of rivets in front of my seat extending out across the nose of the plane. This was my bombsight. As that row of rivets seemed to scoop over the bridge abutment, I released the bomb. In 12 runs I got 11 bombs right on the target, winning for my flight engineer a case of beer from the ground crew. Other pilots had similar success. With delayed-action 500-pound bombs and the diving attack with the B-24, the railroad bridges of Burma fell with astounding success.

We flew overwater flights 12–18 hours long against targets on the Malay Peninsula. At 50 feet above the water we would fly down the Bay of Bengal, cross the Andaman Sea, and bomb the railroad bridges in single-plane attacks. On heavily defended, multispan bridges, with Allied prisoners of war forced to camp around the land abutments, we used a decoy plane to draw ack-ack fire while six B-24s flew up the river and dropped bombs on the abutments built in the water. We used this method on two missions, and I flew the decoy on both.

Although our decoy 24s had self-sealing wing tanks, the bomb-bay tanks were extremely vulnerable to any kind of enemy action. If we had not needed the tanks to fly back home, we could have dropped them out the bomb-bay doors. As it was, we dodged flak for 30 minutes before diving for the Andaman Sea. Halfway back to India there was usually a PBY flying boat cruising around to pick up any of the crews in trouble.

Most crews avoided ditching a B-24. Most of us felt it was much safer to dump the life rafts out and have a few crew members try to parachute close to the raft. We learned this lesson after flying search missions over water. The B-24 apparently broke apart rapidly (just aft of the bomb bay) upon ditching and sank before crew members could get out. On the search missions I flew, only oil slicks were found.

The four Pratt & Whitney engines were extremely reliable, but even if only three engines were going, the B-24 flew well (but slower). I have flown alongside pilots who had to fly all the way home from a bombing mission on three engines—a distance of 1,000 miles. During the evacuation of the air bases in eastern China I saw B-24s take off on three engines and fly to safety. I never witnessed anyone who flew very far on two engines. Some landings were made that way, but they were few. In training I flew a 24 on one engine to see what happened. It had a pretty fast rate of descent. Even empty, with no gun turrets, you were on your way down if you tried one-engine operation.

The B-24 had a definite vibration when it stalled, but it recovered easily with the addition of power. With rudders used properly, the plane would fall straight down with no tendency to drop a wing even though one prop might be feathered. I never put the plane into a full spin, but in training we did try recovery from ¼- to ½- turn spins. The plane would recover in a very tight spiral which could lead to trouble if the pilot was not able to recognize a high-speed stall. In spite of the increased speed, the pilot still had to push the control column forward to recover. On the landing approach, the plane would stall out gently, allowing the pilot to "grease" the plane down onto the runway.

The plane was considered an "ugly duckling" in design; the narrow, high-speed Davis wing was the only part critics thought beautiful. Some pilots remarked that the designers simply hung a bucket on the Davis wing. Considering the designs of foreign planes of the same era, I never felt the B-24 designers had to hang their heads in shame. The Davis wing was designed with Fowler flaps that slid back and down from the trailing edge to give greater area for better landing stability at lower speeds. Even though designers considered the wing beautiful, the pilots knew it was designed to be "alive," because it would really flap when we bounced around inside the Hump thunderstorms.

Because the B-24 was not a pressurized plane, it was necessary for all crew members to wear face-type oxygen masks. When we ran out of oxygen in China I flew the lower Hump twice without oxygen. I did notice my depth perception was off when I started to land, and thus I had a tendency to drag the plane in and feel for the ground.

After 50 missions in the CBI my crew was given R & R, but I was kept on in the squadron to fly new crews on their first bombing mission. When I had completed 9 more missions I was retired and given the job of flight-testing planes and flying damaged planes from our base at Asansol to the depot at Bangalore, India, for repair or junk.

What do I think of the B-24? Let me answer with one more story. When Suichuan (China) air base was under daily attack, I led some P-51s into that base at night with my B-24 loaded with gas. With no radio contact the tower gave me the green light to land—even though some of the runway lights had been bombed out in a recent raid. The 51s landed and then I lined up on what lights I could see through the mist and light rain. With a heavy load and on a bad night I touched down between the first two lights at about 150 mph and was still rolling about 80 mph when I saw the end of the runway. I knew I wasn't going to make it. I also knew that at the end of the runway was a *big* drop-off. So I turned the plane toward a bomb hole and a pile of dirt and we plowed to a stop. The B-24 stood on its nose over an enbankment. The miracle of the whole thing was that the Chinese had just the day before gathered that big pile of loose dirt dug from trenches they were making to defend the field. At any other time it wouldn't have been there. If the dirt hadn't been loose, the plane probably would have exploded, as most gas carriers did on impact. We pumped the gas to the P-51s and they took off at dawn. Because there wasn't a bulldozer for thousands of miles around, I figured my crew and I had a 500-mile walk. Early the next morning hundreds of Chinese came to the runway, each carrying a small grapevine. They wound the vines into a rope, tied it to my B-24, and dragged the plane back to the runway. The plane shook badly as I started down the runway, but as I passed that long line of Chinese they gave me the "thumbs-up" salute and shouted "Ding Hao" (Chinese for OK). And when I saw the old B-24 at the Air Force Museum I gave it a very respectful thumbs-up salute and said "Ding Hao"—it really was OK!

CARL H. FRITSCHE was a pilot on a B-24 in the C.B.I. He returned to Ohio State Univeristy and received a degree in agriculture in 1948. He operated a large poultry hatchery until 1965 and then transferred to the home-building and leasing business. He has a minor in journalism and as a hobby writes children's plays for his wife, who is a teacher.

B-25 bomber on one of its many missions, Barteaux, North Africa, 1943.

B-25 Mitchell

KEITH R. MATZINGER

HOW do you identify an ex-B-25 pilot? Easy: if he doesn't have a hearing aid, he probably needs one.

The combination of the pilot's seat being close to the propeller tips and the individual exhaust stacks made the B-25 one of the noisiest aircraft ever built. But the structural integrity of the pre-World War II design more than made up for the noise.

When the first operational B-25 arrived at Headquarters Squadron of the 17th Bomb. Group (M) at McChord Field early in 1941, it created quite a stir. The 17th, not long out of Northrop A-17As, was then equipped with the comfortable, fast Douglas B-23s. The transition from that docile plane with conventional landing gear to the 25 was quite an experience. (Gen. David Jones, in the late 1970s Chief of the Air Force, was among the group.)

The landings were particularly eventful, and it was a tribute to the forgiving nature of the rugged beast that things went as smoothly as they did. There were nose-wheel landings, tail-dragging landings, too-fast landings, and sickeningly slow landings. The atrocious screeching, throw-you-through-the-windshield brakes (early discs) did little for the nerves of the crew who longed for the cozy, quiet, and spacious cabin of the B-23. Radio operators in particular were disenchanted with the change as they moved from the warm front cockpit to the drafty, cold waist compartment. Most felt they had been demoted.

Pilots who have never flown a B-25 cannot realize the amazing flexibility of this bird. Nothing shows that flexibility better than the legendary Colonel Doolittle leading men of the 17th Group off the deck of the carrier *Hornet* in 1942 to bomb Japan. Few people realize that the original plan called for them to land back on the *Hornet!* The fabulous Doolittle (not exactly a youngster then) characteristically was the first to take off, with less than 400 feet of deck available. Films show that he handled this smoothly and efficiently. Well, for a guy who flew the Gee-Bee maybe it was easy.

During World War II a young pilot in Corsica won a lot of money betting that he could pull a chandelle on takeoff at the end of 5,000-foot runway in a 25. His technique looked daring but actually was relatively easy for someone with the reactions and coordination of a 22-year old.

His method was to pull the control column back into his lap as soon as the throttles were forward. This caused the nose to rise at a sickening angle, and the 25 was ready to fly in just a few hundred feet. He would pull the landing gear just as it was ready to lift, then immediately shove the nose down to stay a few feet off the ground. At this point our young hot dog would dump the flaps, which required raising the nose to offset the sink, then reduce the power to 35 Hgs and 2,500 rpm, close the cowl flaps just as he reached the end of the runway at 175 mph indicated, and—*whammo*—he would rack it up into a steep climbing 180, passing the tower at 1,500 feet.

Actually, all he really did was what Colonel Doolittle had done off the *Hornet* two years earlier, but with a few embellishments.

The arguments still rage among old B-25 pilots over pulling it off the ground or running till the end of the runway on takeoff. The bad booze consumed over that discussion would float the *Hornet*, but few will argue over the amazing flight characteristics of the 25 or its basic structural strength.

One day over the Anzio beachhead, a wing man, flying on a rookie flight leader, slipped his engines into high supercharger ratio (in

B-25 cockpit.

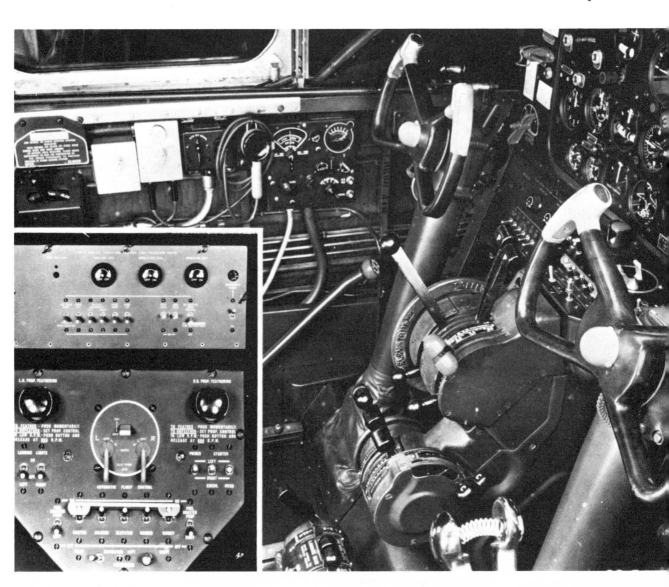

The B-25-H with 75 mm cannon.

defiance of operating rules) because he felt the leader might peel off and dive too fast after the bombs were dropped. The wing man decided he would need all the power available to stay in close for protection against the FW-190s that were circling the beachhead, and that is exactly what happened. In the ensuing wild dive, the wing man ran the manifold pressure past the end of the gauges (55 Hgs) and later estimated he was doing well over 400 mph as they went from 12,000 feet to the deck in 6 miles (VNE was 340 mph). As a matter of interest, he was the only one in the formation who stayed with the leader and came out with only a few flak holes. Three others were shot down, and heavy damage was inflicted on the rest.

A B-25 was fairly easy to fly without a copilot except for raising and lowering the landing gear. That necessitated diving below the level of the instrument panel to reach the gear control on the floor. In fact, the H models, with the 75 mm cannon, had only one set of controls, and the cannoneer-navigator or flight engineer rode in the right seat.

The G and H models with the cannon were, to say the least, an unusual experience when they were first sent to Columbia, South Carolina, to train crews. The cannon was installed in what had been the tunnel to the bombardier's compartment, with the breech extending into the navigator's compartment. The cannoneer-navigator (most were formerly bombardier-navigators) was the loader, and he stood in an almost windowless compartment where the more than 30-pound shells hung in clip racks on the wall.

It was no fun, in a bouncing airplane, to grab a shell off the wall, slam it into the breech, then jump back to await the firing by the pilot while holding onto a handle on the wall, the only support. When the gun was fired, the breech opened, smoke and dirt flew back into the compartment, and the heavy brass shell case ejected against a piece of plywood, thence to roll around on the floor. The cannoneer was soon ankle deep in shell cases. It took a strong stomach to cope with being down in that hole, with no outside reference, while the exuberant young pilots threw the airplane around at tree-top level.

Nightly, the cannoneer-navigators sat in the bar wishing they had been sent to B-17s. They were probably the only commissioned cannon loaders in the history of the U.S. Army.

The more venturesome student pilots had a picnic with the G and H models, as buzzing was not only legal, it was part of the program. All practice missions, even cross-country, were flown at tree-top level, and firing that cannon was great sport.

Early in 1944 it was determined that the low-level cannon missions in Europe were not practical because of the relatively low speed of the aircraft in face of intense ground fire, so the cannon ships were sent off to the Pacific and the Orient where their success, particularly against shipping, was legendary.

The durability of the 25 is well exemplified by one C model that went from North Africa to Sicily to Italy to Corsica with the 321st Group. By 1945 this particular ship had flown more than 300 missions and had been bellied-in four or five times. The bottom of the fuselage resembled the surface of the moon. Painted a desert tan for camouflage, this old bird had been cared for by a crew chief with a macabre sense of humor. Each time he patched a flak hole, he painted the patch with bright yellow zinc chromate. By 1944, the ship had been named *Patches,* and its venerable hide carried over 400 bright yellow blotches. By then it had been bent so many times that it flew with 8° of left aileron trim and 6° of right rudder.

Thus trimmed, *Patches* flew with a pronounced bias. Finally, the bias became so severe that the old bird had to be retired from combat because in formation the sideways flight caused everyone following to trim up on a crab. It was pretty ridiculous to see the first six aircraft in a flight flying straight and the last six flying sideways. When the war ended, old *Patches* was still merrily rumbling along sideways, carrying booze and vegetables from Sicily.

B-25 pilots were often mixed groups. Some came from B-26s, some from fighters (half of one class at Williams Field, a P-38 school, were sent to B-25s, to their chagrin), and the result was often a mixture of hot-rod types with the most conservative characters. Just after releasing his bombs over San Stefano, Italy, one of the Williams Field group, was hit by flak that severed the rudder trim-tab cable. The tab was flopping back and forth, causing violent rudder oscillation. It was obvious that the aircraft would soon shake itself to pieces. The engines were rocking severely and the instruments banged on the limits of their shock mounts. The pilot was unable to remain in formation and was left alone some 300 miles north of the base near Naples. Because the rudder trim control spun loosely, the pilot deduced the source of the trouble and instructed the tail gunner to attempt to shoot the trim off with his .50 caliber machine gun.

Unable to pivot his .50 far enough, the gunner took his .45 pistol, knocked a hole in the Plexiglas, and with his arm thrust into the slipstream fired seven shots, the last of which hit the trim-tab hinge, jamming the tab, and stopping the vibration. With both pilots holding right rudder to keep it straight, the no-longer-shaking 25 limped home safely at 140 mph through 300 miles of fighter-infested territory. The gunner was decorated for his part in the incident.

Single-engine operation was no problem unless the aircraft was extremely heavily loaded. One not-too-brilliant pilot, returning to Corsica from Rome with a nonpilot in the right seat and 15 returning restcampers scattered throughout the ship (a violation of the 8-man maximum rule), stupidly chose the half way point, 1,000 feet over the Mediterranean, to show the nonpilot how to feather an engine. Naturally, the prop stuck in the full-feathered position. Adding power to the good engine, he easily climbed to 2,000 feet and cruised on into an uneventful landing. His only problem was trying to explain to the operations officer why he had feathered it in the first place.

The B-25 was never accorded the recognition or acclaim that was

B-25 Mitchell now flying with the Ghost Squadron of the Confederate Air Force in the colors of the 15th Air Force, 1945.

B-25 MITCHELL   63

given, for example, the B-17. Some believe that was because the 25 was used in less glamorous theaters, but its contribution to the World War II effort was far greater than most people realize. The 57th Bomb Wing flew more than 60,000 sorties in the Mediterranean area.

The B-25 wasn't glamorous, nor was it beautiful; in fact, it was somewhat ungainly looking. It was noisy, drafty, and cold. Heavy on the controls, flying was work, particularly in formation for four or five hours; but it was undoubtedly used in more different fashions, in as many different places, as any other World War II aircraft.

If you want two or three hours of war stories, just ask an ex-B-25 pilot about flying. But be sure to speak loudly, clearly, and distinctly.

B-25 at the SAC Museum, Offutt AFB, Nebraska.

KEITH R. MATZINGER was a Radio Operator Gunner from 1940–1941 in A-17As, B-18s, B-23s, and B-25s. He was a B-25 pilot in the Mediterranean Theater from 1943 to 1945. Currently he is president of Kearny Mesa Toyota, San Diego, California, and is restoring a 1946 Globe GC-1A.

B-26 Invader

WILLIAM CARIGAN

THE Douglas B-26 got to me about the way Juliet got to Romeo. When we met, I dwelt in the house of the heavy bomber and so could only admire those lines from afar.

Shortly after World War II, on a day when I was Airdrome Officer at old Smyrna Army Air Field, Tennessee, Gen. Elwood "Pete" Quesada, then commander of the Tactical Air Command, landed and taxied his B-26 (then A-26) up to the ramp in front of operations. Before he disappeared with the base commander, he told me to prepare him a clearance for Langley. "Make it two hours," he instructed. Inbound, he had filed to cruise at a true air speed (TAS) of 300 mph, and he'd made 300 mph. When he got back, he found I'd made his clearance for 300 TAS, but the 600 miles to Langley against a 55 mph headwind came out at 2 hours and 27 minutes. I added 3 minutes for him to touch down. He shook off my estimated time enroute the way a star pitcher shakes off the signal of a rookie catcher. Grimly, I moved his indicated airspeed up enough to make the ETA 2 hours. The general flashed his magnificent smile, climbed the side of the bird, and departed. I didn't; I sat there at

B-26 cockpit.

operations until Air Traffic Control closed his flight plan upon his landing at Langley, exactly 2 hours later.

A few months later, reporting to the personnel office at Langley for assignment, I learned I had a choice—base supply or duty pilot in the 363rd Reconnaissance Group. I made a show of thinking it over, and two days later I was following Instructor Pilot Roger Rhodarmer's directions about which foot to put on the ladder and which hand to put in which handhold; then and there I was on my first real date with the love machine. I felt the willingness of her exciting skin, and from there things just got better.

Looking at the B-26 was like looking at a classy lassie: good–better–best as you got closer. In 1947, the 363rd had the 162nd Night Photo Squadron, and to suit the night mission the birds were painted glossy lacquer black. Gleaming, exciting black made those birds interesting to everyone on the base, though climbing up the side and onto the wing pretty much excluded the social-security set from the cockpit—which, by the way, you drop into from above, stepping down squarely into the seat, staying off the canopy.

Once in the seat and strapped in, I nearly always set the parking brakes. That item was omitted from the checklists we had in that outfit, and one day I had a ground crew man running alongside waving his arms and pleading with me to stop before something untoward occurred. Brake-setting then became a prechecklist item with me.

No airplane ever had a more convenient cockpit. Everything was within easy reach, except perhaps a stewardess. The airplane was easy to start (but when the engines were hot you could really blow a stack, so looking at the stacks was a common preflight routine on the outside walk-around) and easy to taxi (except that idling rpm would make taxiing too fast, lower rpm sometimes caused the engine to die, and a very little braking heated the drums up too much).

With those early airplanes it was a good idea to pull up the ladder before taking off, because it wouldn't come up once the airplane was in flight. (Later versions had handholds and foot holes up the left side of the nosewheel door and fuselage; earlier models had a ladder on the right side, and this was to be retracted into the fuselage by the navigator or crew chief. But the method of entering the plane was continually being modified.) Warm-up and run-up were the same as for any other reciprocating-engine airplane. On a cold day you might have to wait a minute or two for the R-2800 engines—cylinder-head and oil temperatures—to get warmed up enough for the power check. The operating-limits markings on the instruments are clear and standard. You could stay out of trouble even if you'd never seen the tech order.

Everything is so simple and easy that before you know it you are ready for that big jingle you always get when you mash the throttles forward.

But wait; I forgot to warn you about one little thing. The rear gunner's compartment, usually fitted with two or four passenger seats, for normal operation is isolated from the front end. When you call aft on interphone to see if your passengers are ready for takeoff, they should give you an affirmative. If you get a negative, there are usually too many briefing items, so it's back to the ramp for shutdown and careful rebriefing. The person (or persons) back there is totally dependent on radio and the emergency bell. He has to know how to run that interphone, how to keep up with the flight on command radio, how to reply to the pilot, and

how to behave in emergencies. Nearly every 26 driver has had one trip back to the ramp to get the procedures straight with that stupid ground-pounder back there. You're lucky when you park, shut down, go back, and open the door if you aren't greeted by a compartment full of white nylon parachute cloth. All he knew was to pull the ripcord. After that you are always careful in your briefing to see that your passenger understands. And brief *courteously,* because that guy back there is all too frequently a VIP. I've hauled a lot of stars and politicians and also tucked the lap robe carefully around some pretty WAFs and nurses.

But careful briefing and all, when you call back and ask if the passenger is ready for takeoff and get no reply, all you can imagine is the guy bouncing along the ramp behind you, interphone cord tangled around his leg.

The best A/B-26 story I know is about a passenger in the gunner's compartment whom the pilot didn't check out thoroughly on communication. The pilot took off and climbed through the overcast. As soon as he was on top, he had an engine start backfiring and smoking heavily. He turned back and advised the tower; then he saw a nice big hole which he dived through, coming out under the overcast and heading for the base. Back on the ramp, he shut down and went aft where, to his consterna-

A tight formation of B-26 Invaders do some cloud hopping as they head for their home base in Japan. It is 1951, and they have just completed a devastating, low-level sweep on enemy Communist targets with bombs, rockets, napalm, and .50 caliber fire, and now seek a welcome refuge from dodging mountaintops and other ground objects.

tion, he found that the door had been jettisoned and that his passenger was missing.

Soon base operations got a call from the passenger who requested transportation to the base. When the passenger arrived, he reported on his adventure, which began when the engine started misbehaving. He called the pilot on interphone and got no response (naturally, the pilot was on the command radio). Alone and out of communication, the passenger got nervous. Then the airplane rolled over and pointed down. Deciding that they were crashing, he jettisoned the door and bailed out. Then the airplane leveled out and flew away toward the base.

The 162nd had a couple of dual-control airplanes (except that there were no brakes on the right side). Because it is easy to overheat the brake drums, the IP (instructor pilot) usually puts the student in the right seat for the first ride. Thereafter, the apt student sits on the left. Roger Rhodarmer put me on the right, and I followed through on everything. Every minute I liked the bird better. Cleared to line up and hold on the takeoff runway, we completed the checklist and closed up the cockpit. The tower cleared us to go, and Roger mashed the throttles. That airplane sucked me back in the seat harder than I'd thought possible, and in ziptime the airspeed was at 90. He had the nosewheel slightly up and power stabilized at 52 inches of manifold pressure and 2,700 rpm.

In another few seconds the airspeed was reading 130 and the wheels were off. Roger moved the gear lever to the "up" position and held the nose down for maybe five seconds until we were above safe single-engine speed. Then he backed the power off to 42 inches and 2,500. At 160 he let the nose rise and the bird started climbing at 1,500 feet per minute. He pulled up the flaps, letting the bird assume its new attitude, set the power at 37 inches and 2,300, then let the airspeed rise to 230, still maintaining the rate of climb above 1,500 fpm. Climbing at low airspeed (160–200) keeps the nose so high that you have no forward visibility. Naturally you are soon at cruising altitude, where you let the airspeed rise to 260 or 265, reduce power to 33 inches and 2,100 rpm, and pull the mixture controls to "auto lean."

At this speed the airplane takes a good, tight, level sit in the air, and the controls respond immediately. If you want to cruise at higher speed, the best way to get it is to go above cruising altitude and build up the airspeed in descent to altitude. If, for example, you want to maintain 400 or 500 mph indicated airspeed for a bombing run, you can't do it in auto lean. And power will probably be up around 38 inches and 2,400 rpm. In the early-model airplanes you weren't supposed to open the bomb-bay doors above 240 indicated. Later models were equipped with bomb-door spoilers which changed this airspeed limitation to 425 mph. The spoilers were three heavy, flat fingers about 3 inches wide and perhaps a foot long that extended from the underfuselage just forward of the bomb bay.

Cruising at 33 inches and 2,100 and indicating 260 consumes roughly 175 gallons of high-grade aviation fuel per hour. The bird holds 925 gallons in the wing tanks and bomb-bay tank, but the bomb-bay tank is only filled to 100 gallons; high-cruise endurance is just more than 5 hours. By reducing the power to 30 inches and, say, 1,900 rpm, one can extend endurance by about 3 hours. I don't like to fly this spirited bird at airspeeds below about 230 because the controls really loosen up and feel sickeningly sloppy. In fact, at 200 the nose rises and the controls feel mushy (in reality that is still more than 60 miles above single-engine speed). I even like to fly single-engine well above 200. Bomb-bay ferry tanks, tip tanks, and external tanks extend ranges significantly.

This airplane gets its 52-inch takeoff kick from two Pratt & Whitney R-2800 engines and two-speed two-stage interval gear-driven superchargers—no turbo, so manifold pressure drops off at standard rate as you climb to altitude.

The highest altitude at which I ever flew the 26 was 27,500 feet; at that altitude operating at maximum continuous power, the nose sat quite high, and I couldn't get more than 170 on the airspeed indicator. I don't stay above 17,000 feet if I can help it. The airplane is cold, even though that glass canopy has you in the bright sunlight, and the oxygen mask bugs me. (I had my nose broken once and the mask shuts off the air on the side of my deflected septum.) I hate to be cold. One winter night at McClellan, I walked from operations to the airplane in a heavy downpour, getting totally soaked. Now, I don't have to tell any flyer how cold it is above the high Sierras in winter or how I felt a few minutes after pointing east.

So if you ever buy a 26 for sport flying, plan for fair days at altitudes below 12,000 feet. You'll get that deep suntan.

The airplane is restricted from aerobatics and I never tried any, but I did investigate a fatal after the driver tried to make a loop. Stalls are clean, never vicious, and you have to stand the airplane straight on its tail practically to get a power-on stall. There is plenty of warning, and the airplane almost recovers itself unless you are taking a nap.

Fuel management is simple because you can feed either engine from any tank. Usual management is to use up the bomb-bay tank as soon as you settle into cruise. To speed the consumption and to keep the left and right tanks in balance, I used to run both engines on that tank. In about 30 minutes the tank will empty. If you're sightseeing, you get momentary cardiac arrest when both engines quit. You're sitting there between those two noisy Pratt-Whitney R-2800s when suddenly they both quit at the same time. Because you are in normal cruise there is no problem getting back on tank-to-engine on each side. You soon realize what has happened; that silent moment will bring you back to reality. The navigator is no help about this—a crew chief is better—but someone has to sit watching the fuel-quantity and fuel-pressure gauges. When they start fluctuating, simply turn on the fuel booster pumps and switch the fuel selector valves to tank-to-engine on each side. But look away, think of something else, and there's that jarring moment of silence.

The airplane has no dirty tricks. You're almost as safe as if you were in God's pocket. But wait. One time I declared an emergency. I was instructing a student on a clear day, flying at about 10,000 feet over the Great Salt Lake. Suddenly the airplane controls came all over queer—and I mean queer. The airplane didn't respond properly to the controls. I asked the tower at Hill to clear me in because I had a strange creature on my hands. I went over everything, could find nothing. When I pointed down at the field, pulled the power back and slowed down, the controls began to respond normally. Trouble again. This stable airplane behaved as if it were a ball trying to fall off a pointed stick—weird and frightening. Another search and this time I found the landing-light switches in the extended position. When I retracted the landing lights, the trouble disappeared and the airplane was a 26 again. The tech order warns you not to extend the landing lights above 190, but doesn't say why. Now I know why. With the student doing things and me doing things, I never

B-26 Invader in flight.

figured how the lights got extended. But I repeat: Don't extend landing lights at airspeeds above 190.

The chief problem with engine failure is keeping airspeed above 140 mph so that directional control can be maintained. On takeoff, the bird passes through that speed very rapidly and the problem is largely academic. Fortunately, engine failure is very infrequent. But if you ever lose two engines, there will be no time for pondering through the tech order. That's a time for psalms and prayer and a long runway right under you.

Emergencies are rare, but one fine day I lost an engine while in the landing pattern. I was in the right seat checking out a pilot who was catching on fast, and—would you believe—I was ready to give him a simulated single-engine landing. On the downwind, as I reviewed the procedure with the student pilot, I noticed oil-pressure fluctuation. Behind me in the jump seat, the crew chief began to punch me and point over my shoulder at the warning instrument. The engine was also suggesting heavy loss of oil. On the base leg, the chief shouted in my ear that if I didn't feather the engine it might freeze (I didn't and it did, but not until we'd touched down). I told the student to keep following his simulated single-engine procedure, but that it was real. As we turned final I told the tower we were losing the engine. The student performed perfectly, and when we touched down and slowed down, the engine froze. Off on the taxiway we turned, but that was as far as we could taxi. When we climbed out of the plane, I told the student he'd passed the test; but from the way the crew chief was shaking his head, I assumed I'd failed mine.

The normal way to bring the B-26 in starts with a 1,000-foot overhead approach. If cleared, you can complete the preliminary checklist: mixtures rich, props 2,400, fuel on the main tanks, fuel boosters on, and throttle back to kill off airspeed. When the cat dies to about 220, start a smart 180° turn to downwind, rolling out, still slowing. Drop flaps 15° at this point to further slow the airspeed. As the airspeed slows to 160, lower the gear and push up the power to maintain airspeed at 160.

On base, establish 150 IAS, set props full high, and maintain 1,000 feet; turn final, dropping the nose and reducing the power. When level on final approach, reduce airspeed to 140 and start the flaps down to 38° (or, in the 363rd, 52°). The easiest landing is 38°; 52° is not quite so easy: it is more difficult to keep the nosewheel from popping onto the runway. This sweet bird of my youth drills straight down the runway on the landing roll, requiring very little effort on the driver's part. But stay off the brakes until you're way down the runway and well slowed down. Those brakes heat up fast if you're heavy footed, and you must have brakes to stop the aircraft safely. There are emergency air brakes, but they simply go full on and lock the wheels. They can be released, but there are only about four applications in the system. And remember to save the last one for the full stop, or else be prepared to field some embarrassing questions.

If you don't manage to stay off the brakes, normal or emergency system either, you'll have smoking wheels when you stop and you'll get contemptuous looks from every ground-crew man in sight, as well as from iron-butted commanders who chance to be in the area.

Always use the simple checklist. It's not hard to follow; and reading it off makes the crew chief feel important. If that man can also read maps, manage radios, and give position reports, you have an important gem. That's the kind of a guy who'll also learn to handle the plane and provide you with a chance to relax during the mission. In my travels I have seen many bad crew chiefs (or flight engineers if you wish): lazy, dull, afraid of the airplane, natural slobs, alcoholics, and the like. But I don't remember ever seeing a bad B-26 crew chief. Maybe it's because nearly everyone loves the bird. Anyway, I always had expert and enthusiastic help with the B-26.

I never bailed out of the Invader, and came close only once, at night, when I was in the aft compartment. The pilot planned too long a night VFR flight that wound up at destination in a thunderstorm, without fuel to go to another base. Fortunately, we landed on fumes. But I thought over the bailout procedures. From aft you can go out the right-hand side door, or out through the bomb bay, if the pilot opens the doors for you. The pilot and the crew man in the right seat go out the top after jettisoning the canopy (being careful to duck because the windstream tends to make the canopy dish in slightly). Each man goes out on his side of the plane, face down and headfirst back over the wing. But—a testimonial to the reliability of the airplane—I never knew a pilot who bailed out.

I did manage a midair collision over Biggs Field at El Paso. Nobody was hurt, but the other pilot was practically in shock for a couple of hours. My right prop cut off his one and only prop. Flight-safety people absolved me completely because of my attempts to avoid the cluster of light planes in the area. But one of them came up almost from under my belly and flew into my right propeller while I was in a steep turn away and to the left. The strength of the B-26 made it, for me, merely an incident.

Before concluding this reminiscence, I must mention a modification that seemed somewhat hastily engineered. I refer to the FA-26, a photo modification that was mounted under the tail and included a parabolic flash reflector about four feet in diameter. It also boasted a bomb bay full of high-voltage generators to make the huge flash work. I went west to Sacramento to pick up the first of these FA-26 models, and upon my ground walk-around inspection, I kept thinking of Rube Goldberg. I won't tell how many volts that bay full of generators cranked up to run that flash unit because you'd never believe me. I will say that normal power settings left airspeed about 30 mph below usual. I flew that plane back to Langley at 230 mph and the operation pulled out rivets all around the area under the tail, an event that was not confidence-inspiring. Tolerance and decency demand that we say no more of the FA-26.

Recently I had occasion to look at the Flight Manual for the last model of the 26, the B-26A aircraft, which was used in Southeast Asia, and was impressed with the differences the modification embodied. The early 26s had no wing deicers, no heater props, no tip tanks, no drop tanks, no ADI (antidetonant) system, no reversing props, no antiskid brake system, no copilot brakes, no flight instruments, nor anything like as many restrictions and injunctions as the A-26 has. The old airplane wasn't as heavy; everything was computed in miles per hour and the red-line speed was higher. Manifold pressures and rpm are higher in the A-26A. There is still some seat-of-the-pants flying in the A-26A but, I believe, more fun to be had from the old love machine.

A-26 in flight.

I approached the Invader the right way, coming from the B-24 through the B-25 to the B-26. The B-24 is the heaviest, of course, and the slowest. The B-25 is lighter, faster, and easier to handle. The 26 feels so good in the hand, is so fast and so much fun that it shouldn't be compared to the 24 and 25. But the landing approach, the handling, and the touchdown are alike for all three (provided you use 38° flaps).

Weather and instrument-navigation techniques were somewhat sporty on the early 26. Lack of wing-deicing equipment posed something of a problem, but the bird would carry a lot of ice and burn it off rapidly once you got below the icing level. Instrument navigation was dicey in the 1940s—the only aids were a radio compass and a low-frequency receiver (the old coffee grinder that didn't have frying pan reception until there was heavy weather, but that was when the listening became interesting). Sometime in the 1950s, omni receivers were retrofitted, a modification that took the sweat out of instrument navigation. When I was assigned to the Pentagon to work for the Chief of the Air National Guard, I found their deluxe stable contained 26s with two omnis,

McDONNELL DOUGLAS

autopilots, comfortable aft sections for VIP passengers, and super-qualified crew chiefs, among other refinements—not the least of which was superior maintenance.

I was always looking for a reason to visit an Air Guard base and managed to visit 40 states the first year in that assignment. I retired following my tour there, so the B-26 Invader was the last aircraft I ever flew for pay. I had my darkest days with the B-24 and perversely came to love that sweet old beast; but I had my brightest days with the B-26 and will never forget that blithe spirit.

WILLIAM CARIGAN retired from the Air Force in 1965 as a Lieutenant Colonel and since then has taught English at Utah State University. During World War II he flew B-24s in the Fifteenth Air Force in Italy. He flew the A-26 Invader in 1947-1948 and the B-26 Invader from 1954 to his retirement. In 1957 he won the Air Materiel Command Short Story Contest, and in 1958 he won the overall Air Force Short Story Contest. Since then he has published in the *Saturday Evening Post*, the *Saturday Review*, and in various professional journals. In 1974, his first novel, *The Flying Game*, was published.

*Loaded with forty 500-pound bombs
and 5,460 gallons of fuel, the B-32 had
a range of 3,700 miles. Armament consisted of ten .50 caliber machine guns,
mounted in five powered turrets.*

B-32 Dominator

WILLARD S. RULIFFSON

with ROBIN HIGHAM

I first met the B-32 one day early in 1945 when I was assigned to learn to command one at Ft. Worth A.A.F., Texas. My first impression was that it was a very big bird compared to the old slab-sided B-24s I had been flying. With the great round fuselage, originally meant to be pressurized, it seemed to be immense, and, in fact, was a little over twice the size of the Liberator. As impressive as the size of the fuselage were the great dual main wheels and the immense single fin which appeared to be at least 40 feet high.

The Dominator's large Wright R-3550-23 engines had 2,200 hp; the B-24s had 1,200 hp. The 32's wing span was 135 feet; the B-24's was 110 feet. The Dominator weighed 113,500 pounds with 5,226 gallons of fuel, giving a range of 4,450 miles in still air with 20,000 pounds of bombs. (The designed flying gross weight could go as high as 120,000 pounds, with a maximum of 123,000 pounds.) In contrast, the B-24D weighed a maximum of 60,000 pounds with 3,664 gallons of fuel and had a range of 2,850 miles with 5,000 pounds of bombs—or a maximum ferry range of 4,660 miles. So here was an aircraft weighing over twice as much as those I had been used to flying.

The B-32 Dominator, a great successor to the B-24, was created as an insurance policy in case the Boeing B-29 did not work out. Originally, it had the same engines as the B-29. It was also pressurized. Otherwise, it was a Convair aircraft with the twin tails of the PB4Y Coronado flying boat and the dihedral tail plane. This was changed in the production models to the single-tail fin and normal tail plane, which had appeared first on the Navy's B-24 conversion, the Privateer. Before the aircraft got to production, tactics in the Pacific changed, and instead of the remote and aloof high-altitude attacks, those from lower levels were envisaged, so the weighty pressurization system was removed, as well as the remote-controlled turrets housing the ship's 20 mm cannon. Thus, by the time I got to it, the Dominator was more like an enlarged Privateer than anything else. It carried ten .50 caliber machine guns in five turrets. Officially, the Army Air Force considered it overweight and unnecessary. They also said that the view from the bombardier's position was poor.

But this really was not true, at least that is what we pilots felt when we got to know the B-32 during the spring and summer of 1945. We thought it a pity that only 115 of the 1,713 ordered were completed.

Getting into the B-32 was much the same as getting into the B-24, only the climb to the cockpit seemed to be considerably greater. One could enter the forward of the two bomb bays and then climb the ladder to the intermediate deck on which was located the engineer's station and the galley. The latter was a holdover from the aircraft's PB4Y ancestry. We used it only on overnight flights. Still, it would have been nice on those long bombing runs to Japan from Guam and other overseas bases. Also on the intermediate deck was the trolley, fitted in some models, along which a man could haul himself back and forth across the bomb bay to the rear of the aircraft.

Those of the crew permanently stationed back there (rear top turret, tail turret, and ball turret gunners) got into the aircraft through a hatch located just aft of the retractable ball turret on the underside. The pilots, navigator, radar man, bombardier, and engineer climbed the next ladder onto the main deck. The nose gunner and the bombardier could reach their station through a hatch on the underside of the nose or by climbing down through the pilots' compartment. Chest-type parachute packs were stowed nearby for each crew member, but stowage was not always adequate. On one occasion we had a cabin full of nylon fluffing when the navigator caught his chute on the corner of a stringer or some such thing and popped it open. Luckily, we had a spare on board and equally luckily we did not have to jump on that or any other sortie. The standard procedure for bailing out was for the crew in the rear to exit via their entrance hatch and for the rest of us to jump out the open bomb bay or a hatch forward behind the bombardier.

As soon as you entered the cockpit, you noticed the space—it was wide and had many panels in the windows. In fact, it was enormous—the pilot and copilot could barely touch hands in the middle; and I am not kidding about that, as I am over six feet tall. This great space meant that we communicated via the intercom instead of by shouting as we did in most other aircraft of the day. The other feature of the cockpit was what seemed to be the vast array of instruments and switches. There was a special panel for propeller controls, as this was one of the first aircraft fitted with reversible props to shorten the landing roll or to abort a takeoff. And there was a panel devoted to deicing gear, for this aircraft was one of the first to be fitted with electrical deicing on the leading edges of the wings and tail empennage. Deicing of the propellers was accomplished by pumping isopropanol through a slinger ring; the fluid then found its way to the cutting edge and the tips of the props by centrifugal force.

If the B-24 represented the aviation revolution of the 1930s with its variable pitch propellers, high-octane fuel, retractable undercarriage, flaps, and all-metal construction, as well as its high-aspect-ratio Davis wing, it also suffered from being in the early years of transition. This meant that there were numerous versions. For example, I flew models C through J during my training days, and not every one was an improvement over its predecessor. The B-32, on the other hand, was the second generation. Most of the bugs had been worked out and many of the refinements, accelerated by wartime needs and research, were already installed in the early production models. Thus, compared to the Martin B-10 of a decade earlier, or even to the B-17 and B-24, this was a very

Powered by four 2,200 hp Wright engines, the B-32 had a maximum speed of 358 mph and an average cruising speed of 250 mph.

modern machine. Naturally, in a cockpit of this complexity, simply checking that the ground crew had done their job, or that someone else had not, took time. Thus, before entering the B-32, pilot, copilot, and engineer made sure that the pitot tube cover was removed, landing gear and nosewheel tires and oleos were correctly inflated, fire extinguisher discs were intact and had not been accidentally discharged, props were free of unusual nicks and dents, nacelles were securely fastened and free of pronounced oil leaks, no fuel leaks or seepage existed, trim tab positions were correct—and, on reaching the cockpit, remembering to check that tab-control settings were correct; landing lights were fully retracted and flush, and safety locks on main and nose gear had been removed.

After the copilot and I had strapped ourselves in and had adjusted our seats, we started down the pretakeoff checklist printed on a plastic card about eight inches long. One of us would call out the items and the other would look it over and respond "check," as fuel gauges, auxiliary power unit (APU), inverter switch, circuit breakers, propeller selector switches, hydraulic pump, control locks, antiicer switches, *ad infinitum,* were confirmed to be operating properly or in the correct position.

Once all this was done, we would glance out both sides of the cockpit, check to get the thumbs-up signal from the crew chief on the ground, and proceed with engine start-up. This procedure began with #2, the left-hand inboard engine, because it drove the hydraulic system, as did #3—but generally the pilot had better observation and control when starting #2 first. Once #2 was started, #3, #1, and #4 followed, in that order. With all engines running and intermediate checks on oil pressure, cylinder head temperatures, etc., completed, we checked by intercom to

be sure that everyone was in place, and, with hardly any warm-up—because it was early summer in Ft. Worth—the chocks were waved away and we started the taxi run to takeoff.

The B-32's wing span was 135 feet.

    The B-32 was easy to taxi because it had a steerable nosewheel controlled by using throttle and minimum brakes. Normally, engines were set to turn over at 800–1000 rpm—enough to pull the ship at a good clip along the taxi strip. One problem, usually solved by turning on George, the autopilot, was the leg power required to keep the big rudder centralized when taxiing in a crosswind. Once near the runway, we would swing around into the wind and go through the pretakeoff checks. These included running up each engine in sequence to 48–49 inches mercury while standing on the brakes, switching magnetos to watch for more than a 100 rpm drop, and leaving the turbo-boost controls in position to develop maximum takeoff power. The actual pretakeoff check included closing bomb-bay doors; securing all hatches; checking generator, inverter, and booster-pump switches; setting fuel tank selectors at tank to engine, prop selector to automatic, mixture controls to auto rich, various shutters to open or automatic, and wing flaps to 30°; moving all controls full right, full left, or full forward and full rear; noting critical pressures and temperatures (oil, fuel, cylinder head, hydraulic); and checking that crew members were in position and braced and that all guns were trimmed fore and aft.

Once the pretakeoff check was completed and we were cleared by the tower, brakes were released and the airplane was guided onto the runway using light brakes and outboard engines. When aligned with the centerline, the throttles were walked slowly and smoothly forward to full open (2,800 rpm; 49 inches mercury), and the takeoff run was under way.

A fully loaded B-32 took a long time to get rumbling, though a light version had a pretty snappy takeoff with all 9,200 hp available. About halfway down the 10,000-foot runway, the controls would finally begin to bite, and nosewheel steering could be abandoned. At 130 mph IAS it would finally begin to fly, and one could ease back on the stick and begin to climb away. Apart from his sitting higher, for the 24 pilot the 32 had a normal takeoff and climb. It required a fair amount of rudder at the beginning of the takeoff roll, but once airspeed was adequate it was very docile. Off the ground, unlike the B-24, it was not mushy (or at least the lightly loaded planes we flew were not). The wheels coming up made little difference, though you did have to remember to toe the brakes to make sure that the wheels stopped spinning on their way into the wells and the flaps were milked up in the usual small decreases until it was flying clean. The B-32 did not need to be brought down carefully on the step to level out at the desired altitude; you simply flew to the desired altitude and leveled off smoothly right there. With the Liberator, on the other hand, you climbed up to 500 feet above the desired height and then let down gently to it, or, if diving, you leveled off above and then settled down.

We used the automatic pilot more in this ship than in the B-24, even on climb, and most of the time when cruising, as the aircraft was very stable. It may not be entirely fair to say, but I remember the 32 as being much more stable on an engine-out situation, too. I say it may be unfair to put it this way because of the training we got at Ft. Worth; the instructors only cut one of the inner engines and never an outer one. Why? I don't recall. It may be that they were all combat veterans who could see the end of the war coming and they were darned if they were going to risk a student pilot putting their necks in a noose because the aircraft yawed out of control or rolled over with an outboard engine gone. On three engines the Dominator was definitely stable and needed only a bit of rudder cranked in with the trim to maintain course and altitude. This certainly was not true with the Liberators, they had a tough time on three engines and sank like a brick on two. I know, because one night near Savannah we lost both engines on the left side and we barely made it onto the runway!

Normal cruising for the B-32 required about 34–35 inches of boost and an IAS of 180 mph. Very little allowance had to be made for the weight of the aircraft, though like all machines of the day, it probably jumped a bit if all the bombs were let go at once.

We did only limited formation flying in the bird, perhaps because it was so large and visibility was somewhat limited, perhaps because we never got to operations.

Another peculiarity of our training was that we got very little instruction in power stalls. My main recollection is that with the stiff, round fuselage, the B-32 did not give as clear a signal as the B-24, except possibly for a mild tail shake. When a stall went through, the nose dropped gently but quickly straight down. Once you automatically snapped the control column forward and held the plane straight until the speed built up again to 180–220 IAS (how far depended upon weight), it then was easy enough to recover by easing the stick back and easing on power. To give some idea of the variance in speeds with weights and flaps on this aircraft, the manual shows that with 0° of flap, the stalling speed was 131 mph at 80,000 pounds and 156 mph at 120,000 pounds; with 30° down at 120,000 pounds, the stall speed was 133 mph, varying a bit, of course, from airframe to airframe. Cruising speed was normally 180 mph with the aircraft redlined at 240 mph at 118,000 pounds, or 330 mph at 100,000 pounds.

The B-32 was easy to maneuver in the rather straightforward Rate I (30°/min.) turns we did and was no trouble to handle in the corkscrew pattern that was developed early in the war as a defense against fighters.

As for landing, it was no trouble at all. You simply made the usual downwind leg doing your prelanding check: start APU, retract turret, hydraulic pump on, mixture auto rich, generators on, props auto, 2,400 rpm, gear extended, flaps 30°. Then you turned crosswind and reduced power some to set up for the final at 150–160 mph, a little higher (165–170) on three engines, lowered full flaps (40°), and powered right on in with about 30 inches and 130 mph IAS. Once over the end of the runway, you eased the throttles back and slowly brought the nose up until the aircraft settled—sometimes so gently that you were surprised to be on the ground. If the runway was long enough and someone was on your tail, your roll was a little longer; but usually, once the nosewheel was hard down, the propellers were reversed and the throttles shoved forward, and slowing down quickly and evenly was no problem.

One oddity about the Dominator was that the photographs show a tail skid. I have no recollection of this—whether or not it was retractable or what its purpose was. My only guess 30 years after the event is that it was there to prevent poor pilots from scraping the after-fuselage along the runway when landing in a too-high nose-up manner, which I suppose was possible if you were an old B-17 pilot used to making tail-down

Frontal view of the Dominator's nose and inboard engines.

three-pointers. Certainly it was not a problem for those of us who came off the 24.

While at Ft. Worth, we wondered about the shape of things to come as we could see the tail of the B-36 sticking out of the hangar across the field. One day we even got a glimpse of the whole thing. But the war was over, we never went operational, and I walked away from my last flight in the 32, and from the old USAAF, satisfied that I had flown the largest aircraft then available for operations and a worthy successor to the old Convair Liberator.

WILLARD S. RULIFFSON is a biochemist at Kansas State University, Manhattan. He served in the U.S. Army and Army Air Corps from 1941 to 1946 and in the Reserves until 1950.

B-47 Stratojet

EARL G. PECK

THE Boeing B-47, officially the "Stratojet," was one of those airplanes that never seemed to acquire any sort of affectionate nickname. Although pilots may refer nostalgically to the "Spit," "Thud," "Hun," "Jug," or even "Fort," the B-47 remains just that. This probably stems from the fact that although it was often admired, respected, cursed, or even feared, it was almost never loved. In fact, I think it would be fair to say that it tended to separate the men from the boys!

It was relatively difficult to land, terribly unforgiving of mistakes or inattention, subject to control reversal at high speeds, and suffered from horrible roll-due-to-yaw characteristics. Crosswind landings and takeoffs were sporty, and in-flight discrepancies were the rule rather than the exception. All in all, the B-47 was a very demanding machine for its three-man crew.

None of this, however, should seem very surprising when one considers the near-revolutionary nature of the beast. It was, in fact, the first large, swept-wing American jet aircraft. Landing gear consisted of two tandem centerline trucks in the fuselage, so located because there was no room in the thin, high wings, which angled back at 35°. Because the landing gear was directly under the longitudinal axis, outriggers in the inboard nacelles were needed for ground stability. And because neither of the main gear trucks was near the center of gravity, the aircraft was designed to *rest* in a takeoff and landing attitude rather than rotate conventionally. The margin for error in landing attitude was thus extraordinarily small—a front-truck-first touchdown produced an olympic-sized bounce!

Obviously, therefore, great care was required in deploying the 32-foot ribbon-type brake chute which was installed to offset, during landing roll, the relatively poor deceleration characteristics of the bird. It was worse than embarrassing to have that chute blossom about the time you reached the apex of a bounce after thinking you were properly on terra firma.

The brake chute was not to be confused with the 16-foot approach chute designed for use in the traffic pattern. The approach chute enabled

This chapter was revised from an article in *Aerospace Historian,* June 1975, 62–64.

B-47 in flight.

the pilot to keep the engine rpms in a responsive range, both for more precise control of descent rates and to make thrust more readily available for go-arounds.

But, its idiosyncrasies notwithstanding, the B-47 served as a mainstay of the SAC deterrent posture during the darkest years of the protracted Cold War. Thus a typical B-47 mission was comprised of all those activities that the crew had to master if the system was to serve as a credible deterrent. They were also the same things that would be required during a nuclear strike mission if deterrence failed: high- and low-level navigation (celestial, radar, grid) and weapon delivery, aerial refueling, electronic countermeasures against air and ground threats, positive control procedures, exercising the tail-mounted twin 20 mm guns, emergency procedures, cell (formation) tactics, and others I am sure I have forgotten. Crew planning for a mission took up *most of the day prior* and was elaborately precise and detailed. The crew was expected to approach each training sortie with the same meticulous professionalism that would be required for an actual strike launch.

And professionalism keynoted the mission attitude that prevailed from inception to completion. On the day of the flight, the crew (pilot, copilot, and navigator) checked in at the airplane, with all of their personal equipment (parachutes, survival gear, helmets, oxygen masks, etc.), *three hours* prior to takeoff. There followed an exhaustive series of

(Left) Displaying its maneuverability, a B-47 Stratojet bomber wings over on its back as part of an Immelman turn. The technique may be used in the delivery of bombs, lobbing the bomb toward the target just before the airplane starts its half-roll. (Above) SAC B-47s are shown here in their normal high altitude environment. Note the tiny "vortex generators" above the outboard engine of the plane in the foreground. They serve to disrupt airflow over this portion of the wing, which in turn increases the lift factor in the wing-tip area beyond. (Bottom) Cockpit of B-47.

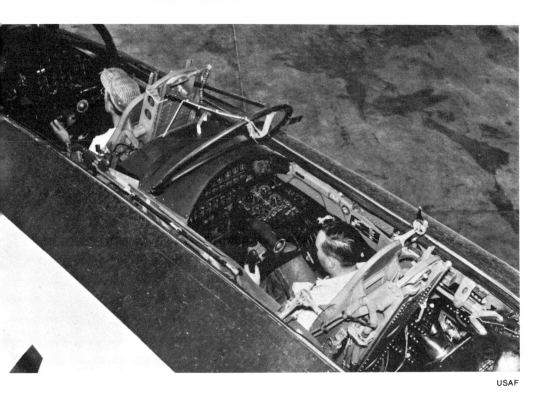

Front and rear cockpits of B-47 with canopy removed.

inspections—station, exterior, and interior—which consumed about an hour and a half and satisfied the crew that the airplane was ready to go.

The station check included the usual perusal of forms, equipment, and safety items, and preceded a rather detailed "walk-around." Normally, the pilot and copilot split the inspection to examine the (for its day) massive exterior (length 107 feet, wing span 116 feet). Generally, they were looking for fuel leaks, hydraulic leaks, loose panels, and tire condition.

Following the exterior inspection, the crew members assumed their respective positions in the crew compartment for a system-by-system interior inspection. Ingress was gained via a self-contained retractable ladder (which according to alert shack rumor cost the Air Force $1,700 each). Pilot and copilot sat in tandem under a Plexiglas clamshell canopy, while the navigator sat in the nose. Virtually nothing escaped the interior inspection—fuel system and loading, hydraulics, flight controls, escape systems (for bailout, the pilot and copilot ejected upward and the navigator downward), switch positions, electrical systems, oxygen, instruments, aerial refueling system, navigation equipment, and so on, through a seemingly endless array of checks.

But we finally would finish and, finding the bird fit, would leave it and wend our way to base ops for a weather briefing and to compute takeoff data and file a clearance.

It should be noted at this point that the SAC B-47 units relied heavily on the crew members' private autos. First, we'd meet at the Personal Equipment Shop, load our gear in the trunk of one car, drive out to the airplane, and unload. After the interior check, we'd drive the car to base ops and then drive back down the ramp and park opposite our assigned airplane. After the flight, the route was retraced, with an added stop at maintenance debriefing. From start to scratch, the crews' own vehicles enabled the system to work!

In any event, we would return to the airplane from ops, strap into the chutes and ejection seats, and run a lengthy "before starting engines" checklist in order to be ready to crank about 20 minutes prior to launch.

Engine start was a frantic exercise requiring dexterous manipulation of switches and throttles beginning with number four and followed by five, six, three, two, and one in rapid-fire sequence. After removing external power, the aircraft hydraulic and electrical systems were energized, the bomb-bay and entrance dooors secured, and the airplane was ready to taxi.

Taxiing the B-47 was relatively easy. Turns could be smoothly negotiated through the steerable front truck with one steering ratio available for taxi and another, less sensitive, for takeoff and landing. Despite the three-point attitude, visibility was good—S turns were not necessary. At heavy gross weights, however, taxi speed was severely limited to preclude undue stress and tire overheating.

When the end of the runway was reached, our heroes would accomplish a routine before-takeoff checklist, recheck takeoff data, and be prepared to cross the threshold precisely on scheduled launch time. Takeoffs were of the rolling variety with all six throttles advanced to 100% rpm shortly after alignment.

Takeoff in a B-47 was, to my knowledge, unique in its day, for the airplane was in effect "flying" shortly after beginning the roll. This was attributable to the flexible wings which permitted the outriggers to lift off as soon as the airflow generated any appreciable lift. The pilot then had to maintain a wings-level attitude through the flight controls, while steering primarily with the front gear truck. In fact, it was possible, at that point, to steer the aircraft by "bicycling" as it would turn left or right on the runway as the wings were tilted.

During the takeoff roll, aircraft performance was checked by timing the acceleration from 70 knots to a precomputed decision speed. At

The prototype XB-47 landing.

that point the pilot made an irrevocable decision to continue the takeoff or abort. Lift-off was achieved at a calculated speed (typically about 160 knots) dependent on weight and conditions and in very nearly the ground attitude.

Gear was retracted immediately and the flaps raised on a schedule linked to acceleration. Normal initial climb speed was 310 knots indicated which was maintained to 20,000 feet and then decreased gradually in accordance with a charted optimum schedule.

Somewhat ungainly on the ground, the B-47 assumed a classic grace in flight. Control response was positive throughout the performance envelope, except at the extremes. At low speeds and high angles of attack, it was possible to induce virtually uncontrollable roll-due-to-yaw, a characteristic responsible for several disastrous takeoff crashes after outboard engine failure near unstick speed. At the other end of the spectrum, indicated airspeeds in excess of about 425 knots produced aileron reversal. This condition was actually due to warping of the flexible wings in which the wing tips functioned as ailerons and the ailerons functioned as trim tabs. In between, however, the B-47 was reasonably docile.

My own experience with outboard engine failure during takeoff was representative except that I was luckier than most. Number six quit about halfway between decision and lift-off, producing a violent yaw toward the dead engine. This was followed by a strong rolling tendency which further aggravated a dismal directional control problem. With rudder and yoke fully deflected, I managed to struggle into the air just prior to leaving the side of the strip. Things weren't looking much better, however, because after retracting the gear, we were headed across the boondocks in an uncomfortably skewed condition, gaining neither airspeed nor altitude. In fact, the navigator, Jim Gravette, said later that he would have ejected except that his downward-firing seat would have driven him into the ground from our precariously low altitude! It's just as well that he couldn't eject, because we were able to gradually nurse a few more knots out of the beast, milk the flaps up, and get the thing flying. From then on, the dead engine posed little problem.

Aerial refueling with the B-47 presented difficulties stemming principally from incompatibility with the piston-driven KC-97 tankers then in use. Very high wing loading and associated stall speeds in the B-47 meant that the KC-97 was taxed to provide any respectable margin above stall while hooked up. On one particularly dark night my airplane stalled off the boom and fluttered gracefully down through 5,000 feet of murk before it became a flying machine again! In retrospect, of all of the airplanes I have refueled in flight—F-84, B-47, B-52, F-4—the B-47 was easily the most challenging.

Also challenging were the combat bombing tactics practiced by the B-47 force. A typical mission involved a low-level, high-speed penetration of "enemy" territory, a pop-up to about 1,500 feet for the simulated delivery of a drogued nuclear weapon, and descent back to the "deck" for escape. It took a skilled navigator and good crew coordination to "hit" (electronically) within the allowable circular error. Although they never dropped a bomb in anger, the ability of the B-47 crews to do so effectively helped make it unnecessary.

Approach and landing were predicted on a "best flare" speed, which varied with the landing gross weight. On a typical landing, "best flare" speed would run about 135 knots, and all other pattern speeds were computed from that base. Thus the downwind leg was flown at

A modified B-47B Stratojet tanker (right refuels a B-47 Strato-jet medium bomber. The B-47 experiment tanker was equipped with a probe-drogue refueling system. The tanker trailed a long hose attached to a "drogue" or large funnel. The receiver plane flew into posi-tion below and aft of the hose so that its spearlike "probe" engaged the coupling in the drogue.

"best flare plus 30," approach chute deployed, and gear and flaps extended. Airspeed was further reduced to "best flare plus 20" during the descending turn to base leg, and again to "best flare plus 15" turning final.

Airspeed was gradually dissipated on final approach in order to reach the end of runway at precisely "best flare" speed. Throttles were retarded when landing was assured and the aircraft rotated in order to touch down on all main gear simultaneously or slightly aft truck first. The situation to be assiduously avoided was the nosewheel-first landing which put you back in the air with something less than desired velocity!

The brake chute was deployed as soon as the aircraft was firmly on the ground and was a great assist in deceleration. It could be extended by either the pilot or copilot, but, for most of us, wisdom dictated that the pilot do it himself to preclude a disastrous, untimely deployment.

Looking back, although much of the flying I did in the B-47 was not particularly enjoyable—it was in fact tedious, demanding, even grueling at times—it was rewarding in terms of professional satisfaction. I felt I was doing an important job and took great pride in doing it well in a machine capable of performing. As with most airplanes, the advertised performance figures (4,000 nautical mile range, 600 mph speed, 40,000-foot service ceiling) didn't mean much to the guys flying the B-47. It was important only that it go fast and far enough to enable a group of professional, dedicated, and gutsy SAC crews to provide the bulk of American deterrent strength during the middle and late 1950s.

At that time the SAC B-47 armada numbered more than 1,400—principally E models. The balance of the inventory included EBs, RBs, and TBs, each with its own specialized role. As the decade waned, the B-47 was gradually supplemented and later supplanted by the B-52 as SAC's "big stick," but the Stratojet had written an important chapter in the history of military aviation.

BRIG. GEN. EARL G. PECK Deputy Chief of Staff for perso nel, SAC, Offutt AFB, Nebrask He is a graduate of the Universi of Texas and the Industrial Col lege of the Armed Forces and holds the master's degree from George Washington University. His 6,000 hours of diversified fl ing experience span 24 years an are evenly divided between fighters (F-80, F-84, F-4) and bombers (B-47, B-52).

B-57 Canberra

ROY J. CARROW, JR.

T HE B-57 built by the Martin Company is the U.S. version of the British-designed Canberra. The original of this twin-jet bomber was designed during World War II but did not become operational until the late 1940s. Various models of the Canberra have been built by Great Britain, Australia, and the United States, and many countries throughout the world have flown and still fly these variants. A unique and perhaps the most ironic event in the history of this aircraft was the Indo-Pakistan War, where the British Canberra and the American B-57 fought on opposite sides.

The Canberra, as originally designed by the British, was built in two versions. One was a tactical bomber and the other a reconnaissance platform. The United States bought the design from Great Britain and built or modified existing airframes into seven different versions. These seven have been further modified to equip the basic airframe for many different missions. The B-57 is truly the ''Gooney Bird'' (C-47) of the jet age.

The basic airframe as acquired from Great Britain has a wingspan of 64 feet and an overall length of 65.5 feet. The basic weight of the aircraft is approximately 29,000 pounds. With wing-tip tanks installed, it will carry 18,700 pounds of fuel. This is sufficient for 4 hours and 30 minutes of flight time at 41,000 feet, cruising at 390 knots true airspeed.

SAF

*B-57B light bomber
near Randolph AFB,
Texas, 1955.*

This gives the aircraft a no-wind range of approximately 1,750 nautical miles, for there is no air-refueling capability.

The aircraft's two Curtiss-Wright J-65-W5B engines originally gave 7,220 pounds of thrust each; today, through modifications, the thrust has been increased to 7,660 pounds each.

The engines are midmounted in the wings approximately 15 feet from the fuselage centerline, a feature that makes flight on one engine a little sporty. If power on the good engine is increased too rapidly, the sudden increase of thrust will result in a violent and uncontrollable yaw and roll. A rudder-power assist system (rudder-power system on B-57E aircraft) was incorporated to lower substantially the minimum single-engine control speed by providing additional rudder deflection when needed by the pilot.

Starting the engines is a rather unusual procedure. A gunpowder cartridge is inserted in the starter, which is mounted in the center of the engine intake. An electrical charge ignites the cartridge and through a gear assembly the starter turns the engine to approximately 20% rpm where it can sustain its own combustion. A clutch then disengages the starter. If the clutch fails, the starter will disintegrate at approximately 38% engine rpm, throwing fragments all around. A starter housing was later installed to contain the fragments from a disintegrating starter.

One of the most unusual features designed into the aircraft is the rotary bomb door. Most bomb doors are clamshell type which open and close like retractable landing-gear doors. On the B-57, the bomb door rotates 180° and actually exposes the ordnance to the slipstream. This allows ordnance to be loaded either with the bomb door installed on the aircraft or on a spare bomb door that can easily be winched into place.

Four high-drag low-lift flaps were installed on the aircraft for lower landing speeds. There are only two positions for the flaps: up for takeoff and normal flight, and down for landing. Additional drag devices are incorporated in the form of wing speed brakes. These are small fingers on the upper and lower surfaces of the wings which extended into the slipstream. Later versions also incorporate two large speed brakes mounted on either side of the aft fuselage.

Flight controls incorporated into the aircraft consist of the standard ailerons, elevator, and rudder. The primary control surfaces receive assistance from the trim devices and the variable-incidence stabilizer. The conventional elevator, rudder, and ailerons have unique mechanisms that relieve the pilot of heavy-control loads. At high speeds, these mechanisms also prevent excessive loads on the structure of the aircraft by indirectly restricting the travel of control surfaces. Rotation of the control wheel, movement of the rudder pedals, or longitudinal movement of the control column moves push rods to actuate the control surfaces directly or indirectly. On the ground and at low speeds, the push rods directly deflect the control surfaces, but as airspeed increases, the resulting load on the control surfaces resists the action of the push rod. Through assist tabs on the control surfaces, the torque tube in the torque-tube-and-blowback-rod assembly twists to absorb the movement of the push rod. This system reduces pilot effort and still maintains conventional control feel at all airspeeds. At high speeds, a large tab angle imposes high air loads on the tab, causing the blowback rod to twist in the opposite direction to the torque tube. This increases the control load felt by the pilot, thereby using the pilot's strength as a limiting factor in maneuvering the aircraft. So don't ever let a B-57 pilot talk you into "arm wrestling!"

The first version built in the United States was the RB-57A. This

model was designed as a reconnaissance platform and was almost a duplicate of the British version. The crew entered the aircraft through a small door on the right side of the fuselage. The pilot's seat was elevated and included a "bubble" type canopy. The navigator sat back in the enclosed fuselage and had only a small 6-inch window. Both aircrew members had ballistic seats for ejection. This version also had a Plexiglas nose. The navigator would move forward and lie in the nose for more exact high-altitude reconnaissance. The British and Australian versions had a manual bombsight in the nose, which the bombardier used for sighting and releasing ordnance. A photoflash cartridge system was incorporated in the wing bays for night aerial photography. Normally 20 M-123 photoflash cartridges were loaded in these bays. Each cartridge had a peak illumination power of 265 million candlepower. An electrical impulse ignited the propelling charge causing the cartridge to leave the aircraft. This also ignited the delay fuse. The cameras were timed with the delay and operated in unison with the cartridge. This model was phased out of the inventory in 1972 after 20 years of service.

The Martin B-57E was the first aircraft built specifically as a target tug. The banner target was contained in a special extension to the after fuselage. This container could be removed and the aircraft converted to a bomber or to other training purposes.

The B-57B was designed as a tactical bomber. The most noticeable change is the forward section of the fuselage (crew compartment). A "clamshell" type canopy was installed and both seats placed on the centerline of the fuselage. The rear seat is elevated slightly to give better forward visibility. Besides the bomb-bay area, this version also includes eight wing stations and a gun-bay area in each wing outboard of the engines.

The B-57C is nothing more than the B model with two sets of controls. It is used primarily as a trainer for checking out new pilots. The instructor occupies the rear seat and has access to all controls necessary for flight. During the Vietnam conflict it was used as a tactical bomber.

The B-57D brought about a rather drastic design change. The wingspan was increased from 64 to 106 feet, and two J-57 engines replaced the J-65s. This version was designed for high-altitude reconnaissance and electronic countermeasure missions. A system was incorporated to allow the aircrew to wear pressure suits for the high-altitude flights. Because this version had problems with the pressure system and flew very few high-altitude missions, it was also phased out of the inventory in 1972.

The B-57E model is basically another version of the B model with a completely different hydraulic system. The two constant displacement hydraulic pumps were replaced by two variable displacement pumps. The rudder-power assist system was replaced with a full-time rudder-power system. This requires an artificial pedal (feel) force to replace the conventional rudder pedal force. This version, like the C model, is dual controlled and was designed originally for sampling and two-target missions. The sampling mission was primarily used in atomic bomb tests in the Pacific.

The B-57F is the "giant" of all the Canberras. General Dynamics converted tactical bombers into high-altitude reconnaissance aircraft. The modifications give the aircraft an increased operating ceiling, greater range, and improved handling characteristics. The conversion, which involved almost complete redesign and rebuilding, makes use of advanced materials, including honeycomb sandwich panels, for the new components. The original 64-foot wing was replaced by a new three-spar wing with a span of 122 feet, 5 inches. The ailerons are inset at about midspan and supplemented by spoilers. New and larger vertical tail surfaces were fitted. All control surfaces were modified to have tightly sealed gaps to reduce drag, and the flaps were eliminated. The J-65 engines were replaced by two TF-33 engines developing 18,000 pounds of thrust each. In addition, two J-60 auxiliary turbojets can be added in under-wing pods. This gives the aircraft the capability to fly at extremely high altitudes. The fuselage fuel tank was deleted to make way for equipment, and all fuel is carried in the wings outboard of the engines. In 1976 two of these aircraft were still being flown by NASA.

The B-57G is the most sophisticated of the Canberras. Again, the tactical bomber version was modified, this time by Westinghouse in conjunction with the Martin-Marietta Corporation. Designed as a night tactical bomber, a slightly modified airframe houses a host of electronic sensors and navigation equipment. Changes visible externally include a broad chin fairing beneath the nose which houses much of the new equipment. A window on the left side provides for a low-light-level TV camera and a laser range finder. The window on the right side contains infrared equipment. Multifunction radar, including terrain-following, is housed in the nose of the aircraft, which also is equipped with VOR, TACAN, and

ADF for navigation. In addition, it has a multipurpose computer that is used for navigation and for weapon delivery. Where most of the B-57s have only one or, at the most, two UHF radios, the B-57G has UHF, VHF AM, VHF FM, and HF frequencies. This gives the aircrew the capability to talk to any place in the world. This is the first aircraft with the capability to drop and track a laser-guided bomb right to the target with no assistance from another aircraft.

The B-57s in the inventory in 1976 primarily consisted of EB-57s. These were previously B and E models modified for use in an electronic countermeasure mission and are under the operational control of NORAD (North American Air Defense). One DC generator on each engine was removed and an AC generator with a constant-speed drive was installed to afford adequate AC power for the ECM equipment. Rocket ejection seats and an improved canopy thruster were later incorporated to give the aircrew a true zero-altitude ejection capability. These aircraft are presently flown by two Air National Guard units and one active Air Force unit.

I first became familiar with the B-57 in May 1963. I was assigned to the 90th Tactical Bombardment Squadron at Yokota Air Base in Japan.

My transition into the B-57 was quite an experience. After instructing pilot training for four years, *I* was the student. Ground school taught me the basics of the aircraft systems and the fundamentals and characteristics of the aircraft in flight.

As in most aircraft, one particular item is stressed, briefed, and practiced so thoroughly that more aircraft are lost simulating the emergency than in the actual event. This is also true in the B-57. Single-engine characteristics were stressed and practiced on almost every flight.

There is a twilight area in the B-57 that occurs shortly after takeoff. If an enpoint, it is almost impossible to control the aircraft. Before the modification that installed rocket ejection seats, this emergency was generally fatal to the aircrew.

Once the plane is airborne and has passed through this twilight zone, loss of one engine does not pose any more of a problem than other emergencies. Good throttle technique and proper airspeeds will result in a safe and uneventful landing. The only bad part of a single-engine landing

Takeoff is smooth, and the aircraft accelerates nicely to the recommended climb speed of 250 knots.

is that if rudder control is lost as the aircraft rolls along the runway, the plane cannot be taxied on one engine except in a circle.

The B-57 is a good flying bird and very stable, but it is completely different from any other aircraft I had flown. The exterior inspection is about the same as for any other aircraft, checking for fuel or hydraulic leaks and overall general condition.

Then comes the interior inspection. The first difference is the spaciousness of the cockpit. Your shoulders don't touch the canopy rails as they do in most aircraft. The rudder pedals can be adjusted to allow full rudder deflection regardless of the length of your legs.

The interior inspection starts with the normal left to right sequence. The armament panel is eye-catching to say the least. There you see an array of 25 lights, one for each bomb that can be loaded. In addition, there is a select switch for each wing station and each section of the bomb bay. The system also incorporates an armament-select switch for releasing rockets and bombs. Through the various switches you can select the weapon you want to expend. The guns are relatively easy to set up. A three-position switch turns on the gunsight light reticle or arms the guns or both.

The fuel panel deserves much attention in selecting the tanks to be used. On takeoff the aircraft is very close to the aft center of gravity limits. Therefore, it is imperative to burn fuel from the aft fuselage tank first. If for any reason this tank does not feed, the aircraft will exceed the aft center of gravity limits approximately 10 minutes after takeoff and loss of elevator control will quickly result.

The rest of the interior inspection is merely turning on and off switches and equipment according to the checklist.

The starter exhaust duct is located on the right side of the engines. This allows the canopy to be closed after the right engine is started so that the exhaust fumes from the left engine do not enter the cockpit area. Normally the right engine is started first and then the left.

After the engines are started, the normal flight control, trim surfaces, and system operations are checked prior to taxiing.

You have to use differential power and brakes to taxi. A standard day takeoff with a 47,000-pound aircraft requires approximately 4,000 feet with a takeoff speed of 140 knots. Brakes are used for directional control until the rudder becomes effective at approximately 60 knots.

B-57 Canberra heads toward an enemy target in South Vietnam.

USAF

Because the nose has a tendency to rise prematurely, a push force of approximately 30 pounds is applied to the control column. At approximately 100 knots, the push force is relaxed to allow the aircraft to assume a level attitude. The nosewheel is lifted off the runway 10 knots below takeoff speed of 140 knots. Takeoff is smooth, and the aircraft accelerates nicely to the recommended climb speed of 250 knots. It takes approximately 17 minutes to climb to 37,000 feet.

The aircraft can cruise easily at any altitude up to 43,000 feet. The cabin pressurization system keeps the cabin pressure below the 25,000-foot altitude level.

On a normal descent, power is reduced to 80% rpm and a descent rate initiated to maintain .70 Mach or 250 knots IAS. At this rate, descent from 43,000 feet can cover 160 nautical miles. For a rapid descent, power is reduced to idle and speed brakes extended. This procedure reduces the distance to approximately 40 nautical miles.

A normal overhead pattern is flown for visual recovery. Airspeed is 250 KIAS and altitude is 1,500 feet. At the "break" point, power is reduced to approximately 65% and an angle of bank of approximately 60° is established. Landing gear is lowered on downwind below 200 KIAS and the flaps are lowered just as the base leg is initiated. Airspeed is reduced throughout the turn with 140 KIAS attained when rolling out on final. Airspeed is further reduced during the final approach to arrive at the runway with a touchdown speed of approximately 100 KIAS.

For instrument approaches the aircraft is equipped with "round dial instruments." The approach is flown at 160 KIAS until the descent is started. Airspeed is then smoothly reduced to the best final approach speed, normally 130 KIAS. When the landing is assured, the airspeed is further reduced to the touchdown speed. The plane is very stable on final, unless turbulence is encountered. Under a minimum landing condition, the aircraft can be stopped in less than 2,000 feet.

I am greatly impressed with the weapon payload this relatively small aircraft can carry. There are 21 stations in the rotary bomb door. In addition, the four inboard wing stations can carry up to 1,000 pounds on each station. The four outboard stations are designed to carry rocket pods containing a maximum of nineteen 2.75-inch FFARs each. These are rockets approximately 4 feet long and 2.75 inches in diameter. The fins fold into the case so that the rockets can be placed into the rocket tube. When the rocket leaves the aircraft, the four fins extend into the slipstream to give the rocket stability. Enclosed in the wings, outside each engine nacelle, are the gun bays. A total of four 20 mm cannons with 1,160 rounds of ammunition can be carried in these gun bays. Some of the early versions carried eight .50 caliber machine guns.

Ordnance is delivered by various methods. High-angle dive delivers general purpose bombs and fragmentary ordnance. The base (or perch) altitude is 5,500 feet above the ground. Approximately abeam of and 1–2 miles from the target a rapid wingover-type maneuver is established. Approximately 110° of bank is used for this entry and the nose is lowered in the final part of the turn. As the airspeed increases, the dive angle is changed to arrive at a release altitude of 2,200 feet above the ground with a desired dive angle of 40° and 350 knots airspeed. A 3½ G pull is initiated immediately upon release. This allows the aircraft to recover from the dive at 1,000 feet above the ground. A total time of approximately 30 seconds from roll-in to pull-out allows about three corrections during the run.

Low-angle dive is used with variations for firing the 2.75-FFARs and for gunnery. Base-leg altitude is the same as for high-angle dive except that it is established 2–4 miles from the target. This gives a release-dive angle of 10–20° at a release altitude of approximately 800 feet and recovery at 500 feet.

Skip bombing is used for delivering napalm and weapons with a delay-type fuse. Base leg is 1,500 feet above the ground and approximately 4 miles from the target. Roll-in is initiated in the same manner as for dive-bombing. You roll wings level on final at 300 feet and then continue the descent to 50 feet for the weapon release. This method is extremely accurate.

LABS and SHORAN are used for delivering nuclear weapons. LABS is used for low-altitude delivery. A release-angle setting is precomputed and set into the LABS release gyro. Normally, an over-the-shoulder toss is used. The run to the target is made at 100 feet and 420 knots. When directly over the target, you depress the bomb-release button and initiate a 3½ G pull. A LABS indicator with two perpendicular needles keeps a constant pull and maintains a wings-level attitude. At the precomputed release angle, the system automatically releases the weapon. The pull is continued and recovery made by executing an Immelman on top. You then dive back toward the ground to increase airspeed and exit the area prior to weapon detonation.

SHORAN is for a high-altitude release. This system is dependent upon a ground station, normally within 100 miles of the target, which is definitely a limiting factor. Here, again, the LABS indicator is used for steering information. When the proper signal is received from the ground station, the weapon is released.

The aircraft is so accurate in all modes of delivery (with the exception of strafing) that we gladly challenged other units for beer events on the range. We knew we would lose strafing but could easily cash in on dive-bombing, rocketry, and skip bombing. The range officers in Japan were friendly, and any delivery within 30 feet of dead center was classified as a ''bull.'' It was not uncommon to go to the range and score a ''bull'' on every bomb and rocket delivered on the entire sortie.

The B-57 was to be phased out of the inventory in 1964–65. The Vietnam Conflict altered this. In April 1964, members of the three B-57 squadrons at Yokota Air Base combined into the 8th and 13th Tactical Bombardment Squadrons and prepared to deploy to Vietnam.

This plan was somehow sidetracked and the two squadrons were deployed to Clark Air Base in the Philippines instead. From April until August, the forces at Clark were augmented with aircrew members, maintenance personnel, and aircraft from the States. Equipment was at a peak, and the aircrews flew daily missions to the gunnery range to improve their delivery tactics.

During May 1964, three aircraft and crews were sent to Tan-Son Nhut Air Base, Vietnam, for combat support missions. We then found we were not the first B-57s in Vietnam. Four RB-57s were already on the ramp at Tan-Son Nhut.

The Tonkin Gulf incident in August 1964 shifted the two squadrons into a semicombat role, and with the bulk of the aircraft and maintenance personnel they deployed to Bien Hoa Air Base in Vietnam. A small contingent remained at Clark to continue the transition and checkout of replacement aircrews and maintenance personnel.

Starting with the deployment to Bien Hoa, the B-57 literally took a beating and the personnel were unable to retaliate. One aircraft was lost in an accident during the deployment, and another ran off the runway on landing. Five more were lost when the Viet Cong launched a mortar attack on Halloween night of 1964. The aircrews had to stand by and do nothing. Due to the political situation, we were allowed to fly only unarmed reconnaissance missions over Vietnam. We were being shot at by the Viet Cong, but our guns were not loaded and the bomb bays were empty. Morale dropped, and for six months we sat in Vietnam and could not do what we had been trained to do and had continually practiced.

Frag orders were the normal means of notification for a mission. They included takeoff time, target, and armament load. These were received daily and then cancelled the next morning. Aircraft were uploaded with various munitions and then down-loaded. We would receive the latest intelligence briefings and then be told to stand by.

This continued until 19 February 1965. On that day, two flights of four aircraft each had been fragged for a mission. The aircraft were loaded with nine 500-pound general purpose bombs in the bomb bay and four 750-pound bombs on the wing stations. The guns were loaded and armed. Aircrews were briefed on the specifics of the mission and the frequencies for the forward air controller (FAC). The aircrews went to the flight line for their normal preflight. The engines were started and before-takeoff checks were performed. This was the furthest we had been allowed to go since our arrival at Bien Hoa. Takeoff time came and still no cancellation.

The commander of the 13th TBS was in the lead aircraft. He took the runway with his flight. The four B-57s took off, made contact with the forward air controller, spotted their target, and delivered their ordnance as briefed.

What followed in the next seven years must surely be outstanding in the history of combat flying. Even though the aircraft were few in number (there were never more than 36 in Vietnam), the ground troops and forward air controllers were always eager to work with the B-57. The original two squadrons were augmented by an Australian squadron flying Canberras.

The capability of the B-57s and Canberras to deliver ordnance with pinpoint accuracy, the time on station, and their maneuverability made them, in my estimation, the greatest air-to-ground jet aircraft during the entire conflict. A flight of four B-57s could deliver ordnance continuously for an hour on any given target. Many of the FACs I talked to would rather have one B-57 to work with than a flight of any other aircraft.

One mission in particular demonstrates the B-57s greatness. An ARVN convoy had been ambushed and pinned down by Viet Cong in a pass near An Khe. The B-57s were to give close air support while helicopters flew into the area, picked up the ARVN troops, and exited out the other side of the pass. When the helicopters started through the pass, the first B-57 started a bomb run. The B-57s flew an extremely tight pattern, and bombs and guns were expended continuously on the area for 35 minutes. The Viet Cong turned their weapons against the attacking aircraft. This allowed the helicopters to do their job. During the withdrawal, not one helicopter was hit by ground fire and not one ARVN soldier was wounded.

Aircrews loved the "old bird" in combat. Its design was the primary reason for the small number of aircraft actually shot down. Two engines located apart, straight mechanical flight controls, and the emergency hydraulic reservoir managed to get most of the aircraft back even when they had to be written off the books after they landed. More aircraft were lost due to accidents and just being old than to being shot down. The greatest loss of aircraft and aircrews occurred on 16 May 1965. An explosion on the parking ramp at Bien Hoa destroyed 10 B-57s and fatally injured 7 aircrew members and 20 maintenance personnel.

The USAF B-57s and Australian Canberras flew continuously in Southeast Asia until 1972. The basic mission remained the same but innovations were incorporated into the aircraft. Night missions became a reality in 1965. Flares were dropped from either another B-57 or a C-130 aircraft to illuminate the target and then B-57s would appear out of the darkness and deliver their ordnance.

Test platforms for new improved sensor and weapon delivery systems were sent to Vietnam. These aircraft were designed primarily for night interdiction. The systems proved reliable, and more airframes were modified. These were the B-57G. With its sophisticated electronic sensors and laser-guided bombs, nothing could hide in the jungle, day or night. These aircraft worked primarily at night, patrolling up and down the "Trail." Spotting a truck, the weapons systems officer would lock-on with one of the sensors, track the target, and drop his ordnance—result, one less truck on the Trail.

In 1972, the last of the B-57s left Southeast Asia, thus ending an extensive, worthy combat history.

My own experience with the B-57 did not end when I left Vietnam in 1965. I was transferred to a Defense Systems Evaluation Squadron. This squadron was equipped with EB-57 aircraft. The mission then, as it remains today, was to play the part of the "friendly enemy." The EB-57s are deployed throughout the continental United States, Canada, Alaska, and as far away as Iceland to fly against preplanned NORAD installations and try to sneak through the defenses. If detected, they direct their ECM equipment against the interceptor sent up to stop their intrusion. In the simulation we were "shot down" many more times than we were able to "slip" through. We wouldn't want it any other way.

In May 1968, I left the Air Force and went to Kansas as an Air National Guard Flight Instructor. I joined the 190th Tactical Reconnaissance Group at Forbes Air Force Base. The unit was equipped with RB-57A aircraft, and I was able to participate in yet another of the many roles in which the B-57 has been utilized.

These RB-57s are primarily equipped with K-17 cameras for high- and low-altitude day reconnaissance, K-38 cameras for low- and medium-altitude night reconnaissance, and P-2 oblique cameras for low-altitude day reconnaissance.

Missions were flown at altitudes from 500 feet up through 43,000 feet. The lenses on the cameras could be varied from a 6-inch to a 24-inch focal length depending on the resolution required for the photographs being taken. These "old" aircraft worked out well on the reconnaissance flights. The missions were fun for both the pilot and the navigator. The Tactical Air Command required the aircrews to fly extensively on low-level (500 feet) routes and to acquire photographs of specified targets along the way.

In addition to the routine daily training, the unit was tasked several times for special projects, which meant deployments to such places as Puerto Rico and the Panama Canal Zone.

Flight of RB-57As in formation.

We retained the RB-57s until March 1972. Then the unit converted to the B-57G aircraft returning from Southeast Asia. I had completed a circuit in the B-57 mission roles: I was back to the bombing mission. The biggest differences for me in this change to the B-57G were the new sensors and ordnance delivery techniques. Before I had only a gunsight for ordnance delivery and a navigator to help spot targets and call off altitudes and airspeed during the delivery pattern. This time we had a weapons system officer with us and he was surrounded by sophisticated electronic sensors. He would track the target, lock-on, and set up the weapon panel for an automatic delivery. The information obtained by the sensors was sent to a computer. The computer analyzed the information, set the weapon panel for the release, and relayed the required steering information to the flight director system. When the systems were peaked up, a weapon could be delivered at night with pinpoint accuracy using only the light of the moon to find the target. We kept the range maintenance personnel busy repairing the pylons after a busy night on the range. For the pilot's fun and amusement, we still had a gunsight installed and a requirement to drop ordnance using the old standby dive and skip methods of delivery.

The unit flew the B-57G until March 1974 when we received the EB-57 aircraft and changed from TAC to ADC. Ironically, we had converted twice in two years and still had B-57 aircraft.

What started for me as a short tour in B-57 aircraft in 1963 has extended into a lengthy and enjoyable career. I have more than 6,000 hours of flying time with more than 3,200 hours in the B-57. I feel I know the "old bird" pretty well and certainly feel at home in it. I still enjoy listening to the fighter pilots relate their stories and add at the end, "You probably wouldn't understand that, being an old bomber pilot." I just sit back and listen and every once in a while tell them, "This old bomber pilot will give you 500 feet of altitude and 50 knots of airspeed and bet you a beer I'll be on your tail in less than a minute."

When the last B-57 finally makes it to Davis-Monthan for storage, I would certainly like to be the pilot that delivers it. Perhaps the B-57 and I will retire at the same time.

LT. COL. ROY J. CARROW, JR., entered Pilot Training in 1957 and received instruction in T-34, T-28, and T-33 aircraft; he received his pilot rating in 1958.

His first assignment was in F-86F aircraft at Williams AFB, Arizona.

He later instructed in T-33 and T-37 aircraft until May 1963 and was then transferred to Yokota AB, Japan, where his career in B-57 aircraft began.

He now flies the B-57 and C-131 aircraft with the Kansas Air National Guard at Topeka.

(Above) C-141 cockpit. (Right) C-141 Starlifter arriving at Hickam AFB, Hawaii.

C-141 Starlifter

ALTON P. H. BREWER, JR.

THE date was 17 December 1963, 60 years to the day after the first powered flight at Kitty Hawk. Leo Sullivan and three members of his test-flight crew boarded a sleek, new, swept-wing aircraft. Minutes later the graceful bird lifted off the runway at Dobbins AFB, Georgia, and the maiden flight of the C-141 Starlifter was under way.

This flight on #12775 was originally scheduled as a taxi test. Only a handful of people were aware that the test crew had a "green light" for flight if all systems appeared stable. Assembled photographers and reporters (an aircraft as well known and as large as the Starlifter attracted media representatives even for a taxi test) were treated to an unexpected and historic moment as the big bird accelerated, then rose into the air.

This flight generated a keen interest in all of us scattered throughout the Military Air Transport Service (MATS) worldwide airlift system. It meant we were one step closer to the day when we would get an aircraft designed explicitly for strategic airlift. Under the guiding pressure of airlift's number one congressional champion, L. Mendel Rivers, two modernized interim aircraft, the Boeing C-135 and the Lockheed C-130, had been purchased for MATS. The C-141 was destined to replace both of these as well as the C-118. On 1 January 1966, the MATS (operational since 1 June 1948 with a mission of cargo and personnel transport) became the Military Airlift Command (MAC) and was placed on a par with other major combat elements. The C-141 was to become the MAC workhorse.

An initial cadre was assembled to learn the operation of this magnificent new machine and then to train crews. Moving from a propeller-driven aircraft into a fan jet requires some reorganization of one's thought processes, even if the transition is from the relatively fast and high-flying C-130. "Getting behind the airplane" is an anxious feeling and a common sensation for almost everyone who has made the transition from either a smaller or a slower aircraft. For this reason, MAC pilots do not spend their first hours at the controls of the aircraft. Instead, the pilots, along with the primary flight deck crew members and the engineers spend four weeks in a classroom learning the aircraft systems. This is followed by two weeks of simulator flying built around ten flights that involve learning normal and emergency procedures and the crew coordination required and getting "a feel for the bird." Only then is a pilot ready to step into the real thing.

Most pilots are introduced to the C-141 on the flight line at Altus AFB, Oklahoma, home of MAC's Transport Training Unit (TTU). The crew bus stops a few feet from the nose of the aircraft and one can begin to visualize the true size of the machine. Huge, swept wings, attached to the very top of the fuselage, droop out and down until they are within eight feet of the ground. The engines, mounted beneath the wing, can be inspected from the ground without the aid of a ladder because the bottom of the outboard engine is only five feet from the ground. The wings betray their size: 3,228 square feet of wing surface housing 153,352 pounds of fuel (25,558 gallons). The fuselage, designed for loading direct from a flatbed truck, is usually about 18 inches from the ground. The aircraft fuselage curves gracefully up and in to form the horizontal stabilizer. Finally, 40 feet above ground level, perched precisely on top of the vertical stabilizer, is the horizontal stabilizer housing the elevator trim motors and elevator actuators. The bullet-shaped leading edge of the stabilizer is the high-frequency antenna. At first sight, head on, I was anxious to be about the business of operating the real machine, yet a bit apprehensive about manipulating those huge wings and powerful engines.

Pilots arrive at the aircraft to find the engineers busy with their preflight chores. On training missions navigators and loadmasters are usually not assigned to the flight. On an operational mission with either cargo, passengers, or both, the minimum crew complement will be two pilots, two engineers, one navigator, and one or more loadmasters. Routinely this complement is augmented with instructors and students to meet the demands for operational mission training.

The Starlifter is a crew-served airplane, with each crew member an expert in his discipline. Operation of the airplane requires each crew member to work in his area virtually unsupervised. All efforts are coordinated by adhering to the copilot's checklist and are keyed to the pilot's commands. A new crew member, or one transferring from a much smaller aircraft, finds the crew coordination requirement one of the top challenges for qualification in the C-141.

Preflight inspection consumes approximately 45 minutes of predeparture time; when complete and the crew has settled into the cockpit, the checklist ritual begins. The pilot commands, "Before Starting Engines Checklist." With that the engineer sets up fuel, electrical, hydraulic, and environmental systems while the pilots tune radios, position flap controls, and select navigation systems displays. Outside, the alternate engineer, called the scanner, signals the launch crew to remove the landing-gear pins and main-gear chocks and to insert nose-gear chocks. The activities of all fuse as the copilot challenges each for his report—"Engineer's report, Scanner's report"—and then reports to the pilot, "Before Starting Engines Checklist complete."

To start the four 21,000-pound thrust engines, bring them to idle speed, and complete the usual hydraulic and electrical checks associated with engine start takes approximately four minutes. This time has been halved very easily in several special circumstances, specifically when the aircraft came under fire in Southeast Asia. The pilot starts the engines by pushing in a starter button, which is automatically held in until the pneumatic starter cuts out, and then moving the Fuel and Start Ignition switch to the run position when the high-pressure compressor section of the engine achieves 15%. The engineer's role in the engine-starting procedure is almost as simple. He positions pneumatic bleed air switches to route the air pressure for starting the engine and then, once it is idling, checks the performance of the engine-driven generator and hydraulic pump.

Taxiing is very easy with proper respect given to the big bird's 160-foot wingspan. A slight advance of power out of the idle range and the plane is under way. On a level ramp, at average weights, taxi seldom requires more than an idle power setting, idle being expressed as a percentage (54% rpm) of the high-speed compressor section. The engine at full power turns at 9,655 rpm. Nosewheel steering for the pilot renders the task virtually effortless. Conversely, for the other crew members the time spent taxiing for takeoff is one of the busier periods. The final checks are run and the copilot makes radio adjustment, copies the flight clearance, sets wing flaps, and arms the spoilers in case of an aborted takeoff. The navigator must program the computer and tune the radar. The engineer is occupied with the environmental systems operation and completes a checkout of the fuel system. The loadmaster, busy with passengers or cargo, is active up to the moment the Starlifter is eased onto the runway to start the takeoff roll.

A pilot's physical exertion in controlling the C-141 is minimal. All control surfaces are hydraulically powered. Trim is either electric or hydraulic motor driven. In addition to the nosewheel steering, a hydraulic-powered rudder pedal steering system allows the aircraft to be steered from either pilot's seat and the takeoff to be made without holding the nose-gear steering wheel.

Taxi in heavy crosswinds even up to 50 knots can be accomplished with ease on a dry surface, using only the nosewheel steering and holding in a little upwind aileron to keep the wing down. The natural droop of the wing helps considerably here.

Lift-off speeds run a gamut from the 110–115 knots used for a light training mission to the 139 knots at maximum gross weight of 323,000 pounds. As the computed speed is reached, a slight back pressure to establish a nose-up angle of 6–8° will find the aircraft airborne and rapidly accelerating to the climb speed of 280 knots.

Stick pressures in the aircraft are surprisingly light: slightly more than the C-130, significantly less than the C-47 or C-54. On a typical mission, only the takeoff, the first several minutes of the climb, and the last hundred feet on approach and landing are hand flown. "George," the pilot's best friend, is put to work for the remainder of the flight. The Starlifter's "George," or Automatic Flight Control System (AFCS), is an immensely capable friend. Coupled to the navigator's computers or ground-navigation facilities, "George" deftly guides the lateral axis. Once cruise altitude is reached, altitude hold will maintain the level within a few feet—even at Flight Level 410 (41,000 feet). With control-wheel steering, the pilot can use the autopilot systems to trim the aircraft by zeroing out the forces he feels on the ailerons and elevators. With the addition of the Category II All Weather Landing System, in conjunction with the Instrument Landing System, the aircraft has been flown to many touchdowns in zero visibility by the autopilot at various airports throughout the world.

The C-141, with less wing sweep than most jet transports and a wing thickness that allows a slower takeoff and landing speed, pays for such features by surrendering cruise speed. We were indeed a curiosity when we first arrived in the high-altitude jet airspace structure! The C-141's optimum cruise regime is FL 350 through FL 410 at Mach .74 (495 mph). Other transport aircraft in this airspace cruise between FL 300 and FL 350 at Mach .82 (707 or KC-135) or even Mach .85 (747).

The C-141 handles like a real sweetheart in engine-out conditions. At 20,000 feet and full power on one outboard engine and all of the others at idle, it will trim out for hands-off flight at 210 knots. A single engine-out approach and landing is flown exactly like a full four-engine normal landing. But with two engines out on one side, the asymmetrical thrust will make the pilots earn their money just as in any other multiengine machine. With fully redundant hydraulic and electrical systems, many problems plaguing earlier aircraft were engineered out of the Starlifter.

The versatility of the Starlifter is impressive. It can carry 154 troops or 123 paratroopers. Outfitted with airline-style seats, it can seat 120 passengers with the comfort pallet (removable lavatories and passenger galley). In its air ambulance dress, 80 litter patients can be accommodated with 8 attendants. In strict cargo configuration it was designed to airlift a payload of 68,500 pounds.

The many missions performed by this workhorse during its first decade in operational service exemplify the theme of airlift.

The C-141 has positioned presidential limousines; carried Arabian horses, musk oxen, and panda bears; transported hundreds of thousands of American fighting men to and from combat zones and served as an "angel of mercy" in airlifting the wounded home; airdropped divisions complete with men and equipment; hosted astronauts and their space machines; trained several thousand crew members; and most dramatic of all flown several hundred Americans and Vietnamese out of Hanoi.

My long association with this magnificant machine has now spanned the years. It began when I was an initial cadre member from the 76th Military Airlift Squadron, based at Charleston, S.C.

The mission of an airlift squadron is to provide fully qualified aircrew members to operate their assigned type of aircraft throughout the MAC system on training, transport, or combat airlift missions. The airlift squadrons receive crew men initially trained in the aircraft from the TTU at Altus AFB. Instructors and examiners of the operating squadrons take the crew men arriving from the TTU and provide on-the-job training in the daily operation of the aircraft on actual missions. At present (1975), an airlift squadron is assigned 18 aircraft and 36 complete aircrews. At the height of the Southeast Asia conflict this ratio was doubled to 4 crews per airplane.

A second aspect of the operating squadron's mission is to provide continuation training in any special mission assigned the unit, such as the Combat Airdrop Mission (CAM). On the East Coast, Charleston AFB owns this mission and on the West Coast, Norton AFB is assigned the CAM crews.

Once a crew member becomes fully qualified in the normal airlift mission, he returns to Altus for the special CAM training. Once qualified in this mission, the squadron has the task of keeping him current by providing periodic training flights to practice the formation and airdrop maneuvers.

On its high-density routes, MAC has made extensive use of the "stage" system, whereby one crew arrives at a station to enter crew rest and turns the aircraft over to a new crew who continue on in the mission

to the next station—a modern version of the pony express. At the height of the Southeast Asia conflict, Yokota Air Base often had 40 crews staging at one time, each waiting its turn to pick up an incoming plane and press on. In those days, a crew was seldom on the ground at Yokota more than 16–18 hours. Such was the flow of Starlifters.

One of the more welcome side effects of the C-141 achieving operational status was the reduction in crew members' time away from home. A C-130 or C-124 assignment to a Pacific mission from the East Coast meant 18–21 days to work around the system. Outbound stages were through Travis, Hickam, Wake, Guam, Clark, Kadena, and Tachikawa; inbound itinerary was Wake or Midway, Travis, and home. The C-141, with its extended flight capabilities, completes the Northern Pacific route (NOPAC) with a stage at Elmendorf, Yokota, Kadena, Elmendorf, then home—a total of 6 or 7 days in all.

A typical mission begins with a phone call from the squadron duty officer, alerting the crew member. "Show" time is usually 1 hour later. A crew usually includes at least one newcomer. After introductions the aircraft commander briefs initial mission routing, altitude, fuel requirements, training objectives (if any), seat assignments, and special duties. Then with baggage in hand, the crew boards a bus for transport to the plane. Preflight duties quickly get under way. Loadmasters and engineers preflight the aircraft, and the copilot checks radios and life support equipment. The aircraft commander and navigator do flight planning at base operations and check through the Airlift Command Post. Upon their return to the aircraft, the loadmaster will be completing his loading duties and the engineers closing up the huge petal doors at the rear of the cargo compartment. The aircraft commander will glance through the cargo compartment to check the security of the load or, on passenger missions, the progress of preparations for their boarding.

As the flight-deck crew members take their seats and fasten in, the engineer delivers a TOLD card (takeoff and landing data) to the copilot. After a quick double-check, the copilot passes the data card on to the pilot where it is fixed into a clip holder on the instrument panel for display throughout the takeoff, approach, and landing. Most pilots will use the few moments prior to starting engines to brief the final departure details such as route and altitude assignments, navigation radio set-up, and emergency procedures for an aborted takeoff.

C-141 mass takeoff from Kadena Air Base for a drop zone near Suwon, Korea.

The loadmaster gives his briefing after the passengers are loaded, showing emergency exits, location and function of oxygen equipment, and the other life-support equipment. As soon as the loadmaster finishes, the pilot starts the engines and taxies for takeoff, calling for the succession of checklists that tightly control the activity of all of the primary crew members. Six checklists—Before Starting Engines, Starting Engines, Before Taxi, Taxi, Before Takeoff, and Line Up—will have been accomplished before the Starlifter becomes airborne.

The big aircraft fairly leaps into the air. With the huge flaps at approximately 75%, the climb immediately after liftoff is relatively flat, approximately 6° nose-up, until gear retraction. I was always an advocate of engaging the autopilot as soon after takeoff as possible for two reasons: to relieve my inside-the-cockpit workload so I could watch outside more, and to allow me to broaden the span of my attention to the monitoring of navigation radios and to interphone coordination as inflight duties progressed. The copilot is the primary operator of the communications radios, traffic lookout, and altitude and heading monitor. The navigator closely monitors the flight path and his radar, alternately checking weather and terrain and updating his flight plan with ETAs based upon actual departure versus the filed anticipated departure time. A scanner, with primary traffic monitor duties is assigned to the jump seat between the two pilots whenever the aircraft is below 10,000 feet. Other crew members are generally seated on the flight deck, which has seat belts for ten. Seating is restricted to a maximum of nine, however, due to the structural inadequacy of the jump seat in the event of a crash landing or ditching. In addition to the regular crew, an instructor or examiner from one of the three aircrew disciplines manning the flight deck is usually on board.

The initial power reduction, to approximately 92%, follows gear retraction and just precedes flap retraction, according to the climb schedule being flown. When 10,000 feet is passed, the power is established at normal rated thrust (NRT), which is the maximum continuous power setting for the remainder of the climb.

As the climb profile is established, the loadmaster begins an initial beverage service for his passengers and the flight deck crew. This service is more than just a courtesy. Fluid intake is necessary to combat the dehydration experienced when working many hours in an environment with an extremely low humidity factor.

The scanner slips back to check the hydraulic service centers and the pressure door, returning to the flight deck to silently indicate all is well. The time required to achieve cruise altitude varies, of course, but usually averages about 25 minutes, or 2,000 feet per minute.

Although the crew refers to a "climb power setting," the power used is really normal rated thrust, the maximum continuous power setting. The parameters of thrust, rpm, and fuel flow change gradually throughout the climb as the engines gain maximum efficiency with altitude. Initially the power is reduced to approximately 90% of the N2 rpm or high-speed compressor at a fuel consumption of 40,000 pounds per hour, but as cruise flight is entered at altitude, the rpm will have increased to approximately 95% and the fuel flow decreased to 22,000 pounds per hour. In cruise flight the rpm is usually 87% at a fuel flow of 12,000 pounds per hour. The Starlifter will enter climb at about 3,000 feet per minute vertical velocity in all but the hottest climates. It will usually pass 20,000 feet at better than 1,000 feet per minute.

During the climb, the engineer has calculated a target power setting and indicated the airspeed necessary to obtain the desired Mach number for cruise. When this speed is reached, the power comes slowly back and cruise flight begins. As an old Gooney Bird pilot I had subscribed to the "step" theory and invariably climbed about 100 feet above the cruise altitude and descended into cruise to find a knot or so extra for the same power setting. However, the Starlifter with its altitude hold and broad power range, has defied application of this technique. In long-range cruise the airplane will traverse several different temperature environments, requiring power changes to maintain constant speed just as gradual power reductions are required as weight decreases. With the increased span of parameters such as weight, altitude, speed, and autopilot control, the phenomenon of the "step" has been lost.

However, another of the "old" techniques of C-47 days is applicable to the operation of the C-141 today. This technique—synchronizing the fans—has proved to be a valuable "carry-over." Prop aircraft developed after the C-47 were equipped with prop-synchronization; thus automation took care of the job. The C-141's engine fans chew their way through fairly dense low-altitude air at high power settings and the resulting annoying vibrant harmonic is loud enough to be heard under the pilot's headset. This noise can be smoothed out by applying the technique used to achieve synchronized props in the C-47 or C-54—just a gentle nudge of the throttle to increase or decrease the engine's power. This procedure in the prop airplane involved moving the prop pitch lever. In the C-141 the only lever to move is the throttle. The results, however, are identical: the harmonic vibration blends into smoothness. The pilot is guided in this procedure by a crew man or a headset stationed to the rear of the aircraft so that he will know when the setting is correct.

The C-141 can cruise for what seems an eternity. The daily route structure features mission segments such as Hickam to Anderson (Honolulu to Guam), usually an eight-hour flight plan, or Yokota to Travis (Tokyo to San Francisco), seldom less than 9½ hours. Longer legs are possible. I have flown as long as 10½ hours, and others have done more than 11. In-flight crew rest facilities for such missions are essential. On the flight deck proper, two people can bunk, one in an upper berth, which is used by the pilots, and one in the lower bunk, which is used by the off-duty engineer. Immediately aft of the flight deck and situated above the comfort pallet or number one pallet position, MAC has added a crew rest facility, containing two additional bunks. The loadmasters, navigators, and any extra crew members rotate through these bunks.

In the cruise flight regime two crew positions will always be manned: one of the two pilot positions and the engineer's panel. Depending on the route location, the navigator may not be required (flying airways for example). During long-range cruise, a specific work-rest plan is used. Although exact duty times vary from one crew to the next, most crew members will work for two to three hours then break for two to three hours. MAC rules require the pilot in command to be in his seat until cruise altitude is reached, 30 minutes prior to descent, and when penetrating an Air Defense Identification Zone (ADIZ). For these reasons most aircraft commanders will take a sleep break at the midpoint in a long flight. During cruise, when beyond the range of VOR or TACAN stations, the navigator must keep the inertial computer programmed through celestial shots or LORAN. This computer output is displayed on the pilot's heading situation indicator (HSI) in place of ground navigation guidance. Coupling the autopilot into this mode reduces the pilot's duties to tending the communications radios, monitoring fuel-range plots prepared by the navigator and engineer, and passing the hourly position report.

MAC utilizes a somewhat unique system for its oceanic position reports. First of all the reports are passed directly to a USAF Global Communications network instead of directly to the controlling civilian air traffic control facility. The USAF Globcom station then relays the report to the civilian controller—an efficient way to reduce frequency congestion. Second, with each position report goes a computer-calculated wind speed and direction report which is forwarded directly to a central weather and flight-planning computer. Thus the flight plans for MAC's worldwide routes are continually updated.

In cruise flight, the C-141 reveals its true luxury to former fighter and bomber pilots: the space to stand and stretch, to go for a stroll, or to use a fairly spacious and comfortable lavatory!

Almost without exception pilots of the Starlifter prefer enroute descents rather than the jet penetration. A penetration, easily accomplished by the C-141, requires spoiler deployment to the maximum in-flight limit and thus produces a noisier ride with more vibration. It does provide for a descent rate of 4,000–5,000 feet per minute, allowing the aircraft to drop from 20,000 feet to ground level in 30 miles and about five minutes of elapsed time. The enroute descent from FL 350 is begun ideally about 110–115 miles from the approach fix and generally about 35 minutes prior to block-in. A descent rate in the vicinity of 2,000 fpm is common. This requires a small amount of engine power, some of which is also necessary to maintain pneumatic pressure for the environmental systems pressurization of the aircraft. During the descent the checklist ritual begins anew with the Descent and Before Landing checklists to be accomplished prior to turning final. Below 10,000 feet the speed is limited by regulation to 250 knots. Above 10,000 feet a descent speed of 280–300 knots is used.

By far the preferred approach is radar vectors to an ILS final. The aircraft, equipped with the all-weather landing system, can be flown to touchdown by the autopilot on runways equipped with the landing system. The touchdown, flown by the autopilot, is slightly harsher than one flown by hand, and for this reason most C-141 pilots will uncouple the autopilot at decision height and hand-fly the remainder of the approach. My personal technique for the fully coupled all-weather approach has been to use automatic facilities available, including automatic throttles for power control and control wheel steering to provide priority guidance to the autopilot which was actually flying the approach. Using this technique I would establish a few degrees nose-high attitude just prior to touchdown instead of the rather flat touchdown attitude programmed into the all-weather landing system. The result is a very smooth touchdown. As the nose gear is lowered to the runway, the pilot calls for spoiler deployment to destroy the lift of the wings and simultaneously deploys the thrust reversers by bringing the four throttles behind idle into the reverse idle position. With full antiskid braking, spoilers and thrust reversers employed, deceleration of the Starlifter requires very little runway ground roll, often in the vicinity of 3,000 feet. Full use of brakes and thrust reversers on a 10,000-foot runway to achieve a 3,000-foot ground roll causes unnecessary wear and noise, and therefore most pilots

In one trip the C-5 Galaxy airlifted all three stages of a huge Titan IIIC booster missile from its assembly line at Denver to Patrick AFB, Florida.

The presidential limousine ready for loading at Moscow and transporting to Teheran, Iran.

deploy thrust reversers, check the brakes, then let the aircraft roll out to runway's end.

Arriving on the blocks at the destination begins another flurry of activity for the crew. As soon as the passengers are off-loaded, the crew baggage comes off to be loaded into the crew bus. Often the outbound and inbound crew's baggage pass on the ramp, separated by a concrete pathway between the bags.

The outbound crew's pilots, navigators, engineers, and load-masters seek out their counterparts on the inbound crew to learn details of the aircraft's performance, load, and any mission peculiarities. A quick-service maintenance team, usually composed of three ground-crew men, receives a briefing by the engineers regarding any repairs necessary, then refueling begins as the inbound crew hustles off in the direction of the MAC command post.

With maintenance debriefed on the aircraft's status, the forecaster debriefed on enroute weather conditions, the command post duty officer advises the crew when their alert call can be expected. This is followed by a short drive to the base billeting facility where once again the baggage comes off the crew bus and goes into quarters. Some MAC troops joke about the old-time crew members whose arms hung below their knees—a result of 10,000 and more baggage drills! A minimum crew rest period is 12 hours; however it usually averages 18 to 24 hours, depending upon the number of crews in stage, maintenance, or the nature of the mission.

The diversity of the big airplane's many missions is perhaps the most gratifying aspect of association with it. For example, between 1970 and 1972 I flew missions to all continents except the Arctic and Antarctic (Thule Air Base in Greenland should give almost Arctic credit). The many varied missions included a routine resupply at Learmouth on the far Australian coast and at tiny Diego Garcia in the Indian Ocean; the round-the-world Embassy run through Thailand, India, Saudi Arabia, and Spain; combat airlift missions; dropping paratroopers and equipment; initial reduced interval formation (on the wing formation); nuclear airlift; Minuteman missile airlift; an extremely exciting presidential support mission through Salzburg, Austria, Moscow, and Poland; and the Med-Evac missions, some of which were nearly overwhelming in pathos and challenged one's most professional capabilities to provide a smooth ride.

One of these missions stands above all others in terms of job satisfaction. Our crew was alerted at Yokota Air Base, Japan (near Tokyo) for a Med-Evac mission direct to Travis, 9½ hours away. We breezed through the flight planning drill using Alameda Naval Air Station near San Francisco as our alternate. Enroute weather was good, averaging 75 knots tailwind following a mid-Pacific routing about equidistant from Midway Island to the Aleutian Islands. To take advantage of this jet stream our planned altitude was 35,000 feet, distance to run: 4333 nautical miles. Any difficulties encountered near the midpoint of our route which precluded returning to Yokota or proceeding on to Travis would require diversion to Wake or Midway Islands in the mid-Pacific, or to Shemya, Adah, or Cold Bay in the Aleutian chain.

With these details accomplished we proceeded to the aircraft to find the medical crew, composed of a Medical Crew Director (MCD)—Senior Nurse—a flight nurse, and three medical technicians busy checking their equipment and preparing for the patient on-load. Our flight crew, finished with their preflight checks, were tidying up loose equipment while the loadmaster supervised the fleet service personnel stocking the comfort pallet with the in-flight meals. The engineers reported full fuel tanks at 153,000 pounds and no significant mechanical discrepancies.

Prior to loading the patients, the pilot, loadmasters, and medical crew director had a conference to review aircraft emergency procedures, the route, weather, and any special patient requirements. Burn patients in Stryker frames are particularly uncomfortable and sensitive to any jostling, acceleration, and deceleration. Our flight nurse informed us that we had such a patient in our load of 20 litter and 30 ambulatory patients. A sparkling little lady in her midtwenties, but a veteran of a year's worth of these Med-Evac missions, our senior nurse asked that we be as smooth as possible. We promised that we would.

In the predeparture crew briefing I stressed our goal to be as gentle as possible in aircraft operation from the physical manipulation of the airframe to the management of the pressurization system. After the patients were loaded and while the nurse delivered her briefing to the patients and passengers, we copied our flight clearance to be ready to start engines as soon as she finished. With engines started, the checklists complete, and taxi clearance received, I slipped the parking brake off and inched the throttles out of idle to build up enough forward thrust to overcome 323,000 pounds of dead weight. As the wheels started to turn forward, the marshaller signaled for a right turn out of parking and we were off the blocks. Almost as soon as the roll was started, the throttles had to be returned to idle to prevent excessive taxi speed—such is the power of these engines, even at idle.

Enroute to the runway the copilot went through the checklist and configured the aircraft for takeoff. Once cleared, the takeoff roll began, using a rolling takeoff technique where power is gradually set as the aircraft accelerates, sacrificing several hundred feet of runway for the extra smoothness.

Our initial climb altitude was 33,000 feet, which we reached about 25 minutes after takeoff. Several hours later, with about 30,000 pounds of fuel burned off, our weight was down sufficiently to permit a climb to 37,000 feet. We maintained 37,000 feet as our final altitude. Using the USAF high-frequency global communications network we phoned ahead to provide information about the aircraft's maintenance status and patient requirements. We learned that Travis had rain showers with cumulous buildups in the area. This meant our navigator with his radar would become a key figure in the descent for landing as we rely on him to thread our way around the buildups to avoid the fierce bumps as we maneuver for the landing runway.

We picked our way past gateway Redwood and established contact with Oakland center, which would guide our descent to 6,000 feet, at which time Travis AFB approach control would assume responsibility. At 135 miles out I eased the throttles back and nudged into a 3° nose-low attitude to find the 2,000 feet per minute rate of descent that I like.

An abrupt change of sound in flight causes anxiety among passengers and when the passengers are patients, the anxiety is intensified. For this reason, when I reduce power for the enroute descent I take most of the power from the outboard engines and leave the inboard engines set well above idle to provide the bleed air required for pressurization, thus avoiding a significant sound-level change.

Throughout the descent the navigator double-checked each heading and altitude assignment for terrain clearance and suggested headings to avoid the areas of turbulent clouds. As we crossed the northern end of Napa Valley, Oakland center passed us off to Travis approach and suddenly we were busy configuring for our landing. The determination to be smooth, plus the wet runway, produced one of those few touchdowns heard but not felt. Taxi into the blocks was as cautious as the taxi out had been. The deep satisfaction of a long day's work done well was realized when the senior nurse came forward after the patients were offloaded and commented, "Colonel, that was the smoothest flight I have ever had!" I never flew with her medical crew again, but that praise had the same effect on my psyche that is produced by the superb golf shot that occurs when everything grooves perfectly—soul-satisfying contentment for today, keen challenge for tomorrow!

COL. ALTON P. H. BREWER, JR., graduated from Aviation Cadets in 1954 and began his USAF flying as a SAC fighter pilot. After a tour in USAFE flying support C-47s and a two-year stint as a Civil Air Patrol liaison officer, he was assigned to MAC in 1963. Since then he has served in five of MAC's Strategic Airlift Wings and has served a three-year tour in MAC's Aerospace Rescue and Recovery Service. He has been a line pilot, instructor pilot, flight examiner, squadron and wing chief of aircrew standardization (chief pilot), squadron operations officer, commander of the 15th Military Airlift Squadron, and presently serves as Assistant Deputy Commander of Operations for the 62nd MAW at McChord AFB. He has 10,000 hours, 7,000 of which have been in MAC, in approximately 18 Air Force aircraft.

*(Above) F-4A with bomb load.
(Right) Phantoms of the USAF
Thunderbird's display team in flight.*

F-4 Phantom II

ALEXANDER H. C. HARWICK

THE F-4 is a two-place (tandem), supersonic, long-range, all-weather fighter-bomber built by McDonnell-Douglas Corporation. Mission capabilities include: long-range, high-altitude intercepts utilizing air-to-air missiles as primary armament; a 20 mm gun as secondary armament; long-range attack missions utilizing conventional or nuclear weapons as a primary armament; and close air support missions utilizing a choice of bombs, rockets, and missiles as primary armament. Aircraft thrust is provided by two axial-flow turbo-jet engines with variable stators and variable afterburner. Airplane appearance is characterized by a low-mounted swept-back wing with obvious anhedral at the tips, and a one-piece stabilator with obvious cathedral. Dual, irreversible power control cylinders position the stabilator, ailerons, and spoilers. A single, irreversible hydraulic power control cylinder positions the rudder. An integral pneumatic system, charged by a hydraulically driven air compressor, supplies compressed air for normal and emergency canopy operation, as well as emergency operation for the landing gear and wing flaps. The wings can be folded for ease of airplane storage and ground handling. A drag chute, contained in the end of the fuselage, significantly reduces landing roll distances and an arresting hook, that is hydraulically retracted, can be utilized to stop the airplane under a wide range of gross weight–airspeed combinations.

The aircraft is powered by two General Electric J79-GE-17 engines. The engines are lightweight (approximately 4000 pounds each), high-thrust, axial-flow turbojets equipped with afterburner for thrust augmentation. Under sea level, static test conditions, the engine is rated at 11,870 pounds thrust at Mil power, while at Max power it is rated at 17,900 pounds thrust. The J79 features variable stators (first six stages), a 17-stage compressor, a combustion chamber with 10 annular combustion liners, a three-stage turbine, a variable area exhaust nozzle, and modulated reheat thrust augmentation (afterburning). A turbine-type starter, operated by air from an external source or by the expanding gases of a solid-propellant cartridge is used to crank the engines for starting. Either the aircraft battery or an external electrical power source is used to provide electrical power during starting. Engine bleed air, taken from the 17th stage of the compressor, is ducted to the boundary layer control system (aircraft without slats), the cockpit air conditioning and pressurization system, and the equipment air conditioning system. From these systems, it is further ducted to supply air to the air data computer, the engine antiicing system, the fuel tank pressurization system, the pneumatic system air compressor, and the windshield rain removal system.

THE preceding paragraphs are from the aircrew flight manual and serve as an introduction to the Phantom and its engines. My own introduction was on a bright summer day in 1963 at Craig Air Force Base. I had finished another day of flight training in the T-33 and was on the way home when I became aware of a distinctive and piercing whine in the visual traffic pattern. The aircraft made several patterns which gave me time to watch it land. My first impression, other than the excitement of seeing the aircraft I hoped to fly one day, was how large and powerful it looked in comparison to the T-bird. After the crew shut the Phantom down, we were allowed to crawl all over it. I remember first impressions of all the lettering on the panels, the brushes on the throttles, and the complexity of the equipment.

As luck would have it, my class, 64-C, became the first allowed to attend back-seat training in the Air Force's newest and hottest fighter, holder of fifteen world speed, altitude, and time-to-climb records. (Only recently have some F-4 climb records been broken by the F-15 Eagle.) Quite naturally, all the alloted slots were taken by the upper portion of the class starting with the top graduate.

In October 1963 we headed to MacDill AFB, Florida, to become GIBs, "guys in back." Our first flight was in February 1964 after completing radar training. At that time the Air Force had 28 F-4Bs on loan from the Navy. The F-4C, the first Air Force version, was just coming into the inventory, so our training was in both types. The first flight was sensational! We were passing 20,000 feet in what seemed only long enough to get the T-bird airborne. After level-off, my commander gave me the aircraft. It felt like a refined sports car compared to the tired T-bird, but it was hard to maintain level flight due to the forward sloping canopy rails and the excess power.

The rear cockpit of the F-4B was designed for a radar operator rather than a pilot. It was cramped by circuit breaker panels on the sides and by pull-out radar controls. The stick had to be removed in order to pull out the radar scope. Needless to say, after two consecutive radar failures, I quit removing the stick prior to flight and learned to work the set in the stowed position. The F-4C was a much better aircraft for the GIB because it was designed with permanent flight controls in the aft cockpit.

The first year after our checkout in the Phantom was spent upgrading to combat-ready status and giving numerous air shows across the United States. These shows were both official and unofficial. It was always a joy showing off our Phantoms. Once, after a hurricane evacuation from MacDill, our entire contingent of 52 aircraft made consecutive maximum performance takeoffs and climbs using one-minute spacing for the benefit of the F-100 pilots stationed at England AFB. That had to be an impressive sight!

In 1965 we deployed to Naha Air Base, Okinawa, to replace the F-102 unit there and provide air defense for the island. During this time, I began front-seat upgrade training. Although I had enjoyed the ''pit,'' the front seat was and is infinitely better.

The aircraft preflight inspection is really nothing more than a check for leaks, cut tires, unexplainable skin damage, engine condition, ordnance security, and condition. The interior inspection consists of a complete check of switch position followed by engine start during which various systems are brought on the line and checked for proper operation.

After the walk-around inspection, both crew members climb up a special ladder or use a boarding step that can be lowered from the aircraft fuselage. Because the parachutes are built into the Martin-Baker ejection seats, crew members wear a special harness that attaches to fittings on the seat. This is a major improvement over earlier systems when fighter pilots had to lug a cumbersome parachute across the ramp. As a result, it is easy to get into an F-4.

After electrical power is put on, the GIB begins alignment of the inertial navigation system. It takes from 5 to 10 minutes to align the system unless the heading memory mode is used. The system is one which gives the Phantom many of its capabilities, so this apparent long wait is worth it. While the GIB is setting up his systems and computers, the GUF, ''guy up front,'' is getting ready to start the right engine.

Engine rotation is brought about by applying air from an external cart or by use of black powder cartridges. At 10% rpm, the ignition button on the appropriate throttle is depressed and held while the throttle is moved forward to get fuel to the engine. The engine then begins to come up to speed. External air is disconnected at 45% rpm, and the engine continues a rapid increase to idle rpm of 65%. The generator comes on the line at 53% rpm, accompanied by a flicker of cockpit lighting and the telelight panel, which has various lights designed to warn of system malfunctions and to relay information concerning fuel transfer, etc. After checking the electrical system and the flight controls, the left engine is started. Again flight controls are checked and all systems including the radar may be brought on the line. Each crew member checks weapons systems, flight instruments, and begins crew coordination procedures which have been briefed beforehand in order to maximize mission effectiveness.

After the inertial navigation system is fully aligned and switched to ''navigate,'' the GIB clears the aircraft commander to taxi. The aircraft commander makes sure the ground crew is clear and gets clearance to taxi from the tower. All Air Force Phantoms have nosewheel steering which simplifies taxi; however, this system periodically has spurious signals, and thus caution must always be used.

Prior to takeoff, the aircraft is generally looked over by a special ground crew to check for cut tires and leaks. Takeoff roll and speed are a function of gross weight, wind, and temperature. Roll may be as short as 2,000 feet for a light takeoff on a cold day or as long as 7,000 feet at maximum gross weight of 58,000 pounds on a hot day. A 3,000-foot roll with nosewheel lift-off at 140 knots and takeoff at 170 knots is fairly standard for a normal training configuration of two 370-gallon drop tanks, a gun pad, and two bombing dispensers.

Afterburner, which had been selected at brake release, is cut off at 300 knots. The standard climb speed is 350 knots calibrated airspeed to cruise Mach. The F-4 actually climbs better starting at 370–380 knots decaying 2 knots per 1,000 feet of climb until reaching cruise Mach. A very steep climb, although not rapid, can be attained at 180 knots. A maximum climb on instruments is performed at 250 knots. The fastest climb can be attained by accelerating to .92–.94 Mach with a constant Mach climb to about 27,000 feet. The nose is then lowered, a slight dive established to accelerate to above 1.2 Mach to open the vari-ramps and close the engine intakes, the nose raised to maintain slightly over 600 knots calibrated at a low G reading until passing the tropopause which is in the vicinity of 37,000 feet, and a slight "dipsy doodle" performed to exceed Mach 2. All this takes about three minutes from brake release. From this point it is easy to pop up to high altitude to engage a high-flying target or to run out to intercept a target at long range.

My first front-seat takeoff was memorable. In the back seat I had the habit of running the rudder pedals all the way forward because of the cramped leg room. Although this was satisfactory in the back, in the front it caused a bit of personal embarrassment, for when the aircraft accelerated on takeoff, I slid down in the seat and had to look out the side to stay aligned on the runway as the nose came up. After vowing never to make that mistake again, I became aware of how much better the visibility from the front really was: no intakes on the sides hinder downward vision; no metal bulkhead or ejection seat in front obstructs forward vision. After a couple of quick intercepts, we spent the first portion of the mission on stalls and aerobatics. Then we found a large rock jutting out of the Pacific and proceeded to make multiple simulated air-to-ground deliveries. The next mission was an air-to-air training sortie in a clean aircraft against another GIB also on his second front-seat mission. At that time there were no GIB upgrade programs in existence, so we were trained to be fighter pilots in the old tradition.

After this introduction to the front, I was reassigned to RAF Station Woodbridge, to the first USAFE wing converting to the Phantom. Flying in Europe during this tour was not only enjoyable but also excellent preparation for combat. The fun included an exchange with a Belgian F-104 squadron, flying crew chiefs in the back seat at Wheelus, being combat-ready in the front, and cross-country missions to Italy, Spain, Germany, and Denmark. Although the normal cruise speed at altitude is .88–.92 Mach or 310 knots calibrated, on one occasion I returned from Aalborg, Denmark, to Woodbridge in 25 minutes, measured from brake release to touchdown at destination. That's an average speed of just over 1,250 mph or slightly more than double our normal ground speed. And part of that flight was subsonic due to supersonic flight restrictions along portions of the flight path.

The preparation for combat included over 1,500 flight hours in three years, realistic training in all phases of tactical fighter flying, and an opportunity to experiment. During my European tour I had the opportunity to fly against the Lightning, Hunter, F-84, F-100, F-104, Mystere, and Mirage. This experience confirmed two basic facts about the F-4: using proper tactics it can defeat any of these fighters, and any of these fighters can defeat an F-4 using tactics that would be employed against another F-4.

The Phantom is an honest airplane that gives more than ample warning when it is being pushed too hard. When it is accelerated properly, the pilot feels both the seat belt across his lap and the seat cushion beneath him. A very mild rumble is felt in the seat when the aircraft is in an optimum turn, a turn that tends to conserve energy. In a maximum turn the aircraft gives a distinctive buffet. Beyond this rate of turn, it goes into hard wing-rock before it lets go and chases its tail. All that is required to stop the fuss is to release back pressure on the control stick. To spin a Phantom takes an asymmetrical load, an out-of-trim aircraft, a bent airframe, or a ham hand. Should one meet any of these conditions, he needs only to break the angle of attack by putting the stick forward and/or using the drag chute.

We also had ample opportunity to learn about air-to-ground. We flew radar low levels in the fog using crew coordination, the radar altimeter, and *precise* navigation. The land-water contrast, which shows up well on a radar set, aided this effort. England also has excellent low-level flying areas where we practiced flight tactics against abandoned World War II airfields. The F-4C does not have a computing sight or automatic dive-release system as do later versions of the Phantom. It is, however, a stable air-to-ground platform. Proper use of the GIB makes the F-4 superior to the F-100 and to other previous systems because with proper crew coordination it is possible to eliminate certain variables in the gunnery pattern. I know this comment will offend some single-seat jocks; but it is a fact that we never lost a gunnery competition to either the F-100s or the F-105s at Wheelus. On one occasion I scored six consecutive bulls in 45° dive-bomb during a competition. Our wing circular error average (CEA) for all bombs dropped in 1968 was 80 feet, which is considered very good for manual dive-bombing.

My next assignment was to the USAF Fighter Weapons School at Nellis. In addition to honing our air-to-air and air-to-ground skills, we learned how to optimize usage of the F-4 navigation systems on the combat profile missions. The F-4 has a TACAN like most modern aircraft;

The F-4 is not as pretty as the P-51, as smooth in roll as the F-104, as stable at low altitude as the F-105, or as light feeling as the F-106, but it is a beautiful blend of all these and others.

but this may be of little value in a combat environment. The inertial navigation system gives the F-4 the ability to navigate in a hostile environment without emitting any detectable signal. This system also provides information to the weapons-release computer system (WRCS), which can be used to correlate navigation information obtained from the radar set. Some F-4s also are equipped with LORAN. Upon completion of the school, I was sent to the 555th Tactical Fighter Squadron at Udorn Royal Thai Air Force Base as a weapons officer.

Flying fighters in combat has to be the most exciting and rewarding flying there is. During the year tour I flew 800 hours—over 750 hours combat time, of which 500 hours were flown as an F-4 forward air controller. During that year the Phantom proved its versatility, reliability, and lethality.

In general, our missions were flown as a four-ship flight assigned to a Forward Air Controller who would control us in the target area. We generally refueled from a KC-135 on the way to the target in order to extend our station time in the target area. The off-load was generally 3,000–4,000 pounds to make up for takeoff and climb fuel. The forward air controllers took 13,000–17,000 pounds at a time. The higher figure was the result of tankers out of position, working a strike farther away than originally planned on some priority target, or getting involved in a search-and-rescue mission. The F-4 takes on fuel at the rate of 3,900 pounds per minute from a KC-135. During refueling it burns from 400 to 700 pounds. Considering an F-4 with two tanks can hold only about 17,500 pounds of fuel, some of the refuelings were critical. Our normal refueling altitude was 24,000 feet at 310 knots, the standard refueling speed, which meant that as we became heavier with the extra fuel, the Phantoms became sluggish like tired old nags heading for the glue factory. Refueling at night under the above conditions was very tedious.

Our ordnance generally consisted of some combination of 500-pound or 2,000-pound bombs, Bullpups, cluster bomb munitions (CBU) of assorted types, or the Rockeye, which is sometimes regarded as a CBU munition. We also carried the Sparrow missile for air-to-air and electronic jamming equipment. Even though the F-4Ds we flew had dive-toss equipment, we seldom used it.

Dive-toss is an automatic release mode that compares radar range and proper delivery parameters during a diving attack. It integrates input from several sources including the inertial navigation system. Each contributing system must be kept peaked if the dive-toss mode is to consistently deliver ordnance on or near the target. As a rule, dive-toss will put ordnance closer to target than manual dive-bombing in a hostile environment when concentration on exact delivery parameters is difficult. Our wing did as well as the wing at Korat, which had ". . . hot from Korat" as a motto, and delivered almost exclusively using dive-toss. Their bombs were like the little girl with the curl in the middle of her forehead: when they were good, they were very, very good; but when they were bad they were horrid! Some of the best bombing from F-4s I saw while I was a FAC was delivered using dive-toss. Dive-toss was also responsible for the worst bombing I ever saw, including some that missed by spectacular distances, well over a mile on some occasions. As a result, dive-toss was never used when "friendlies" were near or during search-and-recovery missions, when we were recovering downed crew members.

Dropping bombs and CBUs and shooting Bullpup radio-controlled missiles was good sport; but flying FAC missions in the F-4 had to be

F-4 instruction manuals.

more fun than anything except the thrill of downing an enemy fighter. The F-4 was and is well suited to the forward air control role for several reasons. It has good response at both low and high airspeed with very good acceleration. The FAC mission in a high-threat environment is enhanced significantly by the back-seater; tandem seating is the only acceptable arrangement. The inertial navigation system (INS) and the weapons release computer system (WRCS) add a vital tactical capability because it is possible to "memorize" a target position and get steering initially to locate it or find it again without having to hang around the target area and get shot at.

The normal F-4 FAC mission lasted about four hours and included four refuelings, one enroute to the target area and one each hour for the next three hours. The standard load was two external fuel tanks, an externally mounted 20 mm gun pod on the centerline station, two or three pods of 2.75-inch phosphorus marking rockets, fuselage-mounted Sparrow missiles, and a jamming pod. Though not a frisky colt like a clean Phantom, the F-4 with this FAC configuration was a thoroughbred capable of impressive performance. On one occasion, to mark a target for a succession of fighters in dismal weather, I flew seven consecutive loops to score or assess ordnance effectiveness and to be in a position to fire a rocket as the next fighter was attacking the target area with the exact target not yet in sight. That the Phantom could be flown in this manner attests to its performance.

In addition to being agile, the F-4 is durable. An F-4D I was controlling one day had the outer portion of its wing, from the fold outward, shot away during a pass. The pilot recovered the aircraft and returned to base with no further difficulty. I had a tank fail at 5 Gs in a 45° dive while marking a target only seven minutes after a full load of fuel. The aircraft pitched up and rolled but was easily recovered by releasing back stick pressure and applying proper aileron and rudder. On another occasion I had an engine blow apart resulting in little fuss other than a single-engine landing.

My own F-4 was named *The Naughty Lady*. During the course of the war it was awarded a purple heart with three oak leaf clusters, having survived a 23 mm shell through the wing, a 37 mm between the front and rear cockpits that sent the plane out of control and the GIB out via the ejection seat (he was later picked up after a gun battle on the Plaine des Jarres), an AIM-9 Sidewinder missile that impacted the left main gear during a loading accident, and a terrorist attack that resulted in damage to the belly from several hand grenades thrown under it. In spite of all this, F-4D #65–708 flew smoothly and with very few write-ups for malfunctions.

The F-4 seems to have fewer malfunctions the more it flies. When it sits on the ramp for a couple of days, it begins to leak and develop mystical maladies. Although plans call for 35–40 maintenance hours per flying hour, the plane can be turned around rapidly and flown three or four times per day if need be. Unfortunately some of the "mirrors and magic black boxes" are located in out-of-the-way places, requiring removal of the aft cockpit ejection seat bucket when they pack up.

Everyone who has flown combat has memories of his missions. Mine include the joys of watching SAM (surface-to-air missile) sites get blown away, controlling laser bombs on gun pits and seeing direct hit after direct hit, watching large caches of fuel go up in gigantic flames, emptying in two strafe passes all 7,200 rounds on 13 trucks stuck in a ford, and watching the Thuds consistently drop good bombs on whatever target they were assigned. I also saw horses stampede and men fall off bicycles when they became aware of a high-speed FAC looking over a road, as well as a Ping-Pong game in the jungle. It was also great sport on murky days flying supersonic at very low altitude through the mountain passes without ordnance. This scattered repair crews and on one occasion disrupted a picnic beside a waterfall we had created in repeated bombings along the road segment.

After my Southeast Asia tour, I was assigned as an instructor at the USAF Fighter Weapons School at Nellis. During this tour I instructed Southeast Asia-bound crews in the finer points of employing terminally guided munitions. "Smart bombs" as they are sometimes called were and are being pioneered on the F-4 weapons system; they mark a very significant technical advance. These weapons increase the already excellent weapons capability of the Phantom and ensure that the F-4 will be a major weapon system for a considerable time.

During my tour at Nellis, I was able to fly and compare the C, D, and the E—sometimes all on the same day. The F-4 has the same engines as the C but weighs more. As a result it is significantly slower than the other two. In fact, few Ds will reach Mach 2 without running out of fuel, but both the C and the E will reach Mach 2 fairly easily. The C will keep up with the E in a drag race with less thrust because of less weight. The RF-4C, in which I also have a little time, will match the E.

With just over 700 hours in 11 months, I returned to Europe as a weapons officer with the 32nd Tactical Fighter Squadron at Soesterberg Air Base, the Netherlands. The squadron flies F-4Es and is responsible for providing air defense. The flying in Holland can also be quite good, particularly during exercises when targets range from supersonic, high-altitude to Harriers on the deck. The rules require not only gun-camera film, which confirms weapons parameters, but the tail number, which gets sporting when a Harrier wants to try to deny the information. Once again the Phantom proved that if flown properly it is a match for anything other than our very newest fighters such as the F-15 and F-16.

When USAFE created a tactics school at Zaragoza Air Base, Spain, I was reassigned there. During this tour I had the opportunity to fly the "slatted E," which is the latest USAF Phantom variant. This new model has a beautifully redesigned cockpit, made to be used by a fighter pilot to bring ordnance to bear on the enemy rather than by some human engineer who mans a mahogany bomber for a living. The slats were added to improve the turning performance. They do this, but at the price of higher drag with resulting high-energy decay. Because the amount of energy available defines the limits of options available in an air-to-air engagement, it is imperative to manage energy extremely carefully in this new Phantom.

Although not a single-seat, single-engine aircraft, the Phantom is a fighter in the truest sense with a name and a tradition that will long be remembered in the annals of aviation history. I am fortunate to have been able to fly it since its introduction into the USAF. It is not as pretty as the P-51, as smooth in roll as the F-104, as stable at low altitude as the F-105, or as light feeling as the F-106, but it is a beautiful blend of all these and others. It has done its job well in every classic fighter mission and will continue to serve the free world as a versatile and reliable front-line fighter. It has been the standard against which all other fighters in the world have been measured for a decade and a half.

MAJ. ALEXANDER H. C. HARWICK has more time in the F-4 than any other person in the world—3,900 hours. He has flown the F-4B, C, D, E, slotted E, and RF-4C. He has been an instructor at Nellis AFB and the USAFE Tactics School. He was head of the F-4 FAC program at Udorn and flew 257 missions and more than 750 hours in the F-4 in combat. He has spent seven years in Europe flying the F-4.

F-84F Thunderstreak

JOSEPH L. VOGEL

To say the F-84 almost was the cause of my death even before I flew it would be stretching the point a bit, but the incident did help me to tighten my preflight procedures and that helped to save my life on at least one other occasion.

As a fresh, "newly winged" pilot just out of jet training, I was undergoing the required 10 hours of hood (instrument training) time in a T-33 prior to being turned loose in an F-84F at Luke AFB, Arizona. As I sat in the back seat that February morning in 1957, I busied myself getting the many straps and buckles fastened when a flight of four swept-wing Thunderstreaks taxied past with their four 100-pound "blue boy" bombs under one wing and a brace of rockets and a fuel tank under the other. I paused in my set pattern of strapping in and savored a moment of anticipation, dreaming of the time I would be going to the gunnery range in the real fighter. As I continued, I didn't notice that I had forgot-

F-84F being readied for a Dart Tow Mission. Other fighters fired at the "dart" which hung from a cable about 1,500 feet to the rear of the tow plane. Note the radar reflector at the rear of the dart.

ten the leg straps on my parachute. After takeoff, climb, and level-off, at about 80 miles from Luke, the T-33 engine began to vibrate violently from loss of a turbine blade, and it looked like we would have to abandon the bird. In fact, the front-seater even told me to prepare for the ejection. With judicious use of power and the remaining altitude, we managed to land safely at Luke. As I unstrapped, I felt a profound sense of shock when I noticed that my leg straps were hanging freely down in front of the seat. The F-84F had diverted my attention at the precise moment I would have fastened the leg straps. If we had ejected, I would have squirted out of the bottom of a blossoming parachute with only a few moments to contemplate my fatal error. Since that time, I have never allowed my preflight drill to be interrupted nor have I ever forgotten to fasten securely any of my personal equipment.

For the pilots who had the privilege of flying the F-84F Thunderstreak, frustration and fascination rode with them in that single-seat, single-engine tactical fighter bomber. The "Thud's Mother," as it later came to be known, underwent a conventional birth and a fretful childhood and finished its service life without a chance to prove itself in combat. Republic built the F-84F with the strength to live up to the reputation of its venerable grandma, the P-47, the Jug. By sweeping back the flying surfaces, the engineers intended to erase the Mach and maneuvering limits that were a drawback for its straight-wing ancestors, the F-84G and E. [On the flying of the straight-wing F-84, see *Flying Combat Aircraft of the USAAF-USAF* (Ames: Iowa State University Press, 1975.)] With a 33.6-foot wingspan swept back 30°, its length of 43.3 feet, and height at the tail of 15.0 feet, the F was a small aircraft by today's standards. It carried a total of 3,575 pounds of usable fuel internally. During its latter stages in the Air National Guard, it was typically fitted with two 450-gallon (2,925 pounds each) external fuel tanks which nestled close to the fuselage on the inboard wing attach points.

The cockpit of the F-84F was straightforward for fighter aircraft of its day; however, any pilot taller than six feet could begin to feel a bit cramped. After attaching the parachute to the seat survival kit and completing the five-item preflight checklist, the pilot climbed a special aluminum ladder, stepped over the cockpit side, and by twisting a knob ahead of the stick, adjusted the rudder pedals usually to the full-out position. The seat had manual adjustment that had to be locked to ensure successful ejection in case that unpleasant necessity occurred. A left-to-right prestart check insured that the fuel was on, the battery and appropriate warning lights all operating.

The F-84F had several features that only now are again being built into first-line fighters. Fighters subsequent to the Thunderstreak have been tied to complicated ground equipment for starting. With the simple press of a toggle switch on the F-84F, high-pressure air (3,000 psi) and JP-4 jet fuel were fed into a small high-speed turbine that was mechanically linked to the main engine. The mixture was lighted and, with a loud explosion, the engine was spun up to starting speed within about five seconds. The aircraft was even fitted with a utility hydraulic-driven motor compressor which, in about 30 minutes of flight, recharged the high-pressure storage bottle. Of course, as with every good thing, this system had its drawbacks. Sometimes the small starting turbine, which had to spin about 100,000 rpm to bring the engine to idle speed (about 5,000 rpm), would not disengage from the main turbine.

When the pilot ran the engine to 100% rpm, the starter turbine

By sweeping back the flying surfaces, the engineers intended to erase the Mach and maneuvering limits that were a drawback for the Thunderstreak's straight-wing ancestors.

went to astronomical speed and quickly disintegrated. Because the starter was attached to the front accessory case, the pieces were promptly ingested, destroying the high-revving engine in one spectacular explosion. At Luke, the story circulated that during the era when Korean pilots were in training, one hapless individual blew his engine on run-up and started a gigantic fire in the aft section. His instructor, in another aircraft, yelled over the radio, "Kim, Kim, get out; you're on fire!" Because all Korean students were referred to as Kim, two others on that frequency abandoned their undamaged aircraft. Needless to say, the importance of flight call signs was stressed from then on.

No warm-up was necessary unless the engine was being started in extreme cold. Pilots then took the precaution not to move any hydraulic controls until the fluids circulated enough to warm the seals. Premature movement was almost certain to cause a leak in the vital fluids and an abort of the mission. A slight increase in power brought the bird out of the chocks and idle power kept it rolling under most circumstances. Because no power steering was fitted to the castering nosewheel, the pilot kept it straight and turned by judicious use of the wheel brakes which were operated by pressing the toes at the top of the rudder pedals. With a tread of 20.4 feet and power-boosted brakes, the F-84 was very easy to steer.

Pretakeoff checks included ejection seat pins out, canopy closed and locked, parachute low-level lanyard attached, takeoff flaps set at 20°, and engine run-up in less than 15 seconds. If the run-up took longer than that, some malfunction such as dragging bearings or slow fuel control was suspected and the flight was aborted. With full power and a heavy load, initial acceleration was anything but spectacular.

The F-84F, on takeoff, suffered from some of the same ills as the straight-wing version. Notable among these was the lack of thrust from its axial-flow J-65 jet engine. Of the 7,800 pounds of thrust advertised, because of a crook in the tailpipe necessitated by the downward tilt of the engine in its mounts, the F-84F lost approximately 700 pounds when installed. With an operational weight of approximately 25,000 pounds and a hot day, high-altitude takeoff became an affair to remember for the hapless pilot. Typically, at the Mansfield, Ohio, airport, F-84Fs had to taxi into the overrun for run-up and full power check prior to brake release in order to have a safe amount of runway ahead. Takeoff run usually went to 6,000 feet on a 60° day. On 80° days, 7,500-foot takeoff rolls were not uncommon. By retracting engine screens, 4.4% more power was available but hardly noticeable. After flying the F-100 with afterburner and the F-4 with two engines and afterburners, I look back on the Thunderstreak as a very slow performer. The acceleration was slow and smooth compared to the "jolt and go" of burner-equipped aircraft. Early in the life of the F-84F, when I was in training at Luke AFB, Arizona, takeoff rolls were a try-and-see affair. Accurate charts for figuring takeoff distance were not available, and acceleration line-speed checks were devised by the pilot through experience and gut feelings. Later charts showed that 120 knots at 3,000 feet of roll assured a safe takeoff; 165 knots was an average takeoff speed. It was not uncommon for the desert dust at the end of the runway to be churned up by the main gear and tailpipe blast while a very frightened pilot nursed a sagging F-84F out of ground effect. Some did not make it.

Landing gear came up within 8–10 seconds of actuation and had to be up before the speed reached 220 knots. Because the main gear retracted inward, no change of pitch was noted. However with the gear up, the artificial feel unit provided a less sensitive stick movement to stabilator-movement ratio so that large stick movements by the pilot were less likely to over-G the aircraft.

Climb power was always 100% for a single bird. In formation, the leader kept advancing power until the slowest bird began to drop back. He then reduced throttle slightly until the weak plane could keep up. On hot days, it would take as much as 15–20 miles to effect a join-up and get the aircraft up to climb speed of 320 knots.

Cruise was the forte of the F-84F. At 35,000 feet, a Mach of .78 produced a true airspeed of 465 knots at 92% power and 2,300 pounds per hour fuel flow. If you were in a real hurry at 35,000 feet, you could push up the power to 96%, burn about 2,600 pounds per hour, and get almost 500 knots for your effort. Cruising at lower altitudes lowered the true airspeed and raised the fuel consumption figures. In combat, the policy was to run at top speed, never get below 450 knots indicated, punch off the external stores, make one pass, deliver the weapons, and egress as fast as possible.

Early aircraft had a conventional horizontal stabilizer and elevator tail known as the "split tail." In the mid-1950s, an all-moving stabilator, or slab, powered by a dual hydraulic system, replaced the split tail. An electrically powered jack screw provided a third system of control which was dubiously effective even in a dire emergency.

My two-period career with the Thunderstreak began early in 1957 at Luke AFB, near Phoenix, Arizona. My wife and I were driving toward the base on the first of many memorable Fridays and were greeted by a rising column of greasy smoke coming from somewhere beyond the military compound. Soon we spotted a parachute descending toward the hot desert floor. Fridays became memorable because on each of the next five or six someone lost an F-84F at Luke. The Commander was said to have even contemplated cancelling flight operations on Thursday not to fly again until Monday. The major problems centered around the new dual-cylinder hydraulic system. With only hydraulic and no mechanical linkage to the controls, many of the F-51-trained fighter jocks were uneasy when they flew the bird. To them, a loss in hydraulic pressure meant immediate bailout. It was a well-circulated myth that jets blew up immediately after a fire warning light illuminated. A flash of the light or a false indication caused the loss of many a perfectly good fighter.

My only in-flight emergency at the time was subtler and difficult to analyze. Our missions typically ran about 50 minutes in length. On one flight, my fuel gauges refused to budge from full. This situation created a false sense of security until, suddenly, 80 miles from base, the gauges dropped to near zero. After descent with engine idling and some fervent prayer, I touched down and taxied to my parking spot. When the crew chief looked in the tank, only one or two gallons remained. It took several years and a lot more incidents of this type to confirm that the self-sealing rubber tank liners were collapsing as the fuel was pumped out, keeping the float-type indicator showing full until the last moment.

The supervisors of today would blanch if they were forced to handle the crew of aggressive, hot fighter pilots that existed in that more carefree and regulation-free day. In the F-100 which I now fly, air combat maneuvering (ACM) is a carefully orchestrated affair with an aggressor and a defender, very well-defined rules of engagement, and firm limits on who may engage and where. I remember as many as three

flights of eight F-84Fs plotting to meet over the desert about 100 miles from base for a dogfight session. Eyesight and altitude were the trump cards with no FAA altitude restrictions and, indeed, no radar even to know we were in the area. The only rule was that wingmen (new guys) were to stay in fighting wing position on their leader, look back to see that the leaders' tail was clear, and see that no one flew between them and the leader. The fights typically started at above 30,000 feet and ended only when the cactus took a beating from the jet blast or the fuel state (bingo!) called for a turn toward home base. Bingo fuel depended upon the distance from home and rate of fuel consumption. About 3,000 pounds was average bingo anywhere up to 200 miles from home plate. (Total fuel, with tanks, was 9,425 pounds.)

It was said that you could not over-G an F-84F because it would stall prior to reaching its maximum of 8.67. The aircraft handbook did warn about that fascinating maneuver called the accelerated stall pitch-up. If a ham-handed pilot ignored the prestall warnings, he could suddenly find the aircraft trying to swap ends, with the nose rising rapidly and a loud bang announcing a complete stall. If forward stick was not immediately applied, especially at high Mach numbers, pieces of aircraft, including the wings, would soon begin to shred off.

The accelerated stall pitch-up did have one desirable effect. If a particularly aggressive attacker could not be shaken any other way, pulling through the buffet boundary into the pitch-up would scrub off the speed so rapidly that he would zoom right on by. The F-84F pilot then had no choice but to dive straight down to pick up speed to get away, because at low Mach numbers the Thunderstreak was no good at all in combat. Of course, the possibility remained that the old bird would depart controlled flight and go into a spin. Recovery from a spin in the F-84F was a rare event. In fact, the good book stated that if no recovery was evident at 10,000 feet above mother earth, recourse to the ejection seat was the only out.

When a decision to bail out was made, all that needed to be done was raise the seat arm rests and squeeze the triggers. Raising the arm rests released the canopy, slid the elbow retainers forward, and locked the shoulder harness. When the canopy reached full up on the mechanical arms, a squib circuit electrically fired explosive bolts that detached the canopy which then flew off above the tail. Early models had such strong mounting arms that the canopy remained firmly attached to the aircraft when it reached the full-up position. The steel bow was then positioned directly over the pilot's head as he ejected. After several fatal accidents

The Thunderbirds, famous Air Force precision demonstration flying team, land their F-84F Thunderstreaks with parachutes out at Luke AFB, Arizona.

with this bow, holes were drilled in the canopy arm to establish a breaking point. Finally, an explosive squib modification assured canopy separation prior to ejection. A healthy squeeze on either or both of the triggers set off initiators which in turn exploded the charge that shot the seat about 65 feet above the aircraft. An automatic device blew the seat belt open and rolled a web backing tightly against the pilot, his chute, and survival kit, and literally threw him out of the seat. A key device retained the automatic-timer lanyard in the seat belt and if the pilot was above 14,500 feet, he would free-fall to that altitude, delay one more second, and get a chute opening. At low altitudes, the pilot manually hooked and unhooked a lanyard that insured immediate opening if he so desired. Emergency oxygen was provided by a steel bottle about 9 inches long and 2 inches in diameter stowed in the right side of the parachute. A hose piped the 10-minute supply of oxygen to the pilot's mask when he pulled a large round green "apple" on the right side of the parachute. The seat was very reliable, and only the pilots who waited too long were ever disappointed.

Shooting the six forward-firing .50 caliber machine guns (four in the upper nose and one in each wing root) was a fascinating experience. Each gun carried 300 rounds in combat configuration and fired about 1,250 rounds per minute. From the ground, it sounded like an erratic Gatling burping out the bullets. Air-to-air and air-to-ground (strafing, bombing, and rocketry) were fairly accurate affairs with the A-4 gun-bomb-rocket sight and the AN/APG-30 ranging radar. The sight and radar automatically computed the lead for firing on flying targets, but Kentucky windage had to be used by aiming the sight "pipper" upwind for ground targets. Skip bombing was the most fun and the most accurate. The pilot approached the target from about 35 feet (later raised to stay out of ground fire) at about 380 knots. When the sight slid over the target, the bomb button on the stick was pressed and an immediate pull-up was started. I once made 55 consecutive passes over a six-month period without a single miss.

To most pilots, landing was a piece of cake, thanks to the wide landing gear and the powerful control of the stabilator. The pattern was entered at 300 knots, with a break to downwind, accompanied by speed brakes out and throttle momentarily reduced to check the warning system. The downwind speed was 220 knots until gear and flaps were down. On base, 190 knots was used, and the pilots shot for 165 knots (adjusted upward for fuel load) on final. The F-84F was one swept-wing aircraft that had a beautiful flare and landing. Even the tyros were able to make good landings with very little practice if they held the proper airspeed on final. It was possible to over-rotate and scrape the tail skid, which cost the pilot the traditional case of beer for the crew chiefs who had to repair it.

After touchdown, the nosewheel was held high for maximum aerodynamic drag. Drag-chute landings were practiced but usually held to be the mark of a poor pilot who could not hold proper airspeed on final. After the nose came down, brakes were used for steering below 60 knots because nosewheel steering was not installed.

On engine shut-down, only one caution was observed. It was said that turning the battery switch off before the engine stopped might allow hydraulic fluid to leak past the landing gear selector valve and release the landing gear uplocks. Downlock pins were installed by the crew chief to preclude that possibility. It was always a good idea to recheck the installation of the ejection seat pins prior to exiting because an unscheduled trip up the rails, and they happened occasionally, always ended in disaster.

Compared to the T-33, the F-84F was a comfortable, long-legged, reliable fighter aircraft. It was capable of supersonic flight in a dive and could take a great deal of G forces without any fear of coming apart. Many improvements were made over the 17 years that marked my first and last flights in the aircraft. Compared to the F-100, it was slow, did not have enough power, and had considerably less range with a smaller weapon load. The F-100 needed stability augmentation devices such as a yaw damper to be flown safely at high speeds, whereas the F-84F was straightforward and very predictable. With the boom and receptacle-type refueling, it could be flown for long distances with only the oil supply and the pilot fatigue factors entering into the range equation. The refueling receptable was a simple door-type arrangement that flipped up out of the left wing about 4 feet from the fuselage, much like the headlight doors on some modern sports cars. With the receptacle up, the pilot flew about 20 feet aft and 4 feet to the right of the centerline of the tanker and held position. The boom operator "flew" the boom to the right position and shoved the telescoping boom downward into the hole. Electrically actuated latches held the nozzle in place until either the boomer or the fighter pilot pressed a disconnect switch. If that didn't work, an electrical override was available. If all else failed, a brute force disconnect literally ripped the nozzle out of the receptacle. This could be dangerous if the nozzle bolts failed and left the nozzle in the receptacle. The fuel flow would reverse and drain the entire aircraft in a matter of 15 minutes. An immediate landing was the only recourse.

One idiosyncrasy showed up when the large 450-gallon tanks were installed on the pylons inboard of the wheel wells. During the strafing runs, at about 320 knots, the pressure buildup between those tanks would cause the Thud's Mother to give a saucy wiggle to her tail. The cure was to fire below or above that speed whenever possible.

Mission changes seemed to come quite often for the Thunderstreak. It was designed as a day fighter, used by Strategic Air Command as a nuclear bomber, became a tactical fighter for Tactical Air Command, was recalled for the Berlin and Cuban crises as a National Guard aircraft, and finally ended its career with the last flight taking place at the Mansfield-Lahm Airport on 30 June 1972. The aircraft, number 52-7021, was piloted by Maj. William A. Millson, a Guardsman from Cleveland, Ohio. Now painted in the early red, white, and blue colors of the Thunderbirds Jet Demonstration Team, it resides on a pedestal beside the Headquarters building of the 179th Tactical Airlift Group on the Mansfield-Lahm Airport. Its Guard pilots placed it on a pedestal during its flying life and left it on that fitting place when it passed from active service.

LT. COL. JOSEPH L. VOGEL is a former jet fighter pilot with the Air Force and the Air National Guard. He is presently flying the C-130B for the 179th Tactical Airlift Group, Air National Guard of Mansfield, Ohio. Lt. Colonel Vogel, who has been flying various types of military aircraft since 1956, has over 3,800 hours of military flying time, is a command pilot, a civilian-rated flight instructor, and a member of the Aviation/Space Writers Association.

F-84 and F-5

WILLIAM· F. GEORGI

WHEN the comparison of the F-84 in Korea and the F-5 in Vietnam was first proposed, it seemed an easy task. However, when I looked at a model of each fighter, just the external appearances emphasized the complexity of the task. The F-84 was an old functional battlehorse and one of the heavyweights of its day, whereas the F-5 was a sleek "racer" and one of the smallest jet fighters built. Nevertheless, both were good at their particular jobs, and both generated a lot of affection from the pilots who flew them.

There is no simple way to compare different aircraft operating in dissimilar wars. To begin with, their design technologies were separated by approximately 15 years. Of even greater import, each plane was designed to a different primary concept. In one important aspect, however, these fighters were similar. The F-84 was a relatively simple and functional fighter designed for a multipurpose role. Similarly, the F-5 was a reversion to the simple, functional fighter in a later age of more complex weapons.

The F-84 was one of the early production jet fighters and was built in quantity to enter the United States Air Force inventory in 1948. Although it started its career as a long-range escort fighter, the F-84 evolved through its life-cycle into a fighter/bomber. To the credit of the

In flight, the F-5 will do almost everything you have the nerve to try.

designers, it has the built-in capability to take this transition. As it progressed through a normal test and development cycle, it acquired a substantial operational history prior to its entry into combat. Nevertheless, as with many multipurpose fighters, it suffered the usual design compromises that kept it from enjoying the role of a first-line air-superiority fighter.

The F-5 was an entirely different animal. It owed its origin and part of its design to the T-38 trainer. It was designed to meet the demand for a simple, reasonable, multipurpose fighter that could be sold in the free-world market. Unlike the F-84, the F-5 was neither designed nor procured for the United States Air Force inventory.

The environments in which these aircraft saw combat were in many respects as different as the aircraft themselves. The Korean War was fought in a climate and over a terrain reasonably similar to that of the United States. The vegetation of Korea was moderate and supply routes were reasonably well defined. In Vietnam the environmental factors of heavy tree cover and poor visibility produced one of the world's areas least suitable for air attack.

Even the opposition and the tactics were considerably different. In Korea the F-84 was consistently used to strike targets in areas where it was subject to attack by North Korean fighters. It was often engaged by enemy aircraft and could defend itself fairly well. Because the formations were usually large, flights in a "fluid four" configuration could effectively provide low-altitude defense for themselves and for aircraft rolling in on targets. Furthermore, the higher altitude F-86 coverage made the MIGs reluctant to engage the F-84s. Fighters in Korea were also subjected to heavy ground fire, but luckily this was the age AAA (antiaircraft artillery) and SAMs (surface-to-air missiles) were not a part of the enemy defense. In contrast, while the F-5 operated in North Vietnam for ap-

The F-5A can penetrate hostile territory with 5,000 pounds of air-to-ground and air-to-air weapons or an equal weight of reconnaissance and surveillance equipment. Note the GAR-8 Sidewinder missile on the wing tips.

USAF

proximately 2 of the 6 months it was tested, it was not engaged by enemy aircraft or by the SAM batteries; its primary competition was the AAA in the North and the small arms fire and occasional AAA in the South.

Reminiscences of experiences with both aircraft begin at Taegu, Korea, early in 1952. The day after my arrival there I had my first close look at the F-84. I had been flying the F-80, and to me the F-84 looked like a beast. Luckily, first impressions are not always completely correct.

Talking with the rest of the jocks during my first days at Taegu didn't improve my first impression. As in any unit, the new guy gets the horror stories first thing, and the 49th Wing was no exception. I was told how the F-84 was the most ground-lovin' aircraft known. With great elaboration they told how one per week never got off the ground on takeoff and trundled off into the rice paddy, with the usual dire results. I learned there was some fire for this smoke, but it was vastly exaggerated. The F-84, like most early jet fighters, was underpowered for the load of munitions and fuel it carried in Korea. Add two other problems—that the engine in both the D and E models tended to have loose turbine buckets and that Taegu (K-2) had one of the roughest PSP (perforated steel plate) runways existing—and you had all the makings of a catastrophe. Takeoff with a loaded F-84 at K-2 on a hot summer day was probably the "hairiest" part of the entire mission. As the weather warmed up in the spring of 1952, we used two 1,000-pound JATO (jet-assisted takeoff rockets) bottles to assure takeoff. Although JATO got us off the ground, takeoffs were still exciting. Everyone from number three man back in the string was zero visibility and had those added moments of panic wondering if the bottles would light and if the man ahead had lost his radio and aborted. When we progressed to the later models E and G aircraft and finally got a hard-surfaced runway, these problems diminished.

In most respects the F-84 was an honest aircraft. It had little tendency to flame-out, stall, spin, or indulge in other undesirable flight characteristics. To its credit, it had relatively long range for its day, could carry a heavy load, and was an exceptionally stable gun and weapon delivery platform. But it badly needed more thrust.

The cockpit was fairly well organized and large enough to be comfortable, but space for maps, etc., was at a premium and the seat must have been contrived by a sadist. Another minus was the positioning of some of the radio and fuel control switches where they were partially blocked by the canopy rail. Visibility wasn't a plus either. However, the A-14 computing sight was welcome, and most of the important controls were readily accessible.

The F-84 sustained some of the higher loss rates of the Korean War. This is sometimes misconstrued to reflect a weakness in the aircraft. In reality, considering the types of missions the F-84 flew, the deep penetration targets, and the high-density defenses, it was one of the more survivable planes. Most of the losses resulted from heavy AAA during the ground-attack phases; loss rate to MIGs was minimal. Although not precisely recorded, the kill ratio against the MIG favored the F-84. (Of course it probably would have been less favorable had we not had F-86 cover.) The F-84 could defend itself, but because of its comparable lack of acceleration and climb it was very poor offensively.

The F-84's greatest attribute was probably its toughness. In one instance, Tom Titus was hit by a MIG that put three 23 mm explosive cannon shells into his aircraft; one exploded in his tailpipe, another lodged unexploded behind his seat, and the third blew a medicine-ball sized section out of his main fuselage tank and fuselage. Tom had to do some fancy fuel management to get the leaking aircraft back to base. On another sortie I picked up more than a hundred various sized holes from ground fire and the aircraft still made it back. A Captain Barnes demonstrated the structural strength of the cockpit while attempting to recover an aircraft after takeoff. He experienced engine and electrical malfunctions, turned final to K-2 at minimal control speed, lost his high-side tip tank, and spun into the ground. We rushed out to the fireball marking the completely disintegrated airplane to find the cockpit fairly intact and a badly bruised Captain Barnes sitting on a paddy wall trying to light a cigarette. Although mildly nervous the following day and turning several shades of purple and green from bruises, he suffered no other disabling effects and was back in the business within a couple of days. Although the F-84 may not have been the most loved airplane in the world, a number of fighter pilots owe their good health to the ruggedness of this aircraft.

I mentioned that the F-84 was developed and introduced into combat in a conventional manner and that the F-5 had a markedly different history. The usual process is to subject a new weapons system to arduous testing followed by an evaluation in operational units. The F-5's introduction to combat was the first attempt by the Air Force to run a full operational evaluation on an aircraft in combat. Although the F-5 test conditions could not, in all fairness, be described as "controlled," they were at least carefully directed and fully documented.

The test project, formed in the summer of 1965, consisted of a squadron of 12 F-5s to be evaluated under combat conditions in both North and South Vietnam. Lieutenant Colonel Hopkins, the Operations Officer, tagged the project "Skoshi Tiger," and this title was picked up as the official designation. The F-5s were to be evaluated to determine their capability in both air-superiority and ground-attack roles. The evaluation team, operated from Saigon, consisted of an analysis section and field teams with photographic and other technical support.

Because the F-5 was not in the Air Force inventory, we had no prescribed training or maintenance programs and no technical orders or manual. One of our first actions was to devise a training and support program. From July through early October 1965, we trained at Williams Air Force Base, using the Gila Bend gunnery ranges and devising tactics as we went along.

We deployed to Vietnam via Hickam and Anderson, with all 12 aircraft arriving at Bien Hoa in good shape on 25 October 1965. I might also mention that the F-5s we took to Vietnam had a number of modifications to fit our requirements. Principal among these were a refueling probe, armor plate, double-gyro flight-instrument platform, modified engine, and pylons and racks capable of handling a number of munitions as well as the TER.

Bien Hoa was a far cry from Taegu. Although our living facilities were not as good as those in Korea, the runway and other airfield facilities were far superior. All of the personnel involved in Skoshi Tiger had trained together, and morale was exceptionally high. It was an effective unit, with a great deal of initiative and eagerness to get on with the job. I find it difficult not to go overboard in praise of the F-5, for going to it from the F-84 is similar to climbing into a hot Porsche after stepping out of the family station wagon. However, there was one difficulty: as in a sports car, the F-5 has little room for goodies such as electronics,

(Left) Instrument panel of F-5E. (Below) F-5B equipped with 50-gallon wing-tip fuel tanks and three 150-gallon pylon fuel tanks and armed with two Bullpup air-to-ground missiles is shown during a test flight near Edwards AFB, California, 1964.

NORTHRUP

fuel, etc. On the other hand, the F-5 was designed with the pilot in mind. The cockpit has ample space, and the arrangement and controls are as simple as you will find anywhere. Starting and emergency procedures are just as simple. For instance, on an airstart all you need to do is check your fuel selector, set the throttle, and hit the airstart. For that matter, the throttle could be in afterburner and the result would be a normal airstart ending with the engine at afterburner power.

Under normal load conditions the F-5 had none of the F-84's tendency toward extended ground roll to an uncomfortable degree. However, takeoff roll was affected with some of the heavier experimental loads. For example, when carrying TERs and full fuel, the F-5 center of gravity shifted forward enough to make low-speed stabilator control questionable. This forced us to higher takeoff speeds and almost doubled our ground roll. The problem was solved by the comparatively simple expedient of installing a two-position nose strut. Controlled from the cockpit, the extended nose strut was about a foot longer, thereby increasing the ground angle of attack and reducing the stabilator force required for rotation. On gear retraction, the two-position strut returned to normal extension.

Unlike the F-84, the F-5 has sufficient thrust to maintain a good rate of climb after takeoff and can maintain control speed on one engine even when loaded. Whereas the F-84 had no drag chute, deploying the F-5 chute during a takeoff abort brought immediate results. Because the F-5 chute was the same size as that of the F-100, there was no question of stopping; rather the problem was remembering to brace yourself so that you wouldn't end up in the windscreen. Consequently, although we had a few takeoff emergencies in Vietnam, we never had any serious problems like those the F-84 encountered in Korea.

In flight the F-5 has to be forced to go out of control and has no tendency toward surprises. If you keep a little speed on, it will do almost everything you have the nerve to try. At low and moderate altitudes it will fight anything, including the MIG-21. Later versions with modified controls and larger engines should be competitive in any theater.

By the time we got to Vietnam, the Skoshi Tiger pilots were firmly convinced they had the best aircraft in the world, but it was readily apparent that the others in Southeast Asia did not share this enthusiasm. This is understandable, considering the peculiarity of air operations in the

The supersonic twin-jet T-38 trainer is used for pilot training in Germany and the United States and by NASA to maintain flight readiness of its astronauts.

Southeast Asian war. At the time, operations in the South relied heavily on the A-1E with its varied loads of munitions and its notably long endurance. Common practice was to launch the A-1E and, once it was within visual contact, have the spotter point out targets as they were observed. Because the A-1E could spend considerable time in the target area, numerous targets could be struck. In contrast, the F-5 was not capable of long loitering with heavy munitions loads. Operations planned around the A-1E's capabilities did not exploit the best features of the F-5. Nevertheless, the F-5 could carry four 750-pound bombs or equivalent, plus a full load of 20 mm a radius of 200 nautical miles, remain in the target area 5 minutes to deliver its ordnances, and then return to base. Although this was less than the A-1E or the larger jet fighters were capable of accomplishing, it was an average load for many aircraft during this period. Turn-around time in the F-5 also was excellent and resulted in a good sortie rate.

We did find a number of items on the F-5 that needed further work. Many munitions had been tested, but the pylons and racks had not been used under the rapid turn conditions of combat. Consequently, we had instances of faulty releases, in which napalm tanks or drogued bombs struck the aircraft or failed to release. A rapid redesign on the pylons solved this shortcoming.

Another problem we encountered was self-inflicted. A principal reason for the F-5's accuracy was that a small, maneuverable aircraft can get quite close to the target prior to the release. In consequence, pilots often pressed too hard, particularly in gun attacks. Debris blown into the air by 20 mm shells was often ingested by the engines with the usual dire results. On the good side, all aircraft made it back to base, even after engine failure; unlike many other engines, the J-85 had little tendency to disintegrate after ingesting debris. During an attack on AAA positions in Mu Gia Pass, my aircraft was hit by a 14.7 high-velocity shell that penetrated the right side of the forward belly, passed through the aircraft, and entered the left ammunition bay, exploding two rounds of 20 mm. The explosion blew the ammunition door open and dumped links and assorted hardware into the port engine. Although the engine ceased providing much thrust, it continued running in idle range for the 35-minute return to base and still was repairable.

We also found that when operating on the same targets, the F-5 took fewer hits than the F-100 or the F-4. We believed this was because of the F-5's small size and lack of an exhaust trail which gave it low visibility. Although the aircraft took a number of hits during the project, we lost only 1 pilot and plane in action. However, this may have indirectly resulted in the loss of another pilot's services. Col. Burt Rowen, the project Flight Surgeon, was also a fully qualified pilot flying sorties in the F-5. But when the Air Force medical high command discovered this, they forcefully suggested that his duties were not those of squadron pilot and that the project could not afford to lose its Flight Surgeon. So he was grounded. Burt never seemed quite as happy after that.

In South Vietnam, sorties were varied and results were consistently good. In the North we were less successful, not because of the F-5, but because of a number of factors over which we had little control. We lost a good part of the value of our early operations at Da Nang when all bombing sorties to the North were cancelled. This reduced us to escorting patrol aircraft and providing out-country sorties. In the spring of 1966, during our second month at Da Nang, we still encountered problems in attempting to get a complete evaluation. We hit ground targets in the North, in a number of cases within SAM range, but did not have any missiles fired against us.

Attempts to induce a response by North Vietnamese aircraft were a dismal failure. Fighter encounters during this period were fairly low for all aircraft and we had none with the F-5. We escorted patrol aircraft and airborne early warning aircraft, hit some targets close to Hanoi, and tried providing low cover for F-4 and F-105 aircraft on their bombing sorties. At this time the North Vietnamese fighters were flying on the deck into the Red River area then popping up to hit the fighters during their bomb run. In an attempt to counter this tactic, we flew low-level tracks at approximately 500 feet in the mouth of the Red River Valley. No MIGs were launched during the periods we were there; they showed only after we left. Apparently they weren't going to chance an encounter until they found out more about us. On our part, we were confident that we could have scored against the MIGs. The F-5 had been flown against a number of aircraft air-to-air while still in the CONUS (continental United States) and proved very capable, particularly in the lower altitudes. We were greatly disappointed not to get a chance to try the plane in combat. During all our sorties in Vietnam we received many SAM warnings but none apparently was fired against the F-5. We ran into ample AAA, but because of our altitude, flight pattern, and speed of approximately 500 knots, we took few hits.

During these activities, as well as those in the South, the evaluation team continued gathering data. The evaluation eventually confirmed that although it suffered the limitations of a small aircraft, the F-5 could do an excellent job in ground attack or air-to-air roles where long-range and all-weather capability were not the primary considerations. It was a tough bird—durable, simple to repair—and provided a lot of capability in a simple package. More important, it is a pilot's airplane and all who flew it liked it.

How do the F-84 and F-5 actually compare? I would say "not very much," if the comparison is based on physical characteristics and performance. However, in concept and employment there is a great deal of resemblance. The F-5, like the F-84, was a simple design, and both answered the need for a functional and comparatively reasonable day fighter. In fact, from a desk in the Pentagon, both are remembered as fantastically good aircraft.

BRIG. GEN. WILLIAM F. GEORGI entered the service in 1942 as an aviation cadet and served as a pilot and later Commander of the 352d Bomb Squadron in North Africa. In 1952 he served in Korea as the Commander of the 9th and later the 8th Fighter Bomber Squadrons, flying 148 missions in F-84 aircraft. Varying assignments in both operations and Research and Development followed.

During 1965 he served on temporary duty in the Republic of Vietnam as Deputy Commander of Project Skoshi Tiger, test of the F-5 fighter aircraft in Vietnam. He flew 162 in- and out-country missions.

General Georgi went to Ramstein Air Base, Germany, in August 1970 as Vice Commander of the 26th Tactical Reconnaissance Wing and became Commander of the Wing in March 1971. In February 1973 he assumed command of the 86th Tactical Reconnaissance Wing at Ramstein Air Base.

In May 1973, he joined the Organization of Joint Chiefs of Staffs as Chief, International Negotiations Division in the Plans and Policy Directorate.

F9F-2 Panther

CECIL B. JONES

IT was big, blue, and beautiful. As I approached the F9F-2 Panther on the Air Group 11 flight-line at NAS North Island, San Diego, I tingled with anticipation of the greatest natural high a mortal can experience. The pilot, strapped in unity with his aircraft, strains his guts and screams with joy as he flies his bird to the outer limits of its performance envelope. Early in 1950 I did not know that the Panther and I had a rendezvous with war. In two combat tours off a Navy carrier I would become so familiar with the aircraft's instruments of destruction and its reponse to my control that the cockpit would become a place of security and in flight the aircraft would be my perfect and absolute domain. I need not explain this feeling to any other fighter pilot, and no amount of explanation would be adequate for nonpilots.

The carrier naval aviator naturally thinks about his aircraft in terms of its combat capabilities as well as its shipboard handling characteristics. The carrier, as a vehicle to get the aircraft within combat radius of action, may never be relegated to the status of a mere floating airfield. Aircraft and carrier compatibility is so obviously an imperative that the need to reaffirm it periodically with every "joint" Navy/Air Force fighter development and procurement is nothing less than incredible.

The F9F Panther, an early straight-wing Navy jet fighter, provides a classic example of the technological interrelationship of aircraft and carrier and of some of the associated problems.

The first flight of the XF9F-2 on 24 November 1947 was powered by a British Rolls-Royce Nene. A second prototype was equipped with the Allison J-33 engine. Throughout its service life, the Panther name covered a small family of differently powered aircraft. The F9F-2 I flew was equipped with the 5,000-pound thrust Pratt & Whitney J-42-P-6 centrifugal-flow jet engine. The F9F-3, nearly identical with the F9F-2, was powered by the Allison J-33-A-8 with 4,600 pounds thrust. The F9F-4 carried the Allison J-33-A-16, which delivered 5,850 pounds thrust. The F9F-5, which shared the same airframe with the F9F-4, was powered by the Pratt & Whitney J-48-P-4, delivering 6,250 pounds thrust. None of the Panther series was equipped with afterburner.

In all, 1,388 Panthers of various dash models were procured. The first delivery to an operational unit was to VF-51 at NAS North Island,

The Panther was the first carrier jet to enter combat; it carried the brunt of the Navy's Korean jet effort.

San Diego, on 5 August 1949. The last delivery by Grumman was in December 1952. From a numbers viewpoint, the Panther was the most important of a small generation of straight-wing carrier jet fighters. Total production of all the others—the Chance-Vought F6U Pirate, the North American FJ Fury, the McDonnell FH Phantom and F2H Banshee—was less than that of the Panther. This meant that in the opening years of jet carrier aviation, more naval aviators earned their spurs in the Panther than in any other jet fighter.

The Panther was the first carrier jet to enter combat, and it carried the brunt of the Navy's Korean jet effort. Panthers from VF-51, flying off the U.S.S. *Valley Forge,* shot down two prop-driven YAK 9s on 3 July 1950, seven days after President Truman ordered the Seventh Fleet to give support to the Republic of Korea. Later that year, 9 November, a Panther piloted by LCDR Tom Amen of VF-111 made the first Navy contact with a Soviet-built MIG-15 and downed it (see LCDR W. T. Amen, "Scratch a MIG," *Flying,* Nov. 1951, Vol. 49, No. 5).

The F9F-2B, so designated because of its bomb carrying capability, was combat-demonstrated on 2 April 1951, when LCDR Ben Riley and LCDR Ray Hawkins of VF-191 attacked a railroad bridge. Each aircraft carried four 250-pound and two 100-pound general purpose bombs. This was the first Navy combat use of a jet fighter in a bomber role, and it marked the end of a period in which Navy jets had been limited to Combat Air Patrol over the carriers with only occasional opportunities to engage in air operations over the beach. The principal missions over land were fighter escort for Navy prop bombers (F4Us and ADs) and escort for the photographic version of the Panthers. The success of this first bombing was marginal and suspect. The bridge had previously been knocked out and rebuilt. To assure hits, the attack was made from very low altitude. One Panther was severely damaged by its own bomb blast. The "evidence" was nevertheless accepted as establishing that Navy jets had other roles to play besides air-to-air combat. And the incident was glorified by James Michener in *The Bridges of Toko-ri.*

The Navy wasn't being archconservative in its reluctance to use its jets in a ground-support role. The Panther aboard the Essex class carrier in the early 1950s was operating with very little margin for error. In mid-1947 the Navy announced a carrier improvement program, "Project 27A," to modify the Essex class to handle heavier, faster aircraft. Later, as the result of jet-carrier experience during the Korean War, this project was modified in February 1952, and more powerful arresting gear and higher performance catapults were called for. The margin of safe operations for Panthers from an Essex class carrier may be identified by a practice resorted to for catapult launches with low-wind conditions. Following readings from a hand-held anemometer, the Catapult Officer would direct the off-loading of 100-pound bombs or 5-inch rockets, one at a time, until the aircraft weight came down and the estimated minimum aircraft catapult end-speed could be achieved with maximum catapult launching pressures. Under these conditions it was a common experience to settle off the end of the catapult with the stick-shaker (stall-warning device) delivering its omen of apparent impending disaster. One soon became accustomed to this and, provided the nose was not rapidly rotated, the aircraft quickly accelerated out of this situation. The stick-shaker, mounted on the control stick, was operated by signals from an outside sensing vane, which was designed to detect an approaching stall condition.

If the Korean War had not developed in mid-1950 and thus forced new defense funds to be made available, naval carrier aviation would have faced a crippled future. In 1949 when the 65,000-ton supercarrier U.S.S. *United States* was cancelled by Defense Secretary Louis Johnson and $36 million cut in fiscal 1950 research and development funds for naval aviation, a whole generation of planes designed to use the proposed carrier was scrapped. The mortgage on the future of naval aviation may have been more than the naval service, beset with internal feuding between "black shoes" (nonaviators) and "brown shoes" (aviators), would have been capable of paying off.

As *Aviation Week* (11 July 1949) noted in an editorial entitled "Crises in Naval Aviation—An Analysis," the reduction of R & D funds and the cancellation of the U.S.S. *United States* had the effect of placing an artificial ceiling on the technical development of naval aircraft. A comparable case, it noted, would have occurred if Air Force planes had been limited to runways of a certain length and thickness.

It should be recalled that the F9F Panther was developed at the same time as the F-86, the first American swept-wing jet fighter. Prototypes of the two different aircraft first flew within two months of each other. The same swept-wing and jet technology available to North American engineers from German World War II developments was also available to Grumman engineers. The first experimental flight of a Navy jet was the straight-wing North American FJ Fury. Had there been any chance of developing a swept-wing Navy jet fighter that could have operated off the carriers available, the Navy would not have been a half generation behind the U.S. Air Force and the Soviet Union in operational jet fighters in the early 1950s. The practical importance of this was not lost even to a junior naval aviator as he went into combat in 1950 from a carrier platform that was marginally capable of handling his aircraft under certain operational conditions. That the Soviets built from German World War II jet technology and had purchased the Nene engine from the British were also sobering facts. In the early 1950s, the hackneyed vision of Ivan whipping his tractor for better performance was irreversibly replaced with a new respect for Soviet technological accomplishments.

My introduction to the F9F Panther came after a swift familiarization course to jet aviation. On 19 January 1950, I completed seven carrier landings in the Grumman F6F Hellcat aboard the U.S.S. *Saipan*, cruising in the Gulf of Mexico off Pensacola, Florida. This was the culmination of advanced flight training, and the following day, after being designated a naval aviator, I was ready to report to a fleet fighter squadron as an Aviation Midshipman. With the aid of outstanding instructors, reasonable skill, and breaks in the weather, I had completed the training program ahead of the normal schedule and was destined to serve in the fleet as a Midshipman four months before being commissioned. Although this may have been a poor economic fate, the luck of my availability caused me to be sent to the first formal Navy jet training class at NAS Whiting Field, Florida.

After ten days of ground school, this pioneer class was led to the flight line and each student strapped into his Lockheed TO-1 Shooting Star (the Navy's designation of the F-80 never became common parlance in the aviation community). Sixteen days later, after 24 flights totaling 28 hours, I was certified jet-qualified and sent to the fleet, which was still predominantly prop equipped.

My first squadron, the Sundowners of VF-111, was in the process of transitioning from the Grumman F8F Bearcat to the F9F Panther. In those relatively casual days, the process of new aircraft checkout was simple to the point of being hazardous. The naive assumption was that a set of Navy wings was a golden key that unlocked any box a plane came in. I proved this absurdity several times. The most dramatic occasion was when the squadron, equipped with only a dozen F9Fs, was scheduled to move to NAS El Centro for a week of gunnery practice. The natural scheme of things assured that no Midshipman would be assigned an aircraft to ferry over to El Centro. There were two other options: travel on a bus or vie to fly one of the two F4U Corsairs to be used as tow aircraft during gunnery hops. When the Schedule Officer asked for volunteers for this last assignment, one Midshipman, who had completed advanced flight training in F4Us, eagerly stood up. I was a fraction of a second behind him. My speed was unnecessary; no one else in the ready-room had ever flown the Corsair. All others were willing to suffer the indignity of a bus ride rather than challenge the bent-wing eliminator's reputation on a spur of the moment urge.

My total checkout consisted of the plane captain's shocked response to my question, "How do you start this thing?" Not only did I survive the flight over to El Centro, which was highlighted by an unintentional spin coming out of a poorly executed loop, but my second takeoff, my first with a tow target, took place immediately after landing. I was cautioned not to drag the banner along the runway but to get airborne as quickly as possible. The resulting spectacular launch was a subject of considerable squadron discussion, and I was labeled a number one Corsair driver. My reward was six consecutive F4U hops before I was allowed my first F9F flight.

The Panther was a solid beast built in the tradition of other Grumman fighters which had long survived the punishment of carrier operations. It had a feel of strength and stability that the F-80 lacked, but was limited to Mach .83, which could be achieved only in a dive, and was easily recognized by severe buffeting and almost uncontrollable pitch-up.

A more practical limiting Mach number was .79. Beyond this, it was difficult either to fire the guns effectively or to drop bombs or shoot off rockets accurately because of moderate buffeting and lateral wobble and trim changes.

On all missions the standard pilot paraphernalia included a G-suit, whose air-inflatable compartments on the legs and abdomen helped maintain blood pressure to the eyeballs and brain during high positive G loads. In the early 1950s the G-suit was not an integral part of the flight suit, but rather a separate corsetlike garment worn from ankle to stomach under the regular multipocketed flight suit. One issue of the summer flight suit was particularly well received. It was a green, extremely lightweight see-through nylon garment. On low-level summer flights, wearing the required inflatable Mae West, which was festooned with packets of fluorescent dye marker, shark chaser, combination day and night flares and smoke, signaling mirror, whistle, and compass, this suit transmitted a maximum amount of air conditioning. But soon after its issue it was recalled and replaced. In a fire, the nylon welded itself to the body and created a vicious scar on any survivor. Although I was willing to give up this suit for flight, its comfort and status symbolism were too great to part with. Twenty-five years later, I occasionally don its well-worn remains when the car needs washing. This has always seemed a safe utilization of the suit; my only complaint is that each year it seems to shrink a bit more.

An essential flight item was the pilot's knee clipboard. Strapped to the thigh during flight, it contained the shorthand essence of the flight briefing and was used in flight to write down clearances and in combat, if circumstances permitted, to document details that were always required in post-action debriefings.

The pilot in the F9F sat on his parachute, which always remained in the cockpit. Between a seat cushion and the parachute was a compartment that contained a one-man life raft, a chemical desalting kit, a solar still, a radar reflector, and a rubberized poncho. Designed to meet the emergency needs of World War II carrier flight missions, this equipment was of no value to a pilot who survived a parachute descent over land behind enemy lines. During the Korean War, each pilot augmented an issued personal survival kit according to his expectation of the risks ahead. Often this was practically determined by the amount of pocket space in the flight suit and flight jacket. Some squadrons removed the desalting kits from the seat pack and substituted tins of high-energy food such as sardines. Personal two-way mini-radios were not in the Navy inventory at that time. A .38 caliber pistol was issued to each pilot, and it was not uncommon to have a round accidently fired in the ready-room by a pilot who was professionally qualified to handle 20 mm cannon and 5-inch rockets but failed to give proper attention and respect to the simple single-action revolver.

In combat the pilot's personal gear was limited to what he could wear and stuff in his pockets. On noncombat cross-country flights personal gear could be stowed in the sliding nose compartment which provided normal access to the battery and the four 20 mm cannons. The standard-issue naval aviator's green bag fitted snugly in the bottom quadrant of the nose section, an area first exposed when the sliding nose section was opened. The fit had to be tight because the green bag held itself in position while the nose was open for loading or unloading. With care, a two-suit clothes bag could be draped over the rear of the 20 mm cannons and the sliding nose section closed over it. A mark of the successful cross-country F9F-2 driver was a clothes bag scarred with small cuts from the nose assembly and dabbed with assorted colors of paint used to mark 20 mm ammunition. The void area where the green bag fitted had a combat role. The 20 mm brass shell cases accumulated there when the cannons were fired. Their weight maintained the center of gravity within limits. Back aboard ship, the squadron ordnance crews fitted a large canvas bag under the rear of the nose section and when the nose was opened, the brass was neatly collected.

The roomy cockpit was an early and successful example of careful attention to the physical and psychological needs of the pilot. Because the plane was designed strictly as a daytime fighter, the cockpit was not encumbered with displays and instrumentation required by night and all-weather fighter aircraft. Access to the cockpit was a self-contained sliding step, which recessed flush in the fuselage when stowed, and two higher-up toe indents and one handhold, which were flush in flight. Their half-moon covers were spring-loaded closed.

The starting procedure was simple. External electrical power was required for engine starts. When the cranking switch was hit, the starter quickly brought engine rpm up to 8–10%. At that point, the throttle was moved outboard to the "Start" position. This motion opened a high-pressure fuel cock and actuated power to the spark igniter. A normal light-off would take place in less than 30 seconds. The rpm increased to 20% and the tailpipe temperature rose to 400° C. At that point, the throttle would be brought "around the horn" into the "idle" position. Idle rpm was set at 28%, and the generators cut in at 36%. Approximately 51% was required to initiate taxiing. Steering at taxi speeds was done by toe brakes. Because each minute on the ground reduced aircraft range 2½ miles, standard shipboard handling procedures attempted to reduce the deck running time to absolute minimum.

Standard checks of the air-conditioning, electrical, and hydraulic systems were made immediately after start-up, completing the pretakeoff check list, except for placing the flaps in the "take-off" position. The Panther had a water-injection system that provided a one-shot quantity of 22.5 gallons of water-alcohol coolant mixture for takeoff. When this system was to be used, the cabin pressure switch and the air-conditioning were turned off to alleviate the danger of alcohol fumes in the cockpit. When the air-conditioning switch was turned on after the coolant injection had been consumed, it was not unusual for a cloud to form in the cockpit momentarily. Although the experienced pilot would anticipate this, experience was not an adequate substitute for visibility. Many rendezvous immediately after launch were aborted because of this phenomenon.

More spectacular than this transient cockpit IFR condition was a situation involving the F9F-3 pressurization and air-conditioning system. The F9F-2 cockpit was air-conditioned and pressurized via perforated tubes ringing the canopy. The F9F-3 had some of this arrangement, but the main duct was located forward of the gunsight and had a fan-shaped opening approximately 1 inch wide and 8 inches long. With warm outside temperature and maximum cooling selected for inside cockpit temperature, ice would form in the duct until it was obstructed to the point where pressure would launch a small oblong "snow ball" over the gunsight. This missile would strike in the vicinity of the forehead of an average-sized pilot. It was a rule that knowledge of this potential was never divulged to the uninitiated.

A ground launch required steering with brakes until the rudder became effective at approximately 70 knots. Lift-off speed for a nominally loaded aircraft weighing 17,000 pounds was 115 knots. At approximately 105–110 knots, the stick was eased back until the nosewheel was just off the ground. This attitude was easily identified because of the sudden reduction of noise and vibration of the nosewheel on the runway. The aircraft smoothly became airborne in this attitude. Landing gear was immediately retracted and the flaps were raised at 130–150 knots. In this speed regime no sinking occurred, and acceleration was relatively rapid to 330 knots, which produced the best rate of climb. The flap system of the Panther featured a "droop snoot" leading edge, which moved in conjunction with the regular trailing edge flaps. These provided added lift and improved stall characteristics. The F9F with the stick-shaker was very honest about stalls. Practicing stalls at altitude in a landing configuration, the stall warning device would practically mix a cake in the cockpit before the nose fell through. The pilot's handbook warned that without this device there was no natural aerodynamic stall warning. Wing design was outstanding for its generation, and the aircraft performed within its envelope without any abnormalities. It was virtually impossible to overcontrol and stall the wing.

Launch from the carrier was always accomplished via catapult. As the aircraft was brought up from the hangar deck, the wings, which had been folded to allow compact storage, were spread upon signal from a deck plane handler. Weaving toward the catapult, the aircraft became a part of the moving scenery of the flight deck ballet for which carrier aviation is noted. Brown-shirted plane captains were checking and rechecking their aircraft even after start-up. Red-shirted ordnancemen faded wearily into the background to enjoy a short rest until it was time to prepare for the next strike. The green-jerseyed catapult crew tensed to their responsibility—a safe launch with a minimum launch interval. The prima donnas of this ballet corps were the yellow-jerseyed plane directors. Their starring performances were supported by the blue-shirted aircraft handlers and chockmen. This colorful and deadly serious balletdrama approached a climax for the Panther pilot when his nosewheel eased over the catapult shuttle and the cable bridle was attached to the aircraft's fuselage catapult hook and a hold-back arm and ring were connected to the after underfuselage. With feet off the brakes, tension was taken on the bridle. After final instrument checks at 100% power, the pilot's ready-to-launch salute was followed by the catapult officer's sweeping launch signal. The hold-back ring predictably parted and the aircraft accelerated to 115 knots in nearly as many feet. The hydraulic catapults of that era strained at every shot to fling the Panther into safe flight.

Immediately after catapult, a clearing turn away from the carrier's launch path was made to assure a turbulent-free launch for following aircraft. In quick sequence the gear was raised, canopy closed, and flaps raised as the rendezvous evolution began.

The Panther carried fuel in two soft, cell-type, self-sealing fuselage tanks located between the cockpit and the engine (a total of 683 gallons) and two fixed aluminum wing-tip tanks (120 gallons each). Full fuel load from tip tanks could be dumped by ram air pressure in approximately one minute at 340 knots. Many photographs have been published of Panthers in formation alongside a carrier, majestically polluting the air and sea with POL products as they came in for a break. The Panther pilot who ended up dumping fuel should not be branded as wasteful and a poor manager of his consumables. Among other considerations was the requirement to be below the maximum arrested landing weight of 12,600 pounds. If he had been on CAP (combat air patrol) over the carrier at high altitude, he probably kept some fuel in his tip tanks to dump in the event of an actual air-to-air encounter with the faster MIG-15. With a 100 mph disadvantage, the Panther pilot would naturally desire the most favorable weight-to-thrust ratio he could get.

The average combat mission for the Panther in 1950 and 1952 was 1.6 hours in length. (This figure is based upon 150 missions flown, the longest being 2 hours, and the shortest being an over-the-beach hop of one-half hour.) Missions were flown at a variety of altitudes, most of them below 5,000 feet on armed reconnaissance. Following the catapult launch, a running rendezvous enroute to the target area was commonly made. Once together, the division aircraft would visually check each other's external ordnance for general security and for the status of arming wires. In formation, the 20 mm cannons would be charged and test-fired. Once done, the master arm switch would be secured until the aircraft was in the target area. Previously, immediately after takeoff, the gyro gun sight was turned on. In a short time it was up to speed and ready to function. If the mission was CAP, the division would climb to altitude under radar control. On these missions no external ordnance was carried. The division would be positioned between the fleet formation and the threat area. Primarily, for radar control training, the four-plane division would be broken up into two sections and practice intercepts made on each other for an hour. Return-strike aircraft were often intercepted, again for practice, or occasionally to escort a battle-damaged jet aircraft.

The most challenging over-the-beach mission was flak suppression. This required a high order of coordination and precise timing to obtain maximum results. The Panther, with its high speed and excellent ordnance platform, was cast in the role of preceding the more heavily armed and slower propeller-driven AD Skyraiders and F4U Corsairs on target. The Panther's job was to engage the antiaircraft positions, gun barrel to gun barrel, just before the prop aircraft rolled in for their attacks on the defended target. Ordnance for the Panther on these missions included the 20 mm cannons, VT-fused fragmentation bombs, and 5-inch rockets. Properly executed, the antiaircraft positions would be either damaged or destroyed and their crews forced to take cover while the attack prop aircraft steadied into their dives. Poor timing made life exceedingly unpleasant for the slower more vulnerable prop aircraft. Release of bombs and firing of rockets caused virtually no effect on handling the Panther. This was primarily because the largest weapon carried was the 250-pound general-purpose bomb.

A third mission was armed reconnaissance. On this, a two-plane section would cover a preplanned road or rail route at low altitude looking for targets of opportunity. Occasionally and only after considerable experience, some of the usually superb Korean and Chinese camouflage efforts would be detected and a worthwhile target taken under attack. Normally, nothing but foot and bicycle traffic moved by day—sparse, if not insulting, targets for a sleek jet. The night-attack pilots had a much different story to tell, and often the first early daylight strike would be against a train trapped in the open by the efforts of the night-attack group. A common and frustrating sight during daytime armed reconnaissance flights was engine smoke drifting out of the opening of one of the hundreds of tunnels that marked the North Korean railroad system.

All pilots at one time or another attempted to lob a bomb into a tunnel entrance. Many thousands of rounds of 20 mm were shot into these black sanctuaries without any signs of results. The following day's review of such gun-camera film always included at least one hairy pull-up over the rim of the mountain that had been tunnelled through.

The Panther handled extremely well in the air. Maneuverability was excellent and there were no significant restrictions on flight maneuvers, even with external stores and full tip tanks. Only snap rolls and abrupt rudder reversals were prohibited with external stores and tip-tank fuel. Spins were not prohibited but were avoided because of large loss of altitude, 4,000–7,000 feet, associated with recovery from even one turn. Maximum G loads for the Panther were plus 7.5 and minus 3. The envelope for these maximum figures in smooth air was from sea level to 20,000 feet with airspeeds from 315–420 knots indicated. At 40,000 feet, G limits were plus 1.9 to minus 1.7 at 210 knots indicated airspeed.

The Panther was built to battle and acquitted itself well in combat. In 1952, when the Panther was used extensively in flak-suppression missions, it repeatedly proved it could take hits and still perform. The Korean War established that the Panther was not only rugged but was dependable and relatively easy to maintain. For the period April to December 1950, the Navy reported 96% combat availability for the F9F-2. This figure is impressive and meant that even though heavy maintenance work was done at night while the pilots rested, the planes were ready for the following day's missions.

Only once, when I flamed out at altitude on instruments over heavy seas, did I seriously have to consider bailing out. The decision was avoided when my third relight attempt was successful at about 7,000 feet. The ejection procedure required a series of independent manual steps that made the probability of a successful low-altitude ejection very poor. A preejection lever jettisoned the canopy, lowered the seat, and released knee braces on the seat sides. A seat-catapult safety pin was pulled when the canopy jettisoned. The pilot slid his feet back into the seat floor stirrups, set his knees outboard against the braces, and pulled nylon rope handles to bring a cover over his face. This action locked the inertia reel of his harness and fired the ejection charge. Later models of the Panther allowed ejection through the canopy. Separation from the seat was manual, requiring disconnection of oxygen, radio leads, and seat belt. The parachute rip-cord was pulled when seat separation was accomplished.

The Panther was equipped with highly effective dive brakes, which caused a nose-down trim change. A split-S from 40,000 feet to sea level was possible with dive brakes out, throttle retarded, and the aircraft riding the maximum Mach line. When the air speed was below 215 knots, the landing gear was extended. Flaps were lowered below 165 knots. Final approach speed for field landing was 115 knots, with wheels and flaps down, dive brakes up. For carrier landings, the hook was extended by manually pulling the cockpit hook handle 3 or 4 times. Final approach was made at 108–110 knots with 1,000 pounds of fuel. For each 200 pounds of fuel over this weight, an additional knot was added. The optimum cut position with a 30-knot wind and steady deck condition was 300 feet out from the number three wire and 18 feet above the deck.

The break-up for landing normally took place from a right echelon formation with the leader at 500 feet and the division flying down the starboard side of the carrier if it was in the wind. With gear, flaps, and

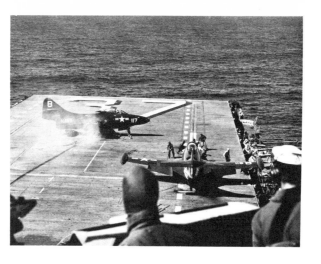

hook down and canopy open, the landing circuit was flown in a conventional racetrack pattern. At the 180° point you called in with landing checklist complete and gave your fuel state in pounds. Visibility was excellent throughout the pattern and the Landing Signal Officer (LSO) usually picked up his paddles as you flew through the 90° position. These were the final years of having the LSO on the port side of the aft end of the carrier personally working each aircraft aboard; the mirror landing system was under development and first installed aboard the U.S.S. *Bennington* in 1955. At the LSO's signal to cut, the throttle was snapped back to the idle position and a landing made. The throttle was not added again until the hook had been disengaged from the wire by the hook-release man and you were being quickly taxied forward of the lowered barriers in order to clear the deck for the next aircraft, which should be less than 30 seconds from touchdown. In the event of a wave-off, full throttle was added and at least 250 more pounds of fuel would be consumed before you could be at the cut position again. The Panther took an easy wave-off, provided the engine was at or above 52% rpm and the aircraft not slow and cocked-up. At the cut, the optimum landing attitude was to have the nose wheel and the tail skid equidistant from the deck when the main gear touched.

As previously mentioned, the F9F-2 aboard the Essex class carrier was not always a comfortable relationship. As might be expected, this was particularly so when a squadron with newly acquired F9F-2s operated off a carrier that previously had handled only prop aircraft. The combination of inexperienced personnel plus the press of operational requirements was often a volatile mixture. For example, when the Korean War opened on 25 June 1950, I had 33 flight hours in the Panther. This included 5 hours in a F9F-3 that had been assigned to the squadron primarily so that hours could be put on it as part of an engine-check program. The air group and the squadron were ordered on immediate deployment. Four flight hours later I had completed field carrier landing practice (FCLP) and qualified aboard the carrier with six landings. Mercifully, the squadron cut the two junior-most pilots with the fewest number of hours in type, and I, along with a squadron mate, was transferred to another squadron just receiving their F9F-2s. From bottom man on the pole I suddenly became a top dog. My 37 hours were puny, but they were more than all of my new squadron mates had together. From my recent rejected status I became an instructor pilot and with a trifle more elan than was justified I checked out the rest of the squadron when the new Panthers arrived. This squadron went through a crash

F-9F-2 deck crash on the USS Princeton. Three Panthers were damaged and one deckhand received minor injuries. The author, who was in aircraft 104, sustained only a minor headache when the canopy squeezed his crash helmet against the side of the cockpit.

training program and in three months qualified aboard a carrier that had never handled jets before, had itself just come out of mothballs, and had a large percentage of reserve personnel as ship's company.

The photographs of an F9F-2 deck crash document the malconjunction of these factors. A major contributing factor to this accident was a hydraulic tail-hook dash-pot that failed to provide adequate stubbing action to keep the tail-hook on the carrier deck as it groped for a cross-deck pendant. The tail-hook of the aircraft involved bounced rhythmically up the deck, avoiding all wires. The final result of this accident was strike damage to three Panthers and minor injuries to one deckhand. The author, who was in aircraft 104 when it was cut into, was highly excited and shaken up but sustained only a minor headache when the canopy squeezed his crash helmet against the side of the cockpit before the canopy was wedged off by the overriding wing of the assaulting aircraft. Three Davis-type barriers were engaged, but they offered no help. The ship, which had never operated jets before, had rigged an incorrect model of the Davis barrier. The model rigged was for the F7F Tomcat, which had a greater distance between the nose gear and the main mounts than the F9F Panther. The result was that the cable designed to engage the main landing gear was thrown up behind it instead of in front.

The Panther operated extensively off straight-deck carriers in every ocean. By the time angle-deck modifications appeared in the fleet, the Panther was giving way to a new generation of swept-wing fighter aircraft.

By a coincidence of fate, when the Panther family was retired from the fleet, I was forced out of carrier aviation by eyesight problems. Land-based antisubmarine warfare aviation, the next step in my naval aviation career, was an incredibly challenging mission, but I look back at my Panther flying days as the zenith of flying joy and adventure. Nearly 600 hours in its cockpit were far too few for the experience and pleasure I gained there. Of these hours, 240 were in combat, and a more dependable aircraft I cannot imagine.

CDR. C. B. "SCOTT" JONES (Ret.) entered the Navy in 1946. Completing flight training in 1950 as an Aviation Midshipman, he joined VF-111, a jet fighter squadron at San Diego. Later, after being transferred to VF-191, he made two combat cruises aboard the U.S.S. *Princeton* (CV-37), in 1950 and 1952, flying the F9F Panther. After a tour as instructor in advanced jet training, again in the Panther, he returned to sea, this time assigned as Intelligence Officer on a Carrier Division Staff. He moved from carrier aviation to land-based antisubmarine aviation in the Neptune P2V-7 as Patrol Plane Commander in VP-18. A series of intelligence assignments in Washington and overseas rounded out most of the remainder of his 30-year career. His last "operational" flying was in the ageless Gooney Bird. As Assistant U.S. Naval Attache to India and Nepal, he flew the DC-3 in and out of 20 countries from Spain to Japan. Now retired, he is currently teaching political science at Casper College, Wyoming.

(Above) Sweep back of the elevator is evident in this photo of the F-94C. The drag chute housing is also readily visible aft of the rudder. (Right) F-94C cockpit trainer locally designed to enhance the conversion of the 179th Fighter Squadron, Minnesota Air National Guard, Duluth, to the new aircraft.

F-94 Starfire

WAYNE C. GATLIN

ONE cannot describe flying the F-94 Starfire without separating the story into two distinct parts—the F-94A/B and the F-94C—for the two aircraft were vastly different with only the center section of the C common to the earlier A model.

The original F-94A was developed in 1949 from the T-33 jet trainer which, in turn, had been developed from the F-80 Shooting Star. The F-94B was nearly identical to the A model except for the A having a low-pressure oxygen system, a 1,000 psi hydraulic system, and a 2.75 psi cockpit pressurization, whereas the B had high-pressure oxygen, a 1,500 psi hydraulic system, 5 psi cockpit pressurization, and windshield deicing, zero reader (the automatic flight instrument that combined all information needed to fly the aircraft on a predetermined flight path), glide-slope receiver, localizer receiver, and automatic cockpit temperature regulation.

Anyone who has had the pleasure of flying the T-33 can readily get the feeling of the F-94 just by remembering what a delight the T-33 was to fly (and still is) and then realizing how great an afterburner would have been on the T-bird. I still fly the T-33 and it continues to be as enjoyable an aircraft as anything taking up ramp space these days— that is, if it doesn't have stuff like pylon racks loaded with Chaff and ECM pods on board, and if .8 Mach is fast enough for you, and if you are satisfied with the 3 G limitation. One's appreciation of the T-33 (or F-94 for that matter) seems also to be somewhat tied to physical size. Both cockpits, being somewhat cramped, made us little guys a bit more prone to sing their praises than did the giants who had to be eased in with a shoehorn and were reluctant to eject for fear of leaving kneecaps under the instrument panel. I understand their fear: I was recently grounded for about six months from the loss of a kneecap sustained ejecting from a T-Bird. My luck ran out over Lake Michigan when my engine failed and, unable to get a relight or find a suitable place to flameout land the bird, I had to "punch out." Unfortunately, I whacked my knees on the windshield bow going out and thus became a reluctant member of the Caterpillar Club after 30 years in fighters. I got back in the T-33 and F-101 on schedule, though.

My first contact with the Starfire came in late 1951 when, as an F-51 driver, I got a class assignment to the F-94 All-Weather Interceptor School at Tyndall AFB, Florida. Before that, my jet experience had consisted of about 20 hours of T-33/F-80 time at Williams AFB earlier the previous summer. The course at Tyndall consisted of 22 sorties for a total of 37 hours. Afterwards I returned to my outfit, climbed back in the F-51, and forgot about the Starfire for about two years. During this time, my 179th Fighter Squadron, ANG, completed its 21 months of Korean Conflict service and was returned to States control, and it was back to the Air National Guard for most of us. Then, in July 1954, the first F-94s arrived on our ramp, the first of 15 A and B models we were to receive. At this time, the F-94A/B was to receive my undivided attention until April 1957 when we ferried all 15 of the original birds to the 109th Fighter Interceptor Squadron (Minn ANG) at Holman Field, St. Paul, Minnesota, and the F-94C became our new "bird" in hand.

The F-94A/B had the same wingspan as the T-33 (38 ft., 9 in.) but was longer (40 ft., 2 in. versus 37.7 ft.) to accommodate the radar in the nose and the afterburner. The top of the fin was also higher (12 ft., 2 in. versus 11.7 ft.) because of the afterburner. Its loaded weight was 16,675 pounds versus the T-33's 15,330 pounds. Armament consisted simply of four .50 caliber machine guns in the nose, though late in the life span of the aircraft some were modified to carry a wing pod under each midwing span. Each pod, weighing 420 pounds, contained two .50 caliber machine guns and ammunition capacity of 265 rounds per gun and upped the gross weight to 17,615 pounds. Naturally, the addition of these pods reduced the maneuverability and performance of the aircraft.

The F-94A/B engine was the Allison J-33-A-33, a centrifugal compressor designed for use with an afterburner for thrust augmentation. Normal rated thrust was 4,600 pounds, but use of afterburner increased it by about 30% to 6,000 pounds. Afterburner was used for takeoff and for periods of climb or level flight when rapid acceleration was required.

Fuel was carried in four groups of tanks. Internally, two leading-edge tanks (52 gallons each), two wing tanks (77 gallons each), and a fuselage tank (65 gallons) totalled 323 gallons. Externally, two centerline tip tanks (230 gallons each) upped the total fuel to 783 gallons. Early models had underslung tip tanks; however, they were all eventually modified and the centerline tank became standard. Normal fuel sequencing was from the tips, then from the leading edge and wing groups, and, finally, from the fuselage tank. If one tip tank failed to feed or only partially emptied, a very serious wing-heaviness condition resulted and it was necessary to jettison the heavy tank; if this failed, abandoning the aircraft was recommended.

The Starfire had conventional stick and rudder controls, and the ailerons were augmented by a hydraulically powered aileron boost. The stick mounted a gun trigger, trim-tab controls, bomb (tank) release switch, and the emergency hydraulic pump switch. The aileron boost provided a 15:1 ratio; without it the ailerons were extremely stiff.

Wing flaps were electrically actuated, and when fully extended were at 45°. For takeoff, you used 32° (70%) of flaps; for landing, you used full flaps. Dive flaps located under the center forward fuselage were used for increasing drag and could be opened at any speed. A slight nose-up tendency occurred whenever the dive flaps were extended.

The tricycle landing gear was hydraulically operated and had provisions for emergency extension. The wheel-brake system was an independent manually operated hydraulic system worked by conventional toe pedals; differential braking was required for taxiing—a sometimes difficult task that required a lot of getting used to.

Each crew member sat in an ejection seat. Raising the right arm rest bottomed the seat and positioned the trigger for firing. Raising the left arm rest locked the shoulder harness. The canopy jettison system was not part of the ejection seat system, as it is in ejection systems now in use, and it was necessary to reach forward with the right hand to pull the canopy jettison handle. Squeezing the trigger on the right-hand grip fired the seat. Standard procedure was for the radar observer to eject before the pilot.

Because the aircraft sat fairly low to the ground, entrance to the cockpit could be made by climbing onto the wing; however, ladders were normally available at bases around the country. The cockpit was snug to say the least—especially with winter flying gear on. Starting the engine consisted of pushing the starter switch to "start" for three seconds and releasing. The starter motor would get you about 10% rpm. At 9% rpm the ignition switch was pushed to "normal" and then the starting fuel switch was pushed to "auto." You would get a stabilized speed of about 25–35% rpm, and then you would put the throttle at "idle" and turn the starting fuel off. No warm-up was required; if you had oil pressure and could get 100% rpm, the engine was ready for takeoff. In severe cold, it was usually necessary to allow time for oil pressure to drop within limits prior to takeoff.

You had to taxi using differential braking steering, and forward movement was necessary to negotiate any kind of a controlled short radius turn. Prior to takeoff, your cockpit check included: flaps, 70% (32°); trim, neutral; canopy, closed and locked; controls, checked for freedom of movement and proper direction of movement; emergency fuel switch, set for "take-off & land"; throttle, open; and engine instruments, checked. You needed 98% for a good afterburner light, and after releasing brakes, you maintained directional control using minimum braking until about 65 knots when the rudder became effective. Nose gear was lifted off at about 125 knots, and the aircraft was flown off the runway in one continuous motion. Once definite climb was established, you raised the gear; the wing flaps were raised between 140 and 175 knots. Climb was at 175–215 knots to a safe altitude, and then you accelerated to your best climb speed. Takeoff ground roll distance for a 60° F, no-wind day, with tip tanks and afterburner, at sea level was 2,400 feet. At 5,000 feet above sea level, it was 3,600 feet. Without afterburner at sea level on the same day, ground roll was 3,400 feet and increased to 5,300 at 5,000 feet above sea level.

Best rate of climb was at 100% rpm nonafterburning, which would get you to 30,000 feet in about 15 minutes using 180 gallons of fuel, the aircraft traveling 77 miles. At 100% in afterburner, it took only 6 minutes to reach 30,000 feet, although you used 260 gallons of fuel and traveled only 37 miles. Best cruise at 30,000 feet was with 93% rpm, giving a 287 gallon-per-hour fuel flow and a no-wind ground speed of 377 knots. As your fuel reduced, a cruise climb to 35,000 feet could get your fuel use down to about 217 gallons per hour with only a slight ground speed reduction to 365 knots. You could usually figure about 850–1,000 miles of range for a "no wind–no alternate required" destination.

The Starfire was directionally and longitudinally stable. Uneven feeding of the tip tanks was easily trimmed out, and once the tips were dry the plane handled beautifully. It had a very high rate of roll, and the stall was preceded by a noticeable mushing and buffeting; you could break the stall just by releasing a bit of back pressure. It was fully aerobatic and a delight to fly. Intentional spins were prohibited as well as extended inverted flight over 10 seconds. It had an airspeed limitation of 505 knots or .8 Mach. Above this speed, aileron buzz occurred, and lateral control was difficult and uncertain.

When we first got the 94A/Bs we had no trained radar observers, so initially we had to treat it as a day fighter. Anxious to see how we could do in air-to-air gunnery, we were quick to load the four "fifties" and head out for our gunnery range over Lake Superior. Pegging the range on the gunsight (i.e., setting a fixed range input into the computing gunsight), we were quick to learn that we couldn't do as well as we had in the F-51 Mustang. We did, however, after only three months in the bird, win the F-94 Fighter Interceptor Category of the Air National Guard Gunnery and Weapons Meet in October 1954 at Boise, Idaho. Flying without radar observers and pegging the gunsight, we performed like day fighters, firing high- and low-altitude air-to-air gunnery, panel gunnery (air-to-ground gunnery on a 10 ft. x 10 ft. target), and dive-bombing (the dive-bombing consisting of scoring miss distances of .50 bursts from an overhead dive-bomb run.) It was great sport; however, we weren't really utilizing the F-94 and its weapon system to the best advantage. Once we got some experienced radar observers and began using the weapon system as it was designed, our scores increased considerably and we really attained an "All-Weather Capability."

We still flew our gunnery pattern from a basic "high perch" position to the side and abreast of the tow target as we had in the Mustang days. Once in position, we would peel off into and down toward the target which was a 6 foot x 30 foot mesh material attached to a tow bar with a metal reflector. The reflector gave the radar observer a better radar return to lock on to. This target was towed 1,000 feet behind the target aircraft (another F-94). As we reached a 90° angle to the target travel, we would reverse our turn and smoothly bring the "pipper" through to where we wanted it on the target. During this time, the radar observer would ascertain the target on the radar set and get a "Reno" or separation of radar returns of the tow aircraft and the target. He would complete the pass. He would call range and we would eyeball the range using the size of the pip in regard to the 6-foot width of the target to reach the best firing range (normal, 600 down to 200 yards). The pip was 2 mils in diameter and, when superimposed on the target, would cover two feet or one-third of the target width at 1,000 feet. After we fired our burst, we would roll away and pass on the opposite side and parallel to the target. If we had a good pattern and were firing a bright-colored ammunition, we could see exactly where the burst had gone into the target. The tips of the rounds of ammo were dipped in a waxlike paint that heated and softened when fired and then left the color around the hole in the target as it broke through the mesh. I preferred red because it was so easy to distinguish. A good crew with a well-harmonized aircraft could put 50–75% of the rounds into the "rag" with the Starfire.

We proved this in 1955 and 1956 when we also won the Air National Guard All-Weather Interceptor Phase of the Annual Gunnery and Weapons exercise and our scores were markedly improved from the days of fixed or pegged firing.

We flew up to four ships in a gunnery pattern, each with different-colored painted ammunition. Proper pattern spacing had one aircraft firing on target, one just reversing its turn, another leaving the perch, and the fourth off target and climbing to the perch. In order not to perforate

Rear view of the F-94C. Afterburner "eyelids" are visible inside the tail cone.

the rag too badly, we normally fired only two guns, with each having only 100 rounds of ammo.

Of course, the least sought-out job when we were firing gunnery was towing the target (we called it "dragging the rag," and the target call sign was always "ragmop"). It took a bit of skill to get the target airborne without smashing runway lights or losing the weight off the tow bar (which kept the target vertical in flight). However, once airborne, the target pilot had a rather long, boring mission ahead, towing at low speed the entire time. He brought the target home and dropped it in a "drop zone" so it could be recovered for scoring. He kept pretty alert during the actual firing on the "rag" to make certain spacing in the gunnery pattern was good and that none of the radar observers missed their Reno calls and locked into the tow plane rather than the target. He could readily tell a proper pass by the position of the firing aircraft as it reversed its turn coming off the perch. If the pilot looked at all like he was pulling his nose (and guns) through the tow plane, the target pilot broke him off, pronto.

Being Squadron Operations Officer at the time, I made it a point not to get nailed as target pilot very often; however, it happened occasionally. The one mission I towed that still remains vivid in my memory involved one of our fighters colliding with the target. I was tooling along fat, dumb, and happy as "ragmop." I had Arthur Godfrey's morning radio program tuned in low on the AN/ARN-6 Radio Compass and his orchestra was playing "Don't Blame Me."

On the mission we had a pilot who had little fighter experience and even less gunnery experience; in fact, it was his first (and last) firing mission. In his exuberance to get some hits on his first outing, he pressed a bit too hard and collided with the target, wrapping the tow bar over his horizontal stabilizer. I was unaware of this collision because he had disappeared behind me. However, I learned about it rather abruptly. The tow line did not break at the time of collision but acted like a fish taking the slack out of a fishing line as it hits the lure. The pilot, after realizing he had hit the target, immediately started a climb, and, as I was on the other end of the line at a slow speed, the tow cable just lifted my tail to what seemed to be nearly vertical, and there I was looking straight down at cold Lake Superior some 10,000 feet below. The tow cable finally broke, and I frantically recovered from my unusual attitude as "Don't Blame Me" ended. The bird involved in the collision made it home safely with the tow bar still wrapped around the stabilizer. I guess the relatively slow overtake speed of fighter over target was the only thing that kept that bird from losing the stabilizer and plunging into Lake Superior. I didn't tow for a while after that either.

Toward the end of our 94A/B era we modified some aircraft by hanging the two gun pods, one under each wing. This gave us eight guns. However, we never got to try them in air-to-air gunnery. Maneuverability was so eroded by the addition of the pods that I seriously doubt any decent scores could have been attained in this configuration.

Of course, in the actual application of the F-94 in a true all-weather or night intercept, a stern position with no angle-off was ideal for destroying an enemy airborne target. In fact, the F-94 gained a place in Air Force history when during the Korean Conflict a F-94B became the first Air Force jet to gain a night radar kill over an enemy plane when it knocked down a marauding Russian-built LA-9 fighter.

The 94A/B was a good aircraft to land. You touched down on the main gear with the tail slightly down. Excessive tail-low attitudes got the sheet metal men mad because you'd scrape the afterburner shroud on the runway. A standard 360° overhead pattern was flown with initial approach at 270 knots, 1,500 feet above the ground. Over the end of the runway, you'd go into a 90° bank, chop power, and extend your speed brakes. Continuing your turn, you'd extend your gear when under 195 knots, put full flaps down under 175 knots, and roll out on final about 140 knots. You'd come across the fence with at least 120 knots and touch down between 95 and 105 knots. The F-94 was excellent in a crosswind, and you could put the up-wind wheel on the runway first and then ease the other main on. To quote one of our former pilots, now long-since retired, in a strong crosswind you "get ahold of the runway and don't let go!"—a truism that cannot be denied.

In April 1957 we ferried all 15 of the aircraft we had originally received to the 109th FIS (Minn ANG) at Holman Field, St. Paul, Minnesota, ending the era of the "bird with a gun" for us. Our efforts turned toward the F-94Cs which were appearing on our ramp in numbers.

In 1949 Lockheed further exploited the basic F-80/T-33/F-94A design with a view to improving performance and brought out the F-94C. The F-94C was once known as the F-94B, then as the F-97A, and then redesignated the F-94C when the B model designation was assigned to the improved F-94A. The J-48-P-5 engine with more power was introduced to improve high-altitude performance. A thinner wing was also used. The C first flew in 1951, and when production ended in 1954, 387 had been built. It was the first U.S. fighter to be designed without guns (a mistake, I believe, that has taken over 20 years to rectify).

The wings had been shortened to 37 feet, 4 inches, and had a very definite dihedral. The tailplane was swept back, the intakes reshaped, and the nose lengthened. The C was 42 feet, 6 inches long, 14 feet, 10 inches high, and weighed 24,000 pounds fully loaded with tip and pylon tanks. It acquired another "first" with its use of a braking parachute. For armament it carried 24 2.75 FFAR (folding fin aerial rockets) in the nose and 24 2.75 FFAR in wing pods. It was powered by a Pratt & Whitney J-48-P-5 continuous-flow, centrifugal-type, turbojet engine designed with an afterburner for thrust augmentation. It was a rugged engine and had a good afterburner that gave 33% more thrust at sea level for takeoff and 80% at flight speed. The J-48 produced 6,350 pounds of thrust without afterburner and 8,750 pounds with it. All in all, it didn't look, shoot, or fly like the F94A/B. It went faster and higher, but not farther.

The C (as I'll call it) had a more aesthetic design than the earlier model. With the marked dihedral and swept-back tail, it had a "cocky" look.

Fuel was carried internally in two wing tanks, a fuselage tank, and an engine feed tank, which together carried 366 gallons of usable fuel. Centerline tip tanks added another 503.8 gallons, giving 963.8 gallons (6,064.7 pounds) of fuel for normal operations.

Should you elect to carry pylon tanks, another 460 gallons (2,990 pounds) of fuel could be added, giving a total of 1,329.8 gallons (8,643 pounds). The added weight of the pylons combined with the vastly diminished handling characteristics rarely warranted flying with pylons. The range increased a bit, but the bird really got "doggy" with pylons.

All of the fuel tanks except the pylon tanks (which we rarely carried) could be refueled through a single-point filler well located on the left side of the nose section. Fuel under pressure (up to 50 psi) entered the single point and was directed to the internal fuel tanks and tip tanks through normal fuel transfer lines. This was a vast improvement over the F-94A/B system which required that each tank be filled individually over the wing—a slow, tedious process.

The aircraft hydraulic system operated aileron boost, elevator boost, speed brakes, landing gear, and rocket doors. An emergency system was incorporated to lower the landing gear in the event of normal system malfunction.

The primary flight controls moved manually by conventional stick and rudder pedals or remotely through the electrical and hydraulic systems of the automatic pilot. Hydraulic boosters reduced control-stick forces on the ailerons and elevator. The C was trimmed by electrically operated aileron and rudder trim tabs, ground-adjustable rudder and aileron bend tabs, and electrically repositioned springs to control lateral stick movement. The stick grip mounted a trim switch, external tank release button, rocket-firing trigger, automatic-pilot disengage button, and interphone button.

Electrically operated split-type wing flaps lowered to 45° in the full down position. Two pairs of hydraulically operated speed brakes were used for increasing drag. The forward pair was located in the underside of the forward fuselage and the aft pair in the fuselage behind the wing fillets. The drag chute was packed in a housing above the fuselage tail cone. The 16-foot ribbon-type chute reduced landing roll approximately 40%; however, it would shear if released in excess of 200 knots. The gear and brake systems were essentially the same as on the A and B models.

Ground start consisted basically of placing the ground starter switch to "start" for 2–3 seconds then releasing it, the igniter master switch to "normal" when 7% rpm was reached, and the throttle to "idle" at 9% rpm and of checking that tail pipe temp was within limits and that idle rpm stabilized at 26–36%.

The C taxied easier than the A/B; however, differential braking was still required for turns.

Pretakeoff check was essentially: canopy locked, speed brakes up, AB (afterburner) nozzle closed, flaps 32° (70%), trim neutral, elevator and aileron boost on, engine checks complete, and you were ready to go. With brakes depressed, you'd advance to full power, then release brakes, using minimal braking for directional control to 40–60 knots when the rudder became effective. You'd move throttle outboard to afterburner position and check for proper afterburner light, which was a momentary loss of thrust (interval between cock of afterburner nozzle opening and ignition) and then a definite kick in the pants as the afterburner ignited. The afterburner nozzle opened during afterburner operation to prevent excessive tail pipe temperature and pressure from building up in the tail section. This, in effect, gave the tail pipe a larger diameter, and as it opened approximately three seconds before afterburner ignition, there was a resultant loss of thrust.

You raised the nosewheel and flew the aircraft off the runway in one continuous motion at about 147 knots when using afterburner and having full tip tanks and rocket pods. Once definitely airborne—gear up, flaps up to 160–175 knots, and out of afterburner detent for a nonafterburner climb—initial climb was 200–225 knots to a safe altitude and then you gradually accelerated to the best climb speed, which was 315 knots at sea level, dropping off 15 knots for each 5,000 feet up to 30,000 feet where you indicated 225 knots. A no-wind, nonafterburner takeoff distance for a 60° F day at sea level with tip tanks and rocket pods was 4,200 feet; at 5,000 feet, pressure altitude was 6,200 feet. With afterburner on the same day at sea level, takeoff roll was 3,800 feet; at 5,000 feet, pressure altitude was 5,100 feet.

For a good many pilots, this was the first jet they had flown that was capable of going supersonic; but to do it, you had to climb to 45,000 feet, plug in afterburner, and roll the nose over and start down. You knew you were supersonic only when the airspeed indicator "jumped" across the Mach meter and you sensed a slight wing drop; when that happened you had to chop throttle, extend your speed brakes, and start back on the stick so as not to put a hole in someone's back yard.

Maximum allowable acceleration for symmetrical maneuvers was plus 8.67 Gs and a minus 3.0 Gs for all configurations except with pylons on. Full pylons installed reduced the G load limitation to 3.85 Gs. Rolling pullout limitations were plus 5.78 Gs and minus 1.0 G, except for aircraft with pylons installed.

We flew the standard 360° overhead landing pattern with the C entering on initial approach at 270 knots; 1,500 feet above the ground and over the end of the runway you would break into a steep bank, chop throttle to 55–65% as you simultaneously opened your speed brakes. Once under 215 knots, you would drop the gear, get full flaps, and maintain 150 knots in your final turn. Holding a minimum of 145 knots on final approach, you would retard the throttle to idle when the landing was assured. The C was peculiar on touchdown for it really "paid off" or quit flying quite abruptly, and no two birds were alike. Obviously, it was best to be near concrete when it did quit flying. After touchdown, you pulled the drag chute handle and braked to a stop. Use of drag chute was recommended for all landings except those in strong crosswinds. In a strong crosswind, the drag chute would weathervane or swing to the downwind side of the runway, causing the nose of the aircraft to swing to the upwind side. To keep the aircraft on the runway took all of the opposite rudder, aileron, and smooth braking one could muster.

The C had deicing boots installed on the leading edge of the wings and horizontal stabilizer. High-resistance wires embedded in rubber provided continuous heat for the leading edge of each boot. Deicing was not often needed in the F-94C. The J-48 engine, a centrifugal compressor type, was relatively free of icing problems. Surface icing was usually avoided and the best system was to place wing and empennage deicer and pitot deice systems in operation before the ice actually formed.

The C was the first jet I flew that had an automatic pilot. It could be used for cruise, coupled ILS approaches, and radar-coupled attacks. I remember the radar-coupled attacks quite vividly as they sometimes gave a really wild ride; and after a few of these, aircrews were prone to prefer steering the attack manually. Once you coupled the autopilot with the radar, the aircraft reacted immediately to center the steering dot on the pilot scope. This more often than not caused high G forces, rapid wing roll, and a rather uncomfortable ride as the controls were trying to respond to inputs from the radar system. A "hot" or jumpy dot was really amplified on the controls, and the pilots much preferred using basic "stick and rudder" techniques to center the dot. The state of the art on "coupled" attacks has improved vastly over the years and now many aircraft automatic flight-control systems (the F-101 in particular) are capable of performing smoother coupled attacks than a highly competent pilot using basic control movements.

The primary armament consisted of 48 2.75 folding fin aerial rockets (FFAR). Twenty-four were carried in closed-breach launching tubes in the nose of the aircraft, and 12 were in rocket pods on each wing. Rocket firing was normally controlled automatically by the E-5 rocket-firing control system employing radar tracking and computing combined with a rocket-firing computer. A standby fixed optical gunsight for manual firing was available in the event of a radar system malfunction.

The nose section had four circumferential doors hinged at the forward end that moved inward simultaneously by hydraulic pressure, exposing the launching tubes prior to firing. The doors opened when the trigger was squeezed and closed three seconds after the trigger release by an automatic timing delay. Each rocket pod had 12 rocket tubes. A rocket pod nose of plastic was shattered by the rocket exhaust gases when the rockets were fired. Rocket selection was in salvos of 6 or 12 from each pod, and they could be fired manually or automatically, in conjunction with a corresponding number of 12 or 24 nose compartment rockets.

The F-94C brought us into a new arena for weapons firing. Instead of the usual aerial gunnery pattern where we combined radar tracking, a gunsight, and eyeballs to put bullets into a towed target, we were vectored on to a 90° beam rocket attack by ground radar control.

We fired at a Delmar target which was aerodynamically shaped, made of lightweight Styrofoam, with a radar reflector built into it. It was about eight feet in length, looked like a large bomb with fins, and weighed only a few pounds. We carried it cradled in a basket under the left wing of a T-33, and once airborne, it was reeled out to 5,000 feet for the firing runs.

Uniquely, the F-94C enabled us to fire over an undercast: once we ascertained that the Lake Superior range was free of vessels, we could be on top of the clouds and the Ground Control Intercept Station could set us up on firing passes and keep both fighters and target aircraft within the confines of the range limits by radar vectors.

The target ship would normally traverse the length of the range, and the ground controller would space the fighter so that each one turned in on its firing pass at about the time the fighter ahead had broken off of the target. Once the radar observer got an initial contact on the target, he would establish a "Reno" or separation between target and tow ship and then "lock on" to the target. After the "lock on" was solid, the pilot would then steer the aircraft to center the dot on the pilot scope. The pilot of the target plane was the only person who could give clearance to fire, for he was the only one able to ascertain absolutely that the fighter was in fact "locked on" to the target and not the tow ship. He, of course, would have to get a visual sighting of the fighter and then watch for movement of the fighter to the aft as it closed in range. There was a standard radio call "20 seconds to go" when pilot radarscope presentations started shrinking, and it was about this time that the target could detect the fighter drifting aft toward the towed target. Once this drift was perceived, then and only then would the target pilot give a "cleared to fire." Once cleared to fire, the pilot would concentrate on centering the dot, getting the wings level, and trying to make a smooth firing pass. You'd squeeze the trigger and the computer would fire the rocket salvo at the optimum range. You would then break up and into the direction from which the target came. Normally, the rockets would create a good pattern, and we destroyed a number of Delmar targets; but occasionally a fin would hang up on one of the rockets and they would gyrate all over the sky. If no "kill" of the target was made, the tow reel operator could retrieve the Delmar into the basket and bring it home for another mission. The retrieve took skill and deftness, for if the target came in just a "tad" fast, it was knocked off as it banged into the basket.

You could always tell when a flight was returning from a successful rocket mission, for with the plastic nose covers off of the rocket pod and the rocket tubes empty, the F-94C made a weird sound that someone likened to the "howl of the banshees."

As with the A/B model, we were equipped with the C for about three years; then as our ramp started to tilt from the weight of our newly arriving F-89J Scorpions, we ferried the fleet of Cs to the "bone yard," except for those that stayed in the local area to be mounted on pedestals. [For more on the F-89, see *Flying Combat Aircraft of the USAAF-USAF* (Ames: Iowa State University Press, 1975.)]

Thus ended the F-94 days for us. However, we have retained the T-33, and it is still providing great service. We use it primarily as a target aircraft carrying Chaff and Electronic Counter Measure (ECM) pods in our daily intercept training. It is still a delight to fly, and I can still hear my instructor pilot yelling at me (from way back in 1951), "Dammit Gatlin, you are done with that yank and bank flying, now you've gotta be smooth!" Nor will I ever forget the sensation of smoothness and the quietness of that first jet ride.

The T-33 has been to jet fighter flying what the T-6 was to conventional fighter flying during World War II. Its progeny, the F-94 A/B and the F-94C, fulfilled a vital role in air defense and earned a place of honor in the exacting mission of all-weather fighter interceptor flying.

The T-33s and F-101s are now gone and we are into a conversion to the RF-4C and the Tactical Reconnaissance Mission. As for the RF-4C, all I can say is, "What a beautiful bird to fly!"

COL. WAYNE C. GATLIN, a World War II veteran, is commander of the 148th Fighter Group, Minnesota Air National Guard, stationed in Duluth. He has logged nearly 6,000 flying hours, mostly in fighters.

KC-135 Stratotanker

PHILIP C. BROWN

READY for contact,'' reported the boom operator over the refueling frequency. Slowly the B-52 Stratofortress edged forward, guided by the ''boomer's'' instructions.

"Forward ten, up six." Delicately, the aircraft commander of the B-52 advanced the eight throttles to bring his aircraft to the position at which the boom operator would effect the final contact. On the top of the giant bomber's fuselage, behind the cockpit, the slipway doors were open, forming a V-shaped access to the refueling receptacle.

In the cockpit of the tanker, the pilots were alert for the radio call of "breakaway" in the event that the bomber should overrun the tanker or collision appear imminent. Then it was up to them to add power and, when advised by the boom operator that they were clear, to climb straight ahead. Over the interphone, the boomer had been advising the remainder of the tanker crew of the position of the receiver aircraft.

"Fifty feet and closing, thirty feet, twenty feet." The pilots of the KC-135 felt the rear of their aircraft rise as the bow wave of the B-52 exerted its upward push on the tanker's tail. Because most refuelings were done with the tanker on autopilot, this upward movement was noted by the stabilizer trim wheel taking a few turns to the rear as the autopilot sought to maintain level flight.

LLOYD S. HATHCOCK, USAF

A-7D refueling from a KC-135 tanker in the Dallas area, silhouetted against the sunset sky.

Although the presence of fighters and smaller bombers on the boom was hardly noticeable, a B52 was another matter. While the tanker pilots attempted to maintain a constant airspeed during refueling, an increase was usually noted shortly after contact with a B-52 as the giant bomber started to push the tanker. It was truly a case of "the tail wagging the dog."

As the bomber stabilized in the refueling envelope, aided by the pilot director lights on the underside of the tanker's fuselage, the boom operator made the final contact. Lying on his stomach on a couch in a pod on the underside of the tanker, the boomer flew the boom with a stick in his right hand while his left hand controlled the boom telescope lever that extended the boom to the receptacle. At night, and particularly in rough weather, keen depth perception and a steady hand were required.

"Contact," reported the boomer.

"Contact," acknowledged the crew of the B-52. With a yellow "contact-made" light on the fuel panel in the cockpit, the copilot of the tanker activated the pumps to start the fuel flow. Through bumpy cirrus and with turns to avoid bad weather, a good bomber pilot would hang on for the 30 minutes or so necessary to receive over 120,000 pounds of fuel. Then, with the refueling complete, the bomber would back off, receive a refueling report from the navigator of the tanker, and be on his way. This drama is enacted many times a day in all parts of the world as the Strategic Air Command fulfills its global mission.

In the summer of 1959, as a pilot trainee in Laredo, Texas, I had my first look at the KC-135. As I taxied out in the front seat of a T-33, my instructor, Lt. Carl Wheeler, said, "Brown, if you're lucky, someday you might fly that aircraft." Three months later, I was one of three in my class chosen to fly the KC-135.

In 1959, the KC-135 was regarded by many as the "Cadillac" of the Air Force. It was an outgrowth of the development by the Boeing Company of a four-engined jet transport originally known as the Dash Eighty that had its first flight on 15 July 1954 and was to attain recognition as the 707. Later, the prototype aircraft was fitted with a refueling boom and associated controls, and 350 flight hours were spent to test and demonstrate its feasibility as a tanker. The KC-135 joined the Air Force inventory in January 1957 and set many records in early 1958, climaxing on 8 April 1958 with a record nonstop flight of 10,228 miles from Tokyo to the Azores.

Crew training consisted of ground school at Castle Air Force Base, California, with flight training at Castle or Roswell Air Force Base, New Mexico. Coming from pilot training where the largest plane I had flown was the 15,000-pound T-33, my first impression of the KC-135 was of its size. It was 136 feet, 3 inches long with a wingspan of 130 feet, 10 inches. The top of its fin towered 38 feet, 4 inches above the ramp. It had a maximum takeoff gross weight of 297,000 pounds and could carry 31,200 gallons of fuel, which gave it an endurance of over 19 hours. Although its top speed was .90 Mach, normal cruise was .78 Mach.

It had a large cargo door on the forward left side, but normal crew access was through a crew entry door on the lower left side abeam the cockpit. Climbing a ladder brought you to the flight deck just behind the pilot's seat. Here the crew of four was normally seated. In addition to the two pilots there was a navigator and the one enlisted man on the crew, the boom operator. A small folding jump seat could be let down between the pilots, just aft of the control pedestal. To the rear of the cockpit door was a lavatory and an area in which the crew could live aboard during a wartime situation. In this well-insulated compartment was an oven, two seats, and six let-down bunks. Farther to the rear was a large 6,000-cubic-foot area for cargo or troops, with center-facing let-down canvas seats along the side and cargo tie-down provisions on the floor. A traveling hoist on an overhead beam could be installed to aid in the handling of heavy cargo. At the rear of the aircraft was an auxiliary power unit that provided electrical power and heat while on the ground.

Almost all of the fuel was carried in the wings and beneath the main deck. At the rear of the cargo area and beneath the level of the main deck was the refueling pod from which the boom operator worked the boom during refueling operations.

The aircraft was powered by four Pratt & Whitney J57-P-59W engines that developed just under 13,000 pounds of thrust with water injection when installed on the aircraft. Although I was impressed with what I thought were four rather large engines, takeoff performance proved to be critical at the heavy weights at which we operated. Commercial transports of this type were then limited to maximum weights of about 245,000 pounds. At our normal takeoff weights of from 275,000 to 285,000 pounds, 9,400 to 9,800 feet of runway were required to get airborne.

All crew members were kept quite busy with their duties, particularly during refueling. Without a flight engineer in the crew complement, the pilots acquired many of his duties such as running the fuel and electrical panels and controlling the pressurization and heating systems. Normally the copilot handled most of the communications, often obtaining clearances for the bombers involved in refueling. Besides his normal navigational duties, the navigator was the quarterback of the refueling rendezvous, locating the bombers on radar and vectoring both groups to effect the join-up.

The boom operator, who rode up front during most of a flight, was also the loadmaster for cargo operations and aided the navigator by doing all of the celestial "shooting" with a periscopic sextant that was extended through a sextant port in the ceiling of the cockpit. This was an area in which most boomers took particular pride, usually surpassing the navigators in their ability with the sextant. Usually the boom operator was also pressed into service as the cook of our in-flight meals and here their abilities were not so universally revered.

On our early aircraft we had a fuel-air combustion starter on the number 4 engine that would allow the crew to start that engine without outside aid and then use air bled from that engine to start the remaining three. Later this was replaced with a cartridge-type starter that utilized a ballistic charge that was fired with a resultant cloud of smoke to start number 4, with the remaining three engines again started with bleed air from this engine. Provision was also made for the utilization of an external source of air.

As the starter was engaged, the engine began to rotate, as indicated on a tachometer. At about 15% rpm, the throttle was placed to the START position and fuel was introduced to the engine. A successful start was indicated by a rise in egt (exhaust gas temperature), reflected on an egt gauge. Other engine instruments, all of which were on the pilot's center instrument panel, were an oil pressure gauge, a fuel flow indicator (which read in pounds per hour), and an epr gauge (exhaust pressure ratio), the primary power instrument which reflected the difference between the pressure at the inlet of the engine and that at the rear.

KC-135 Stratotanker in flight over Vietnam, 1965.

After number 4 was started, a matter of a minute or so, it was run up to 90-95% rpm to ensure adequate air for starting the remaining three engines. Although normally started in sequence, the air supply was sufficient to start the remaining three simultaneously, as we did when on ground alert. However, initial rotation of the engines was a bit slower with three engines sharing the same source of air.

For a normal training mission, the checklist through starting engines probably took 20-25 minutes. Excerpts from the actual KC-135 checklist, dated March 1960, follow. On alert, the airplane was preflighted daily down to the point of "hitting" the starter so that a start only took 1½-2 minutes. In the alert situation, all of our airplanes were to be airborne within 15 minutes from sounding the alarm. With the airplanes "cocked" and employing MITO (minimum interval takeoff) procedures, this was a realistic goal.

EXTERIOR INSPECTION

1. Equipment—Stowed (All)
2. Safety Check—Completed (P)
   a. Nose Door—Closed
   b. Defueling Valve Cover—Closed
   c. Refueling Valves Handle—FLIGHT
   d. Single Point Receptacle—Checked
   e. Single Point Panel—Switches off, cover closed
   f. Water Quantity—Checked
   g. Ramp Area—Clear

INTERIOR INSPECTION (CP reads)

(Items 2, 3 and 4 for Copilot when Navigator not flying)

1. Crew Inspection—Completed (P)
   a. 781—Checked
   b. Time Hack—Completed
   c. Emergency Procedures—Briefed
   d. Jumpmaster—Designated
   e. Mission and Weather—Briefed
   f. Start Engines Time—Announced
   g. Questions—Cleared
2. Electronics Cabinet—Checked (CP)
3. Navigation Equipment—Checked (CP)
4. Navigator's Oxygen Panel—Checked (CP)
5. Circuit Breakers—Set (CP)
6. BO Interphone Selector—INTER (CP)
7. Instructor's Oxygen Panel—OFF and 100% (CP)
8. Throttles—CUT-OFF (P)
9. Fuel Panel—Checked (P)
10. Starter Switches—OFF (P)
11. Radar Intensity—Full CCW (CP)
12. Overhead Panel—Checked (P, CP)
13. J-4 Panel—Checked (CP)
14. Anti-Icing—OFF (CP)
15. Pilots' Data Cases—Complete (P, CP)
16. Crossover Valve—NORMAL (CP)
17. Alarm Bell—Checked (P, GC)
18. Battery Switch—EMERGENCY (P)
19. External Power—Checked (CP)
20. External Power Switch—CLOSE (CP)
21. T-R Voltage—Checked (P)
22. Battery Switch—NORMAL (P)
22A. Battery Charging Current—Checked (CP)
23. Instrument Gyros—ON (P, CP)
24. Oxygen System—Checked (P, CP)
25. Crew Report—Completed (BO, N, CP, P)
26. Omni, TACAN, Command Radios and VGH—ON (P, CP)
27. Wheel Well Doors—Clear (P, GC)
28. Inboard Spoilers—CUT-OFF (P)
29. Hydraulic System—Checked (P, CP)
30. Pitot Heat—Checked and OFF (CP, GC))
31. OMNI, TACAN and Command Radios—Checked (P, CP, BO)
32. Autopilot—ON (CP)
33. Fuel Dump—Checked (CP, BO, GC)
34. Lights—Checked and set (P, CP)
35. Fire Switches and Warning Lights—Checked (P, CP)
36. Generator Circuit Open Lights—Illuminated (CP)
37. Synchronizing Lights—Illuminated (CP)
38. Inboard Spoilers—NORMAL (P)
39. Speed Brakes—Checked (P, GC)
40. Control and Trim—Checked (P, GC)
41. Inboard Spoilers—CUT-OFF (P)
42. Flap Warning Horn—Checked (P, CP)
43. Fuel Quantity—Checked (P, CP)
44. Autopilot—Checked (P, CP)
45. Instruments—Checked (P, CP)
46. Cabin Pressure Release Handle—In and Safetied (P)
47. Air Cond Override Switch—OVERRIDE (P) 71 > 97
    Left Alternate Pressurization Switch—ON (P) 98 >
48. Emergency Heat and Pressurization Switch—DECREASE (P) 1 > 70
    Aux Pressurization and Heating Switch—DECREASE (P) 71 > 97
    Right Alternate Pressurization Switch—DECREASE (P) 98 >
49. Air Cond Override Switch—NORMAL (P) 71 > 97
    Left Alternate Pressurization Switch—OFF (P) 98 >
50. Air Cond Crossover Switch—OPEN (P) 98 > plus
51. Cabin Temperature—Set (P)
52. Cabin Manual Pressure Control—OFF (CP)
53. Cabin Pressure—Set (CP)
54. Cabin Rate of Change—Set (CP)
55. Auxiliary Pumps—OFF (P)
56. Hydraulic Pressure Switches—OFF (P)

BEFORE STARTING ENGINES
(CP reads)

1. External Power Switch—CLOSE (CP, GC)
2. Battery Switch—NORMAL (P)
3. Pedals, Belts and Harnesses—Adjusted (P, CP)
4. Navigation Lights—As Required (CP)
5. Auxiliary Pumps—OFF (P)
6. Hydraulic Pressure Switches—OFF (P)
7. Locks and Pins—Removed (P, BO, GC)
8. Nose Gear Door Actuators—Connected (P, GC)
9. Wheel Well Doors—Clear (P, GC)
10. Hydraulic Pressure Switches—ON (P)
11. Auxiliary Pumps—AUTO (P)
12. Radio—Request Area Coverage (CP)
13. Gear Warning Light—Extinguished (CP)
14. Air Cond Master Switch—RAM AIR (CP)
15. Bleed Switches—OPEN (CP) 1 > 426
16. Windows—Closed (P, CP)
17. Deleted
18. Fuel Panel—Set for Takeoff (CP)
19. Fuel Heater—Check (P, GC)

20. Inboard Spoilers—NORMAL (P)
21. External Power—OFF (P, GC)
22. Battery Switch—OFF (P)

STARTING ENGINES (CP reads)

1. External Power Switch—CLOSE (if auxiliary power available) (CP)
2. Battery Switch—NORMAL (P) (EMERGENCY if no auxiliary power available)
3. Reserve Brake Pressure—Checked (P)
4. Parking Brakes—Set (P)
5. Radio Call—Completed (CP)
6. Check with Ground—Ready to Start #4 (P, GC)
7. Fuel Air Starter—GROUND START (P)
8. No. 4 Throttle—START (P)
9. Fuel—Air Starter—OFF (P)
10. Oil Pressure—Normal (CP)
11. Check with Ground—Ready to Start #3 (P, GC)
12. No. 4 Throttle—90-95% RPM (P) (Do not exceed MRT)
13. No. 3 Starter—GROUND START (P)
14. No. 3 Throttle—START (P)
15. Oil Pressure—Normal (CP)
16. No. 3 Starter—OFF (P)
17. No. 3 Throttle—IDLE (P)
18. No. 3 Generator Breaker—CLOSE (CP)
19. Check with Ground Controller—Ready to Start #2 and #1 Simultaneously (same procedure as No. 3) (P, GC)
20. Starter Switches—OFF (P)
21. All Throttles—IDLE (P)
22. Flaps—UP (CP)
23. Auxiliary Pumps—OFF (P)
24. Copilot's Instrument Power Switch—START (CP)
25. Electrical Panel—Checked (CP)
26. Battery Switch—NORMAL (P)
27. Aileron Lockout—Checked (P, GC)
28. Flaps—Set for Takeoff (CP, GC)
29. External Power, Chocks and Interphone—Removed (P, CP, GC)
30. Taxi Report—Completed (N, CP, P)
31. Engine Anti-Icing—Climatic (CP)

TAXIING (CP reads)

1. Brakes and Steering—Checked (P)
2. Window Heat—NORMAL (CP)
3. Flight Instruments—Checked (P, CP)
4. Cargo Door Light—Extinguished (CP)

BEFORE TAKEOFF (CP reads)

1. Parking Brakes—Set (P)
1A. Pitot Heat—ON (CP)
2. Stabilizer, Aileron and Rudder Trim—Set for Takeoff (P)
3. Speed Brakes—0 degrees (P)
4. Fuel Panel—Set for Takeoff (CP)
5. Flaps—Set for Takeoff (CP)
6. Attitude Indicators—Adjusted (P, CP)
7. TACAN—OFF (P)
8. Radio Call—Completed (CP)
9. Takeoff Data—Checked (P, CP)
10. Takeoff Report—Completed (BO, N, CP, P)

LINE-UP (CP reads)

1. Brakes—Holding (P)
2. Directional Indicators—Checked (P, CP)
3. Throttle Brake—Set (P)
4. Landing Navigation Lights—As Required (CP)
5. Beacon Lights—Both ON (CP)
6. Starter Switches—Climatic (P)
7. Throttles—Advance for Dry Thrust Check (P)
8. Throttles—Set Water Start EPR (P, CP)
9. Water Boost Pumps—START (CP)
10. Engine Instruments—Within Limits (CP)

TAKEOFF

1. Brakes—Release (P)
2. Throttles—Adjust (CP)
3. Engine Instruments—Monitor (CP)
4. Control Column—Hold Forward (CP)
5. Stab Trim Indicator—Monitor (CP)
6. Airspeed Check—Accomplished (P, CP)
7. Decision Point—Checked (P, CP)
8. Critical Engine Failure Distance—Checked (P, CP)
9. Rotate—Called Out (CP)
10. Airplane—Rotate (P)

RUNNING TAKEOFF (CP reads through Item 9)

This checklist will be used in lieu of the normal line-up and takeoff checklists, during running takeoff operations.

1. Landing, Navigation Lights—As Required (CP)
2. Beacon Lights—Both ON (CP)
3. Starter Switches—Climatic (P)
4. Directional Indicators—Checked (P, CP)
5. Enter Runway—(P)
6. Water Boost Pumps—START (CP)
7. Throttle Brake—Set (P)
8. Throttles—Set Takeoff EPR (P, CP)
9. Takeoff Roll—Started (P)
10. Throttles—Adjust (CP)
11. Engine Instruments—Monitor (CP)
12. Control Column—Hold Forward (P)
13. Stab Trim Indicator—Monitor (CP)
14. 70 Knots—NOW (CP, N)
15. Time—HACK (N, CP)
16. S1—NOW (P, CP)

17. Rotate—Called Out (CP)
18. Airplane—Rotate (P)

ENGINE SHUTDOWN (CP reads)

1. Parking Brakes—Set (P)
2. Electrical Equipment Except Command Radio—OFF (P, CP)
3. Air Cond Override Switch—OVERRIDE (P) 71 > 97
   Left Alternate Pressurization Switch—ON (P) 98 >
4. Emergency Heat and Pressurization Switch—DECREASE (P) 1 > 70
   Auxiliary Pressurization and Heating Switch—DECREASE (P) 71 > 97
   Right Alternate Pressurization Switch—DECREASE (P) 98 >
5. Air Conditioning Override Switch—NORMAL (P) 71 > 97
   Left Alternate Pressurization Switch—OFF (P) 98 >
6. Boost Pumps—OFF (CP)
7. Battery Switch—EMERGENCY (P)
8. Throttles—75% RPM, then CUT-OFF (P)
9. Oxygen—OFF and 100% (P, CP)
10. Hydraulic Pressure Switches—OFF (P)
11. Command Radio—OFF (P)
12. Lights—OFF (P, P)
13. Battery Switch—OFF (P)

While taxiing, the aircraft commander steered the aircraft by means of a small wheel mounted on the left side wall of the cockpit. Practically all takeoffs were made with the aid of water injection. A tank in the right wheel well held 670 gallons of demineralized or distilled water. Turning onto the runway, the copilot actuated a switch that started two pumps that delivered the water to the engines. This gave added thrust to the engines for approximately 2 minutes and 5 seconds. Unfortunately, one pump fed the left engines while the other fed the right side. Failure of a pump, therefore, gave quite a yaw as well as a loss of power.

At some of the bases we transited where the KC-135 was not a common sight, we would sometimes get a laugh when we said we needed distilled water. Some well-intentioned staff officer would finally locate a quart or so at the base hospital and ask us how much more we needed. At the heavy weights at which we operated, the KC-135 was noted for its long takeoff runs and gave the B-52 pilots who sometimes rode with us many anxious moments as they watched the green lights marking the end of the runway coming up at us with the aircraft still showing no inclination to fly.

V-speeds varied with weight and they approximated those of the 707, which are:

	Aircraft Weight	
	295,000	200,000
V-1 (at which you can safely stop or continue on three engines)	144 knots	116 knots
Vr (rotation speed, nose gear raised from runway)	149 knots	120 knots
V2 (takeoff speed)	166 knots	137 knots

Acceleration was checked by comparing actual performance from 70 knots with a precomputed speed that should be attained after a run of so many seconds. Although I am a bit hazy on the details, I do recall that you started the time at 70 knots and at the end of the precomputed interval you should have accelerated to a certain speed with an allowance of 3 knots. If you were not accelerating properly during this interval, you discontinued the takeoff.

High above the clouds, a Strategic Air Command B-52 heavy bomber is refueled by a KC-135 Stratotanker.

Although loss of an engine at high gross weights did not present much of a directional problem, it certainly could not be taken lightly because of our high gross weights and the loss of thrust that resulted. Our already lengthy takeoff run was lengthened further. Normally after the loss of an engine one thinks of getting the gear up as soon as airborne to reduce drag, but the first thing that takes place in the gear retraction sequence is that the gear doors that have previously been closed drop open, the forward edge of them adding even more drag. Therefore, trying to "suck" the gear up quickly resulted in the aircraft trying to settle back in until the gear was retracted and the doors again were shut.

Particularly at light weights, but also at the heavier weights, the loss of an engine, especially an outboard, resulted in deviations of up to 75 feet from the runway center line. Full rudder and up to 5° of bank were employed to keep the aircraft on the runway.

Takeoff procedures called for us to climb 500 feet and level off, accelerating to 280 knots as the water ran out. Because the surrounding terrain was often higher than the field elevation, a midnight takeoff of three KC-135s was not unheeded by the local populace as we roared overhead at 200–400 feet and rattled the dishes from their shelves. In North Africa, areas quite close to the runways were cultivated by local people using camels to draw their wooden plows. I can still see the camel who bolted when our water cut in with its resultant roar as we turned onto the runway. For all I know, he's still running, digging the longest furrow in Africa.

In an attempt to get the SAC Alert Force airborne in a minimum of time, a technique known as minimum interval takeoffs (MITO) was developed. This called for aircraft to take off at 15-second intervals with three aircraft on the runway at the same time. One would be lifting off, another accelerating through approximately 100 knots, and a third just starting his takeoff run. With the smoke resulting from the use of water injection, visibility was severely restricted, and the most desirable takeoff condition was to have a slight crosswind that would clear this smoke from the runway and disperse the turbulence that would be churned up by the preceding aircraft. Although a 15-second interval was desired, occasionally someone would tap his brakes and you would find the interval shortened even further. Needless to say, optimum conditions did not always exist, and a nighttime MITO takeoff under calm wind conditions could provide quite a thrill. However, using this technique, eight B-52s and eight KC-135s could be launched in four or five minutes—an awe-inspiring sight.

The early aircraft were fitted with an unboosted rudder that required quite a high pedal force in the event of the loss of an outboard engine at low weights and low temperatures. Both pilots had to be properly seated and prepared for the directional control requirements, and even then large excursions from the runway centerline could be expected. Later, three feet of length was added to the fin, and power boosting was incorporated to make a much more satisfactory system.

Dutch roll, a characteristic of swept-wing aircraft (the KC-135 has a 35° sweep back), was a possibility in the KC-135. If you encountered dutch roll while hand-flying the plane, engaging the rudder axis of the autopilot dampened it out quickly. The aircraft handled well at high altitudes but did tend to wallow a bit if flown above the optimum altitude for the particular weight and not kept in trim.

Stalls presented no particular problem, as there was quite a margin of warning. Buffeting preceded a complete stall so that you had sufficient time to take corrective action before getting into an aggravated condition. Smoothly lowering the nose and adding power soon drove you out of trouble.

One inherent advantage of the KC-135 was its ability to reduce weight rapidly by dumping fuel through the boom. At least 6,500 pounds of fuel per minute could be jettisoned in this manner.

The boom itself was a telescoping four-inch pipe the boom operator flew by means of a stick that positioned control surfaces known as ruddervators at the end of the boom. A telescoping lever allowed the operator to extend the boom to a maximum length of 45 feet, 11 inches. When in contact with the receiver, toggles engaged the boom, holding it until certain position limits were exceeded by the receiver. Thus, if the receiver got too far to the left or right, too high or too low, too close to the tanker or dropped too far behind, the boom would automatically disconnect and retract. If the receiver aircraft separated from the boom, a poppet valve slammed shut preventing the additional flow of fuel. The copilot of the tanker then turned off the pumps until contact was reestablished.

For refueling certain types of fighters, a funnel-shaped drogue could be attached to the boom to accommodate their refueling probes.

All the fuel on the tanker was available for transfer, with the exception of approximately 1,000 gallons beneath the standpipes in the main tanks. Or the tanker could consume all of the fuel itself. In an emergency the tanker could even take on a small amount of fuel from a B-52 through a procedure known as reverse refueling. Also, in an emergency the KC-135 was capable of towing a fighter on its boom, and in Vietnam at least one case was recorded of a disabled fighter carried in this manner to an emergency base where it disconnected and glided down to a successful landing.

Emergency egress was through the same crew entry chute that served as the primary entrance. An actuating lever known as the "chinning" bar was stowed on the ceiling above the chute. Pulling this bar down jettisoned the crew entry door and extended a spoiler at the forward edge of the crew entry chute to disrupt the slipstream. The crew member then hung on the bar and dropped through the chute. Although there have been successful bailouts, films of dummy drops in tests did not instill much crew confidence, as they showed the subject passing within a few feet of the boom. Needless to say, the "wheels" should be retracted or one might find himself meeting the left main gear at a very inopportune moment.

During approaches and landings, the aircraft handled very easily. Lowering the flaps unlocked outboard ailerons which then gave the aircraft a fine roll response even at slow airspeeds. Although the KC-135 did not have reverse thrust, braking was good on the long runways from which we normally operated.

One shortcoming was the use of engine bleed air to remove rain from the windshield. Just as we rounded out over the end of the runway and closed the throttles, our area of unimpaired vision would disappear because of inadequate engine bleed air available to keep the windshield clear. We attempted to correct this by retaining some power on the inboard engines for as long as possible.

All the time I flew this aircraft I felt it was a fine airplane. Despite the hard usage to which we put the engines, failures were few; more than one every two or three years was more than your share. Between 1956 and 1965 the Air Force purchased 806 KC-135s and used them in a number of roles—as a tanker, as a transport, as an airborne command post, and for various test projects such as simulating weightlessness for astronauts. The aircraft has performed admirably.

Yet, when I went to work for the airlines in 1965 I realized how much more sophisticated the later 707s are than our early "water wagons." Practically the only thing that I recognized in the cockpit was the window latch. Reverse thrust, fan engines with a much greater thrust rating, engine fire extinguishers, advanced flight director systems and instrumentation, Doppler navigation systems, and the addition of a flight engineer, all made our tankers seem simple by comparison.

Still, the KC-135, endowed with the same dependability and ruggedness that has established the Boeing 707 as the flagship of most of the world's airlines, has proven a valuable addition to the inventory of the United States Air Force.

After graduating from the University of Connecticut, PHILIP C. BROWN entered the United States Air Force, winning his wings in October 1959. His first assignment was as a KC-135 copilot at Wright-Patterson Air Force Base, Ohio. During a four-year assignment there he represented his unit in the Strategic Air Command's Bombing, Navigation, and Refueling competition and served as an Instructor and Maintenance Test Pilot, winning the Air Force Commendation Medal for his work. He flew the tanker during the initial refueling tests of the F-105 fighter at Eglin Air Force Base, Florida. Following 14 months at Ramey Air Force Base, Puerto Rico, he left the Air Force to join Pan-American Airways as a 707 pilot on their international runs out of New York. He has written several articles on early aviation.

P-26

ROSS G. HOYT

I reported for duty at Barksdale Field, Shreveport, Louisiana, in September 1937 after my second four-year tour in the Office of the Chief of the Air Corps and was assigned to command the 20th Fighter Group. It was equipped with P-26s and retained them throughout the remainder of 1937, and during the 1938 Air Corps Exercises based at Roosevelt Field, Long Island, New York, until they were replaced by P-36s in late 1938 and early 1939.

The P-26, designed and built by the Boeing Aircraft Company, Seattle, Washington, was a low-winged, open-cockpit monoplane of metal construction with faired, fixed landing gear, swiveling tail wheel, horizontal stabilizer adjustable on the ground only, elevator trim tabs adjustable from the cockpit, left aileron and rudder trim tabs adjustable on the ground for roll and yaw, toe brakes, hydraulic shock absorbers, hand-operated landing flaps, and a 52-gallon main fuel tank in the fuselage with a 20-gallon reserve standpipe and two 26-gallon tanks, one in each wing. A small bomb rack could be attached, but was rarely used except for magnesium flares for emergency night landings. Power was provided by a Pratt & Whitney R 1340–27 engine in the first 111 aircraft.

Of the final 25 aircraft, the first two had R 1340–33 engines with fuel injection and were designated P-26B. The remaining aircraft were completed with the original R1340–33 engine without fuel injection and

P-26As in combat formation in elements of three planes.

This chapter was revised from an article in *Aerospace Historian,* June 1976, 62–64.

USAF

were designated P-26C, differing only in minor control changes from the P-26A. The delivery of P-26Cs began in February 1936; they were all later converted to P-26Bs.

A two-bladed, fixed-pitch propeller was used. The engine was fitted with a ring cowling and was started by a hand-energized inertia starter with removable crank inserted on the left-hand side. Streamlined brace wires ran from a few feet inboard on the top of the wing to the fuselage and from the bottom of the wing to the landing gear. Streamlined cross brace-wires ran from a few feet inboard of the top of the wing to the fuselage and from the bottom of the wing to the landing gear. Streamlined cross brace wires ran between landing-gear struts. This increased strength, but it also increased parasitic resistance. With the fixed landing gear and other parasitic drag, the top speed was considerably reduced.

Armament, in the first several P-26s, consisted of two .30 caliber fixed machine guns, cocked from the cockpit, synchronized to fire through the propeller, aimed by an exterior sight mounted in front of the windshield, and fired by pistol grip on the control stick. In further production, armament was changed to one .30 caliber and one .50 caliber gun. Synchronization reduced the rate of fire about 50 percent. With bomb rack, the P-26, with a stretch of imagination, might be considered a forerunner of the fighter- bomber.

Communication was provided by an SCR 183 radio with 7 watts output on phone, MCW, and CW.

The instrument board included oil pressure and temperature gauges, tachometer, fuel pressure gauge, fuel gauge (quantity—main tank only), altimeter, compass, rate-of-climb indicator, bank-and-turn indicator, turn indicator (gyro), ammunition counter, and manifold pressure gauge.

With the addition of an improvised cockpit hood, instrument flying training could be conducted with a second plane trailing with the pilot acting as an instructor, giving warning of any dangerous situation.

The first time I saw a P-26 I thought, "Well, here is the big brother of the Sperry Messenger," which, for the benefit of those who don't know or remember, was a little toy-sized, low-wing monoplane powered by a small, 3-cylinder radial engine produced experimentally for use by the ground forces for the purpose its name indicates.

A short-coupled, sturdy, low-winged monoplane, the P-26 was the nearest in appearance to a fighter pilot's conception of what a fighter aircraft should look like at the time of its introduction into the inventory of the Air Corps.

Getting into the cockpit of the P-26 entailed placing the right foot on the left wing next to the fuselage, grasping the rear edge of the cockpit, hauling oneself up onto the wing, and stepping into the open cockpit through a longitudinally hinged door which dropped down to facilitate the process. After being seated in the cockpit, you lifted, shut, and latched the door.

The engine was started by a mechanic standing on the left wing to hand-energize the inertia starter by means of a crank inserted into the starter shaft. When the starter was "wound up" sufficiently, the pilot turned on the ignition switch and engaged the starter. If good luck prevailed, the engine started on the first try.

Because of its short coupling, brakes, and swiveling tail wheel, the airplane was very easily maneuvered on the ground. However, because of

(Above) P-26 cockpit.

(Left) P-26 in a bank.

(Below) P-26B with flaps down.

the sensitivity of the hydraulic landing gear, a wing would go down on turns. As a result, the plane gained the sobriquet "limber legs." It was also known jocularly as the "peashooter."

After taxiing to takeoff position, the brakes were applied and the throttle opened to maximum allowable manifold pressure at sea level. The throttle quadrant had a "gate" that could be set for maximum allowable manifold pressure so that it was not necessary to look at the manifold pressure gauge each takeoff. After checking engine operation and condition, the throttle was closed, brakes released, and throttle opened gradually until flying speed was attained. It was important that the throttle was opened slowly. As stated earlier, the airplane was equipped with hydraulic shock absorbers. If the throttle was advanced too rapidly, the engine and propeller torque might compress the left shock absorber to the extent that the left horizontal stabilizer could strike the ground, causing an abrupt turn. This situation was to be avoided at any time, but especially on takeoff in formation, when collision would probably occur. One such minor accident occurred in the 20th Fighter Group during my tenure of command.

Visibility in flight was good up, to the right and left, and to the rear. Visibility down was obscured through a wide angle by the wings. Visibility forward in level flight was good.

The P-26 responded readily to the controls and was capable of performing all the aerobatic maneuvers, but it was not stable in flight to the extent that it could be flown "hands off."

Landing flaps were used habitually in the 20th Fighter Group for formation landings. Sideslips were employed in individual landings if desired but were barred in formation landings, obviously.

I am informed that, because of its tapered wing (in both thickness and form), the P-26 had a dangerous stalling characteristic. Fortunately, I did not encounter that trait. But if pulled up into a stall, the P-26 would slip back down tail first and then fall into a dive with little or no tendency to spin. This trait proved helpful in shaking an enemy off one's tail in combat.

As Air Force Representative on the American Military Mission to China, I was at Toungoo, Burma, from 9 to 20 October 1941 for a conference with Claire Chennault, commanding officer of the American Volunteer Group, to determine, in detail, the situation pertaining to personnel, training, and materiel in the group and to obtain his recommendations and conclusions. During the course of the conference, my notes show Chennault stated that in 1937 the Chinese Air Force had three fighter groups: one equipped with Curtiss Hawk-3 biplanes, one equipped with Curtiss Hawk-2 biplanes, and one equipped with two squadrons of Fiats and one squadron of P-26s. There is also a note stating that the P-26 proved excellent in combat.

Although compared to present-day aircraft the P-26 was deficient in armament, it made a good showing in combat with contemporary aircraft—that is, the pre-Japanese Zero.

Performance data and specifications for the P-26 were obtained from the Headquarters United States Air Force, United States Air Force History Division, as follows:

Landing speed	73 mph
Maximum speed	234 mph
Cruising speed	199 mph

Range	360 statute miles
Rate of climb	2,360 fpm
Service ceiling	27,400 ft
Wingspan	27 ft 11½ in
Length	23 ft 10 in
Height	10 ft 5 in
Engine	500 hp Pratt & Whitney

Landing procedure was simple. If planes were in formation, the landing area (usually a grass field) would be circled in a counterclockwise direction at about gliding distance from the airport to allow all pilots to obtain a view of the area. Landing then could be made individually, by elements (3 planes), flights (2 elements), or squadron (3 flights). Modern airports with runways would probably restrict landings to formations no larger than an element.

Approaching crosswind on the downwind side of the landing area about gliding distance away, a turn into the wind could be made, throttle closed, landing flaps placed down, and flying speed maintained to set down. There was no tendency to ground loop during landing roll. It was, therefore, a safe airplane to land in formation and to use in training newly rated pilots.

In the hundreds of hours of formation and individual flying in a P-26, it was never necessary for me to bail out. However, I often contemplated what the best procedure might be for abandoning ship if the occasion arose.

If the pilot had control, he could roll over on his back, unfasten his safety belt, and fall out. If not, he could stand up, and while grasping windshield and headrest, step out onto the wing, fall prone, and slide off. He could stand up and jump to the side, hoping he would clear the vertical fin and horizontal stabilizer.

I led the 20th Fighter Group, equipped with a total of 48 P-26s from Barksdale Field, Louisiana, to Roosevelt Field, Long Island, New York, participated in the extensive Air Corps Exercises of 1938, and returned with all 48 airplanes to home station with only routine maintenance of engine and airplane performed by the crew chief of each plane. For ease of maintenance no better evidence than that of the above performance exists.

The P-26 was, I believe, the first low-winged monoplane fighter aircraft procured by the Air Corps and the last fighter plane with fixed landing gear.

It was a good interim airplane for use in all-around training: individual and formation flying, aerobatics, simulated combat, gunnery, navigation, and instrument flying. It was employed on extensive and widespread Air Corps maneuvers in conjunction with ground forces.

I enjoyed flying the P-26 and appreciated its performance, but I always looked forward to the day of closed cockpit, retractable landing gear, free-firing guns of larger caliber, cannon, and engines of greater horsepower with resultant increase in fighter performance. All these came in the late 1930s and during the 1940s.

BRIG. GEN. ROSS G. HOYT, USAF (Ret.), was active in military aviation since 1918 in the Aviation Section, Signal Corps, and in both lighter-than-air and heavier-than-air craft. He was a versatile pilot and commanded fighter units—Squadron, Group, and Wing—in peace and war. He flew the P-26 airplane, of which he writes, while commanding the 20th Fighter Group, Barksdale Field, LA.

He participated in or led many pioneering flights in the 1920s and 1930s including the mid-air Refueling Endurance Flight of the airplane *Question Mark*, as pilot of a refueling airplane, and night and day flight in a fighter airplane from Mitchell Field, N.Y., to Nome, Alaska, 18–20 July 1929, among others.

Between duty in the Southwest Pacific and the UK during World War II, he commanded the Single-Engine Advanced Flying School, Luke Field, Arizona, the largest in the world.

(Right) A P-40 of the 9th AF Fighter Group based in North Africa takes off on a mission to Russia, 1943. (Below) P-40s of the 80th Fighter Group lined along the runway at Nagaghuli Air Base, Upper Assam, India, 1944.

P-40 Kittyhawk

DONALD M. MARKS

DOUBTLESS, many military aircraft of the United States could qualify, in one sense or another, for the appellation "winged institution." But for being a breakthrough aircraft in its time, for being on hand and delivering in an unavoidable world conflict, for numbers produced, for pilots trained, and for theaters in which it served, few U.S. military aircraft can compete with the record of the Curtiss P-40. Tomahawk, Kittyhawk, Warhawk—call it what you will, this schooner of the sky entered full-scale production in the summer of 1939 and continued (although always under modification) until late in 1944. Over 15,000 P-40s were eventually produced, and although it was both praised and damned, it served in virtually every theater of World War II and, of course, gained an almost histrionic fame as the shark-toothed aerial weapon of Gen. Claire Chennault's China-based Flying Tigers.

I first met the P-40 in the summer of 1944 at Napier Field, Dothan, Alabama. Having just graduated from advanced flying school and feeling myself lord and master of the AT-6, I was elated to learn that I was one of a small group to undergo transition training in the P-40E. Of course, checking out in a new aircraft in those days did not entail the highly formalized training programs we have today, which employ much ground school, large dosages of simulator time, and dual-seated aircraft. Ground school we had, but it was fairly casual and even superficial by today's standards. The Pilot's Aircraft Handbook was certainly abridged in comparison with the Dash Ones for today's aircraft, and instructor pilots (IPs) always seemed to have other duties and/or concerns. In my case, my IP's wife was pregnant and his anxiety concerning her condition far exceeded his interest in teaching me some of the mysteries of the seemingly awesome P-40.

Being familiar with only radial-engine aircraft, the pointed spinner and long nose of the P-40 gave each of us a bit of a start. Then, too, we had heard many rumors about the Allison V-1710 in-line engine; its vaunted horsepower coupled to the huge, three-bladed Curtiss electric propeller gave us fledglings a weak-in-the-knees feeling. Finally, weight and size were eye-catching, in that the P-40 weighed some 5,500 pounds empty and had a wingspan of 37 feet, length of 32 feet, and stood almost 11 feet.

I recall that the preflight inspection was stressed by my IP and he graphically proved his point on a number of aircraft parked on the ramp. There were usually several loose Zeus fasteners; a myriad of leaks from coolant, water, fuel, oil, and hydraulic fluids; rust and corrosion; trim tabs out of alignment; and, due to humidity and summer thunderstorms, excessive condensation in the fuel tanks making it necessary to drain the fuel strainers prior to each flight. Also, a very hot Alabama sun shining on exposed metal surfaces could render those same surfaces absolutely untouchable.

If just viewing the P-40 from the ramp was small cause for consternation, climbing up the left wing root, throwing the seatpack parachute into the seat, and easing oneself into the cockpit was indeed real cause for dismay. First, you were forced to wend your way through an ingenious control-lock arrangement only to find that the wing itself substantially formed the shallow pilot's seat. Being short of arm and leg, I found the control stick much too far forward, as were the rudder pedals and instrument panel. Consequently, I immediately became probably the only "four cushion man" in the AAF. But once buckled in, and with my somewhat distraught IP standing on the wing root, I was privileged to attempt starting the elongated Allison. This procedure was not too complex. Battery switch was turned to "on," proper fuel tank selected, and mixture turned to idle cutoff. You then depressed the heel of the starter pedal to energize, the toe to engage, and once the Allison caught, vigorously primed until moving the mixture control forward sustained combustion. Once warmed up to where the coolant needle registered in the green, one was reasonably ready for the headier demands still awaiting him.

It is difficult for a flyer attuned to a radial engine to adequately describe the sinister harmony of the Allison engine, for once warmed up it had the snarl and purr of a giant tomcat. But it had its demands, too, in that you had to constantly address positioning the manual coolant shutters. In flight, many a new P-40 pilot learned this requirement the hard way because in moving the coolant shutter-control lever it was easy not to position it in the proper indent position. Airflow on the shutters forced the lever sharply back, and the unwary pilot had barked knuckles for a souvenir. This quirk of the P-40 forced many pilots to wear gloves, a custom still adhered to in today's USAF.

I can still remember mechanics wincing from the Allison's snarl as they pulled chocks. And taxiing out did nothing to increase confidence as the long, black-striped nose looked more like the runway than part of the aircraft itself. With such poor visibility, it was necessary to continually "S" the aircraft, and a fair share of the unwary were guilty of running into mobile fire carts. Then, too, there was an interconnect between the rudder and the tail wheel which sometimes resulted in almost wild rudder kickings—especially when we were forced off taxiways onto natural turf. It was also apparent during early taxiing that the throttle control was uncomfortably close to the side of the fuselage. This engineering aberration was especially maddening during formation flying, as a tightly clenched fist around the throttle would rub against the fuselage wall during throttle movements.

In our training situation, we tended to bunch up during taxiing out to take off, and a common occurrence was to have the engine overheat, percolate, and thoroughly splatter the windscreen. In fact, the P-40 could be depended upon to bathe the pilot in at least one of the aircraft's vital fluids. At Napier, in an effort to combat the overheating, fire trucks would position themselves near the takeoff point and hose down the engine areas as the P-40s approached number one—not too effective really, but it was an effort to keep the Allisons cool and the aircraft mission worthy.

Taking the active runway for the first time in a new and more challenging aircraft is always an adrenalin-producing experience. With aircraft behind you and the brusque urgings of the tower, there is scarcely time to savor the unreality of the situation. On opening the throttle of the P-40, two factors were immediately apparent: I forgot that there was no automatic boost control and I blissfully exceeded the designed manifold pressure—even though the throttle gate was purportedly designed to thwart such violations; more frightening was the pronounced torque I encountered which necessitated tapping the right brake pedal to stay within the general runway dimensions. With over 50 inches of manifold pressure and some 3,000 rpm, we were airborne in about 1,000 feet.

Thrill followed thrill. The Rube Goldberg gear design required moving the gear handle up and then depressing a button on the stick which actuated an electric hydraulic motor. About 30 seconds were required for this cycle, and I came to believe that every P-40 pilot ought to have a third hand. Moreover, the gear rotated 90° as it retracted, and because it was not always symmetrical during the process, the long nose took some fright-inducing wanderings before the gear nestled into the wing wells.

With a little altitude and growling along about 300 mph IAS, one experienced a sudden sense of euphoria and, for a moment, actually felt as though he were master of the aircraft. I could not help but remember my IP's parting words as he had waved me out of the chocks: "If you get confused, climb it in the red and cruise it in the green!"

Trying to trim the aircraft gave me an opportunity to wax profane and as I experimented with various speeds and altitudes, I found myself literally a slave to the rudder trim. The elevator trim knob was especially difficult to deal with in that it was small and awkwardly positioned directly beneath the rudder trim tab. Thus, a moderate amount of digital dexterity was needed simply to trim the bird.

The need to constantly monitor the rudder trim produced its share of victims. Toward the end of the course, and while flying in a three-ship formation, the number two man apparently attempted to reset rudder trim while in normal formation. With his head in the cockpit, he fell back but drifted into the lead ship so that lead's empennage suddenly became a flapping, shredded mass of metal and canvas. Amazingly enough, lead managed some degree of control, but elevator action was virtually nonexistent. A hasty airborne conversation resulted in the lead pilot electing to bail out—which he did. I remember him slowing the aircraft down, sliding back the canopy, carefully stowing the Form #1 in his flight suit, crawling out on the wing root, and sliding down the trailing edge to blossom just before entering a thin, partial undercast. And for what seemed like an eternity, that pilotless P-40 continued in flight before the left wing finally drooped and the machine eventually entered a steep, pseudospiral before vigorously merging with an Alabama peanut field. Thereafter, our lead pilot was, for days, the hero of the base and a man who commanded much awe and respect.

The most noteworthy in-flight characteristic I can recall about the

P-40 was its slight, effective, and agile ailerons. With the long nose, sharp spinner, and highly responsive ailerons, slow rolls or barrel rolls were pure delight. Indeed, the T-38 of today has astounding roll characteristics, but it is a jet and the controls are boosted. That old P-40, however, in many of its aerobatic maneuvers, reminds me today of similar aerial antics in the T-38. Also, as I recall, stalls in the P-40 came on with celerity but no real deceit; however, the aircraft would roll to the left with an accompanying sharp dip of the nose. The aircraft also had a pronounced tendency to be somewhat tail heavy.

At medium altitudes the P-40 was reasonably fast, as it had a maximum true airspeed of around 330 mph at 15,000 feet. And for those more adventurous souls who like really "creative" flying, the Bendix-Stromberg injection carburetor system allowed rather sustained periods of negative Gs; however, after about 15–20 seconds, the oil pressure began to waver, signifying that it was time to right oneself.

Loops commenced around 250 mph at 5,000 feet and would gain about 3,000 feet in the ensuing arc—much better than the AT-6 and no need at all to play back pressure at the top and backside as demanded by the Texan. But much rudder was needed—all the way around.

Snap rolls were fun in the AT-6, but the few I did in the P-40 always seemed to be harbingers of some forthcoming structural failure, as I would hear strange murmurs throughout the airframe. The aircraft seemed to resent the maneuver.

I never spun the P-40, although it was a common adventurism in the AT-6. Also, in mock dogfights, I found the P-40 to be fairly good on acceleration, somewhat lagging in climbs "back on the perch," and reasonably responsive in heavy G maneuvers. The normally light ailerons became quite heavy in a high-speed dive.

As with any reasonably successful flight, there must be a landing. My return to the field the first time was concerned more with doing just that than with the problem of inserting myself into a mixed pattern of floundering P-40s and AT-6s.

The lengthy nose of the P-40 still bothered me, and, of course, there were higher traffic pattern airspeeds to consider as well as the unsettling memory of tales about how difficult it was to three-point the aircraft. Notwithstanding these nagging doubts, I was committed to

USAF

P-40 cockpit.

P-40Fs in flight.

merging with the landscape in some fashion, and I fervently hoped that the aircraft shared the same concern.

Weaving my way down through Alabama cumulous buildups and attempting to dodge other P-40 and AT-6 aircraft, I went through a hurried prelanding check consisting of advancing the mixture and rpm plus selecting for proper fuel tank, slowed the aircraft to about 220 mph, and entered a 45° leg to the downwind. Turning on base was around 180 mph, and I initiated a reverse of the gear-up procedure previously accomplished after takeoff. The gear indicator, although graphic, really didn't give the assurance that the gear was down and locked, so a crosscheck was accomplished by attempting to actuate the emergency hand pump on the right side. Of course, there was a horn check when throttle power was sufficiently reduced. Lowering flaps was a pleasure; you could move the flap selector to the "down" position and then just squirt down the desired amount of flaps by depressing the button on the control stick.

Naturally, I overshot final while mumbling "gear check" and performed an erratic "S" turn to line up with the runway. Final airspeed was around 110 mph, and as I crossed the fence and began groping for the ground the whalelike nose blotted out the entire airfield—and there I hung. I have a formula for such moments in flying. When inordinate stress is upon you, simply commit your soul to God, consign your better judgment to the devil, and comfort yourself with a tight shoulder harness and a fervent soliloquy that you are indeed in control of the aircraft. With these matters arranged in a sequence of importance, your mind is suddenly unfettered to contemplate such trivia as airspeed, drift, lineup, height above runway, gear down, touchdown point, etc. In this case, touchdown was around 80 mph and, predictably, a bit long. Because I could not see the runway's end, it passed my mind how nice it would be if someone were in front of me spreading concrete. Subsequently, I learned there was less heartburn in making wheel landings and then judiciously using the brakes once the tail wheel lowered to the runway.

Turning off the active, I manually opened the cowl flaps, raised the wing flaps (how close that handle was to the gear handle!), and began to "S" my way back to the ramp. Understandably, the crew chief was surprised to see me, my IP was nowhere in sight, and I shared my uncommon elation with myself. As the huge prop spun to a stop and the noisy, metallic murmur of the Allison ended, I could not help but feel a genuine sense of accomplishment. There have been many airplanes since the P-40, but for me it was a love affair I never really erased from memory—nor wanted to.

Unfortunately, or so it seems, when fighter pilots convene and converse, the talk revolves around the joys, thrills, and dangers of a particular flight; seldom do the aircraft actually receive their due. But candidly, what is it that makes any aircraft great? Such a question spontaneously and understandably triggers several responses. Aircraft are great because they are truly superior flying machines; others achieve stature in the hands of skilled pilots or superb tacticians; others simply have a good press—the P-40 probably falls in the last two categories. It *was* inferior to the Zero, but in the hands of AVG pilots, it compiled an enviable record. And its colorful air intake, plus its AVG role, produced for it the stuff that projects legends. I have flown a number of different conventional fighters and whistled about the sky in a few jets, but in the recesses of my memory there remains that long-nosed demon that gave me my share of anxious moments—and pleasurable thrills.

Unavoidably, the P-40 gave way to the Mustang, the Thunderbolt, and the Lightning. The latter aircraft all achieved eminence in the aerial battles of World War II but they were not even on the horizon in 1940. The P-40 was present for duty and it met challenges and tests until giving way to the new breed. In a sense, it was the mother fighter for the future USAF, for it spawned new fighter versions and trained countless pilots in the rudiments of flying a genuine fighter plane. Unequivocably, it was, and remains, a winged institution.

COL. DONALD M. MARKS, USAF, flew the P-40 at Napier Field, Dothan, Alabama, just after graduating from flying training at the same airfield in the summer of 1944. Since that time, he has flown a variety of conventional and jet aircraft—most of which have been in the fighter category. He has been Professor of Aerospace Studies at Kansas State University and is now teaching high school social studies at Manhattan, Kansas.

The Republic XP-47H was constructed as a flying laboratory for testing a new 2,500 hp Chrysler Motors liquid-cooled inline engine. Only two of these Thunderbolts were built, having been converted from two P-47D-15s with major modifications to enable them to house the new engine.

P-47 Thunderbolt

MARK E. BRADLEY with HELEN PORTER

IT was big for its time—16,000 pounds and up—6,000 to 7,000 pounds heavier than World War II's other single-engine fighters, the P-51, Me-109, Spitfire, and FW-190. Officially, it was known as the P-47 Thunderbolt, but that's not what the pilots called it. With the large 2,000 hp Pratt & Whitney engine up forward, in the air it looked like a milk bottle with wings. The men who flew it affectionately called it "The Jug."

An all-metal airplane, sturdy and durable, the Jug could stand up to 16 Gs in pull-outs. Its air-cooled engine could take unbelievable punishment and still get the plane home. Capable of well over 400 mph at 30,000 feet, the Jug also had superlative fire power, including eight free-firing .50 caliber machine guns in the wings. It would carry a bomb load of up to two 2,000-pounders. But its size and weight prevented maneuverability equal to that of the lighter and smaller fighters. For this reason pilots took advantage of the speed and diving capability and generally avoided close-in-turning combat. The Jug was only a fair high-altitude fighter. Its specialty was ground attack. At this it was superb.

The first American production fighter (then called a pursuit airplane) with a completely cantilevered wing structure was the Seversky

REPUBLIC AVIATION

P-35 in flight.

P-35. Its predecessor, the Boeing P-26 (see Chapter 19), had been a monoplane with metal wings supported by external brace wires to absorb landing and flying loads. Close behind the P-35 came the Curtiss P-36, the Air Corps' second fully cantilever-winged fighter.

The P-35 had good range and top speed of something under 300 mph, probably about 280. The P-36 had less range but was a bit faster and, according to Col. Charles Lindbergh, was superior in flight stability. (Lindy had flown both planes as an Air Corps colonel just before the start of World War II in 1939.) I had to agree with the Lone Eagle that the P-35 would snap into a ground loop during the landing roll if not watched carefully, but in the air, with a properly balanced load, I thought its stability was pretty good. True, a mechanic or a deer in the large rear baggage compartment could create a condition of imbalance. Sasha Seversky used to carry his mechanic around in this fashion but was well aware of the hazard. I personally found out the effect of a deer on my way back to Wright Field from a hunt near Williamsburg, Pennsylvania.

The Seversky AP-4 was a new design similar to the P-35 but bigger and modernized with flush rivets and a turbosupercharger to boost its 900 hp Pratt & Whitney engine to achieve more power at altitude—a critical need. The supercharger was placed below the fuselage at the rear of the pilot, the same positioning to be utilized later in the P-47 design.

The Curtiss YP-37 had the same wing, engine, and empennage as the P-36, with the addition of a turbosupercharger like that in the AP-4. To balance the heavy engine and supercharger up forward, the pilot was moved far back in the tail, just in front of the vertical fin. I can vouch for the fact that this *can* be done and the airplane *can* be flown, as I flew the YP-37 from Buffalo to Wright Field in a snowstorm one February night so that it could participate in the upcoming flight evaluation. But it was definitely doing things the hard way. Putting the supercharger and not the pilot back there in the tail was a lot better way to go. Later I flew the YP-37 several times trying to measure its performance but was never able to get satisfactory operation out of the supercharger.

In January 1939 a competition was held for the first big (over 500) production order for U.S. Army Air Corps fighters. Competing were the Seversky AP-4, the Curtiss YP-37, and the Curtiss XP-40. The XP-40 had a P-36 airframe with an Allison 1,000 hp engine substituted for the previous air-cooled Pratt & Whitney engine of somewhat less power. The Allison was a conventional 12-cylinder, liquid-cooled V; the Pratt & Whitney, an air-cooled radial. The XP-40 won the competition almost by default. The AP-37 engine-supercharger combination was never made to function properly and, because the extra altitude performance obtained from the supercharger was its main advantage, the airplane really never had a chance. Over 10,000 P-40s were produced before the end of the line in 1944. In spite of its shortfall in speed and performance at altitude, it put up one hell of a good fight.

Later in 1940, George Price and I took part in some trials of the XP-40 vs. Spitfire III at Ottawa, Canada, competing with RAF and RCAF pilots. The XP-40 held its own very well in all of the main fighter characteristics—speed, climb, and maneuverability. But that was before the addition of about 1,000 pounds of combat essentials. Small wonder that the P-40 declined in performance. Everything was added except horsepower. We were stuck with not over 1,000 hp in the P-40 for all its long life.

The reason the early P-40 did not keep up with the Spitfire in performance is not hard to find. First, the horsepower of the Rolls-Royce engine in the Spitfire was progressively increased whereas the Allison stood still. Second, the British were able to hold the weight of the Spitfire down, whereas we had to encumber the P-40 with six .50 caliber guns in addition to armor protection and bullet-sealing tanks to make it combat-worthy.

In 1939, as a gesture of appreciation to a talented and loyal contractor, 13 YP-43s had been ordered from Seversky (to become Republic after a reorganization). The YP-43 was very like the AP-4 that crashed. Because it had only two .50 caliber machine guns and no armor or bullet-sealing tanks, it was not a really combat-worthy design. Nevertheless, the lessons learned while producing and testing the YP-43 were to prove invaluable.

Being aware of the old P-35's ground-loop problem, we insisted that the Republic engineers provide the 13 P-43s with a good, strong tail-

Curtiss XP-55 Ascender in flight.

wheel lock—a device that prevented the tail-wheel strut from rotating. It was locked during takeoff and landing, but set free for turning and taxiing. No one seemed to know what caused certain aircraft to ground loop, but it seemed logical to me that the tail-wheel lock was our best chance to prevent it. How wrong I was!

Republic followed orders: the first YP-43 had a fine, strong tail-wheel lock. Nevertheless, on an early landing by an expert test pilot, the airplane ground looped so violently that it dug in a wing tip at high speed and flipped completely over, breaking the fuselage in two behind the cockpit. The pilot, luckily, was unhurt. But after this near tragedy, a concerned and embarrassed project officer set about grimly to find the cause and the cure of this violent maneuver once and for all.

The next P-43 was ready in a few weeks and I went to Farmingdale on Long Island to begin my search. It was midwinter, so we moved over to the Floyd Bennett runways where there was better snow clearance. I began by landing damned carefully. I soon found the tendency to "snap the nose" to the right, at the same time dropping the right wing, to be definitely there at a point during most landing rolls. I found, as I had previously on the P-35 and at times on the P-40, that quick application of the toe brakes away from the turn at the instant it started would correct the snap and prevent disaster—all of which called for an extremely alert pilot with his foot ready on the brake pedal. A small delay or a push of the rudder instead of the brake, and Katie bar the door!

At this point the weather forced us to move to Langley Field in Virginia, and it was there that we were to find the answer we were seeking. I had had some previous dealings with NACA, the predecessor organization to the present NASA, so I asked them to help us find out what cooked with landing a P-43. Bob Gilruth, a young engineer who much later became the man behind the people in the Apollo project, was assigned as the scientific side of the house. In a try for "no wind" conditions, I had been getting up well before daylight to be ready for takeoff as soon as light came. Working alone, I'd found that the ground loop was worse at no wind and that at more than 10–20 mph wind the tendency disappeared altogether. Then along came Gilruth. From there on, I bow to the scientific side, a procedure I have not always made a practice of following over the years.

In the meantime, Republic had placed tufts all over the vertical tail and wing for photographing during landing and the start of the ground loop. The pictures showed the tufts waving in all directions. But why? In addition, the company had built a new vertical tail of considerably more surface. This we put on and flew; but with no wind there was no improvement, just the same violent snap to the right.

Then one day after a period of considerable frustration Bob casually said, "I think if we raise the tail higher off the runway, it will help." So we took the tail-wheel strut off, took it to the NACA shop, put in a 10-inch extension, and put the lengthened strut back on the airplane. The next morning there was no wind and no ground loop. From then on, observant people probably wondered why all the P-43 and P-40 tail wheels remained hanging out in the breeze, even after retraction of the main gear. Because the P-40 had also had ground-loop problems, we fixed both planes at once. We lengthened all the tail-wheel struts, but since there was no time to redesign and change the fuselage and doors, we let it all hang out!

About the time it chose the P-40 for production by Curtiss-Wright, the Air Force, facing the need for capacity production by all our capable fighter producers, appointed a board of officers to decide what fighter Republic would produce for the war. I've been unable to get the names of the board members, but I have a strong hunch that Lindbergh was an adviser. When the board met sometime during the summer of 1939, the XP-47 was born. It was decided to start with Pratt & Whitney's latest highest-powered engine, the 2,000 hp R2800, equipped with a turbosupercharger similar to the P-43 installation, then to make the airplane large enough to accommodate the big engine, plenty of fuel, armor protection, bullet-sealing tanks, and, most important, four .50 caliber machine guns in each wing. Republic quickly came up with the design and the XP-47 was ordered.

By the fall of 1940, the XP-47 was in its early flight testing. It looked great, handled well, and had good altitude performance. It was the heaviest and most powerful single-engine fighter ever built, and the test pilots at Republic were creeping carefully up on the performance envelope. We did not want to lose our single prototype. I say we. Col. Mish Roth was Project Officer on the XP-47. I was assigned to the production program. However, because production was released long before the XP-47 flew, we were both in effect the project officers.

One day we had British visitors. They were outstanding RAF officers who had weathered the Battle of Britain and had come over to work with and advise their inexperienced counterparts in the USA. A few names come to mind: Boothman, Broadhurst, Malan, Tuck. These gentlemen flew all our newer fighters and bombers. Boothman and Broadhurst later became Air Marshals. Wing Commander Tuck, a fearless fighting and flying character, took the XP-47 up while visiting the Long Island factory. He ignored the untried areas of XP-47 performance. He took the one and only at full power to 40,000 feet, turned it over, and dived it to terminal velocity to 15,000, pulled it out successfully, and landed, full of enthusiasm for the future of the aircraft. When he told us of his treatment of our war baby, we were in a state of shock. We could have lost them both right there. The speed and gravity forces Tuck had put the plane through were much greater than its previous pilots had yet attempted. Later we too had pilots like Tuck, but they did not begin to appear until we were at war. I'd say Dave Shilling, Buzz Wagner, Dick Bong, Tom McGuire, Bob Hoover, and a lot more took over in the United States where Tuck and his friends left off in the RAF.

After our struggle with the P-35, P-43, and the P-40, we were well prepared for any ground-looping problems we might find in the XP-47, but to our great relief there were none. The Jug's landing roll was as stable as the landing roll of nosewheel aircraft in which all ground-looping tendencies are completely eliminated. Why? Because it had a low ground angle. The plane was longer and had relatively short main landing-gear struts so that when sitting on three points, its wing to runway angle was considerably less than that of the P-43 and P-40, even with their tails raised 10 inches. The fact that the P-47's main gear was spread quite far apart undoubtedly helped, too. But the ground angle was the primary reason for the stability. Had we understood this sooner, we could have retrofitted the P-35s as well as the P-43s and P-40s.

Testing the XP-47 proceeded and we were finally ready to start production. Tail troubles developed in some of the early production models, and a few planes were lost. No such problem had been encountered in the XP-47, which we must assume had a stronger tail. Unfortunately, adding a stronger tail and making other necessary changes had increased the weight of the rear part of the airplane, resulting in a shift of the center of gravity to the rear and a consequent deterioration in stability. It goes without saying that with the loss of stability, an aircraft becomes dangerous. In a high-speed dive when a pullout is attempted, the airplane may tend to tighten up the pullout to the point of failing the wings or tail because of over G and resulting overstress. This, then, was the problem facing the P-47 in late 1941.

We had nothing we could remove. Every item of equipment in the P-47 was essential. (I can personally vouch for that.) Relocation of the battery was studied but was deemed to be of insufficient effect. We tried a "bob weight" installation, a lever with a heavy weight on its end, fastened to the control stick in such a way that gravity acts on the weight to push the stick forward; at the same time, during a pullout from a dive, because the center of gravity is at the rear of the plane, gravity is trying to pull the stick back. Today's bob weights are electronic, but ours then was strictly mechanical. I did not want to start production with such a weak reed in my bow.

As so often happened in those days, the Republic engineers came through practically overnight. They built a little 5-inch bridge or trestle structure (or engine mount) to fasten the engine to the front of the airframe, moving the heavy engine forward 5 or 6 inches. We had it made. We had a solid, stable airplane with no tricks and no gimmicks. Production went full speed ahead.

Now, a bit of philosophizing. I want you to know that while I am not an inventor, during this period I did, with some help from Republic, outdo the developmental capabilities of the General Electric Company. Most of our fighters had only three handles on the throttle; the power lever, the mixture control, and the propeller control. However, the P-47 had an additional lever for control of the turbosupercharger. In general, it could be said that all of these levers move from the rear to the front as they go forward. It was obvious to me that we needed an engine control mechanism that would give us proper performance of all four functions by moving one handle. I gave the powerful and talented General Electric Company a contract to produce such a control. Unhappily, General Electric worked on the problem until all the money was spent but failed to produce a workable control.

In the meantime, I had talked the problem over with the Republic and asked them to try the idea of a mechanical link between the control levers. As an interim measure, we came up with a way of interconnecting the levers mechanically so that with the proper rigging at least the change from idle to full power and back could be done by pushing only one lever. This we did by adding some retractable ears to the throttle-control arm so that, when down, the ears moved all controls forward and backward. When the ears were pushed upward out of the way, the control levers worked separately. As far as I know, all P-47s delivered, except an early few, had this throttle control. The pilots used it and General Electric missed a bet for some added business. The Air Force had a simple, inexpensive control that never failed, and the pilot could use it or not at his own discretion.

From what I have seen of the wildly escalating complexities and costs of today's aircraft and weapons, we need more inexpensive and simple solutions like this.

At about this time we got into the conflict by way of the Japanese war lords' audacity. The P-47 production line was gaining momentum and a few production prototypes were almost completed. One of these contained the first production-designed armament installation: eight .50 caliber machine guns with 500 rounds per gun, with nicely designed, quickly detachable mounts—the heaviest fire power ever before placed in a production fighter aircraft. The Japs hit us on the 7th of December and by the end of the month I had the armament airplane at Patterson Field for the first firing.

The reason for taking the P-47 to Wright-Patterson Field was twofold. First, the armament experts, a Mr. Ferguson and Earl Hatcher, were there. They knew the .50 caliber machine gun better than anyone in the world. Second, there was an old World War I firing butt down on the eastern edge of Patterson Field where we could do the shooting.

I won't forget New Year's morning 1942. The two of us—my head and I—rose long before daylight and went down to the P-47 parking spot in a pouring rain. I climbed into the Jug and prepared to start the engine for taxiing to the butt. On my first attempt to start the engine, all 2,000 hp of it backfired—an explosion so violent that it shattered an experimental plywood duct that ran from the rear-positioned supercharger through the cockpit floor. In spite of the size of my head, I had been able to don helmet and goggles, but my hands and face looked as though I had gone sliding down a cellar door upside down.

In case you're wondering about the plywood duct aluminum was very scarce at the time. The War Production Board was pressuring everyone to substitute wood for aluminum wherever possible. Wright Field had several lousy all-plywood airplanes built; for, as you know, when the pressure gets high enough people sometimes try to comply whether or not it is possible or makes any sense. That is what happened here. Needless to say, the victim of the explosion was the right man, the project officer. There was no more plywood tested or utilized in P-47s or in any supercharger duct in any planes that he had anything to do with.

Because no flight was required, after taking stock I again started the engine, this time successfully, and proceeded to the butt. The stage was set. The P-47, our cherished hope to defend us from the thousands of Zeros and Messerschmitts, was about ready to show its deadly fire power. We put the tail up on a rack and aimed at the bottom of the old pile of dirt, loaded all guns and fastened the gun covers. I climbed in and pressed the trigger. What happened was one of the greatest disappointments of my life. Instead of eight guns firing 600 rounds per minute, each with a deafening roar, we got a scattered firing of one to ten rounds from each gun, then deep silence. I finally released the trigger. First I was stunned, then depressed. Some gun mounts were broken, several guns had jumped off their mounts, and the remainder were jammed. I sat there for some time visualizing a lost war, somehow holding myself personally responsible.

It took a few days to find that the guns had been freshly delivered to the Air Force by Frigidaire. Because they were just starting production, their first products did not have interchangeable parts. The guns had been fired successfully after assembly, but during final teardown and reassembly, parts were scrambled, as required by the Ordnance Department. Naturally, the guns would not shoot. I should add here that Frigidaire did a great job later on.

It was probably just as well that the guns jammed that day. Of the hundred or so rounds fired, a sizable number apparently went

(Above) "The Jug" in flight. (Center) The early P-47Ds were the first of the Jugs to incorporate a water injection system for increased emergency power. Both front and rear armor protection and bullet-proof glass were provided for protection of the pilot. This model also incorporated the paddle blade propellers. (Below) Republic YP-43 in flight.

through the old butt and scattered over Wright View Heights a mile away. Had we fired the 4,000 rounds, I'd probably be doing time!

By the end of 1942 production was such that the first two Jug wings were in England preparing to enter combat. In January 1943 I was sent over to help get them ready. I took the Clipper to Lisbon just one week before the next Clipper crashed there in landing. I was lucky; mine made it OK. In England I reported to Brig. Gen. O. D. (Monk) Hunter, head of the 8th Fighter Command at Bushey Hall outside London. A World War I fighter ace, Monk was one of our famous fighter generals. He made clear immediately what I was to do: get the P-47 radios to function properly and get more range in both the P-47 and P-51. After a later meeting with Lt. Gen. Ira Eaker, I had no doubt as to the critical nature of my mission.

We first attacked the problem of the radio. It seemed the R2800 engine ignition system and the VHF radio were completely incompatible. When the engine was running, the radio signal was drowned out by the ignition noise. I went to Debden at once and visited the 4th Fighter Group which had previously been equipped with Spitfires and manned by Americans serving in the RAF. It had formerly been called the Eagle Squadron and had an outstanding war record. Col. Ed (Andy) Anderson,

(Above) First production model of the YP-37 in flight.

(Left) Seversky AP-4.

(Right) P-36A in flight.

P-47 THUNDERBOLT "THE JUG" 189

an old friend from our Chanute Field days, was wing commander, and Chesley (Pete) Peterson was the group leader. They were eager to get the P-47s going but were frustrated by the radio performance. Another P-47 wing nearby, commanded by Armand (Pete) Peterson, had the same problem. Both of these Petes were exceptional leaders. Chesley, though downed at least twice in the Channel in Spits, had a notable war record and is now well and happy in retirement in Utah. Armand was lost soon after his wing went into action, and he died leading it to what became a tremendous record of success against the Luftwaffe.

It took several months, but the radio problem was eventually solved by making certain changes in the electrical system of the plane's engine. During this time at Debden I got a chance to do some flying with both the 4th and 56th, but about the time I was considered fairly well ready for a trip across the Channel, I was ordered back to Wright Field.

So I returned to Ohio in June 1943 with the radio mission accomplished with two new goals: immediate installation of bubble canopies on the P-47 and P-51, and extension of the range on both airplanes. In England I had seen what the bubble had done for the pilot's rear vision in the Spitfire. Republic installed a canopy on a P-47 in record time, and I flew the first airplane so equipped to the West Coast to show it to Dutch Kindleberger at North American Aviation Company. It wasn't long before Dutch had one going on the P-51s as well.

In a 1974 article for *Aerospace Historian,* "The P-51 over Berlin," I described at length how we managed to extend the flight range of the Mustang to make that feat possible. It is enough to say here that though the P-51 was already equipped with wing tanks, we were able to bring about a further increase in its droppable fuel capacity and resultant range by placing an additional 90-gallon tank behind the pilot's seat. We had no such luck with the P-47.

There was no place to put more fuel in the P-47 except in droppable wing tanks. Earlier Republic had developed what was called a "slipper tank," usable for ferrying only. Because it made the airplane unstable, it was not suitable for combat. In the end we used the same pylon and tank arrangement utilized on the P-38. The first such installation was made, not at the factory and not at Wright Field, but in Africa by Col. Claire Bunch, an enterprising officer working for Jim Doolittle.

Along toward the middle of 1943, our government allocated 100 P-47s to the Russians. They were to get the airplanes in January 1944, and in making arrangements for their delivery I experienced the kind of Soviet negotiating we have seen many times since. In mid-1943 General Arnold decided we had the war won. It turned out he was correct, but at the time I certainly wasn't sure. Anyway, to show the enemy and the world our confidence, the General ordered all camouflage removed from new production Air Force aircraft. His order became effective in the fall of 1943. With a production rate of 600 a month, it was not possible to make any sort of special arrangement to leave the paint on the ones for Uncle Joe. So I went to the Russian colonel at Wright Field and presented him with the following proposition: they could have their 100 aircraft in January without camouflage, or, if they demanded the paint, we would have to have it done after delivery at the factory and they would get them in February. "Which do you want?"

The Colonel was very polite. He said he would wire home for the answer. In about a week, he came back, "We want them in January with camouflage on." And such was their power in Washington—that's what they got!

By the summer of 1943 I had taken the P-47 and P-51 as far as they were to go when I was transferred from the fighter business and made Chief of the Flight Test Section. There I flew all the foreign fighters we had come by (FW-190, Me-109) as well as the new experimental planes being worked on by our development people, including the XP-59, our first jet, and the B-29 bomber.

All during the war our development people were up against a tough problem. Until the late 1930s aircraft development consisted of three main features: cleaning up drag through sleeker design, adding power (bigger engines with more power at altitude), and increasing size and carrying power for either loads or armament. Improvement in some of these areas tended to level out in the late 1930s. The piston engine was a definite limitation. For example, the Pratt & Whitney 4360 was about as big as a fighter airplane could accept. It had more power; but with its outsized propeller, size, and weight it was unable to provide much more speed than the previous smaller, lighter engines. We were fast approaching a point of diminishing returns in the development of bigger, more powerful, piston engines. Cleanliness of design had gone far, but again the propeller contributed to drag. Faced with doing the job with what we had, the piston engine, our designers began to experiment with rearrangement of the components or the elimination of parts. Toward the end of the war, we saw the XP-55, the Curtiss Ascender (we called it the Assender). It was a tail-first airplane, having the same general power setup but with a pusher propeller and the horizontal tail out front. I had a flight in it. It had about the same performance as comparably powered fighters, but its lack of stability and handling difficulties gave me the feeling of sitting astride a powder keg. I was glad to get it on the ground.

Another innovation was the tailless design. We had a fighter and a bomber. I flew an early model, a small tailless test vehicle, and had an even greater feeling of the powder keg. Once more landing was a pleasure. With apologies to my friend Jack Northrop, it seems to me that a tail is a very fine thing to have on an airplane. It balances the wing and, if of proper size and location, gives the plane needed stability. In addition, the intervening fuselage, which must connect it to the wing, is an ideal place to put things—from people to bombs.

A perfect example of trying to do the job better by rearrangement was the P-39. Larry Bell and Bob Wood came up with the idea of putting the engine behind the pilot and driving the propeller and forward-mounted gear box by means of a drive shaft that ran forward between the pilot's legs. I recall Larry's saying that one reason the P-39 would be an outstanding fighter was the location of the engine, the biggest weight in the airplane, on the center of gravity. But we young pursuit pilots viewed the design with grave apprehension. We did not like the idea of the flex shaft travelling forward between the pilot's knees. What if it broke? Well, to this day I've never heard of one that did.

Although the flex drive shaft always performed well, that is not to say we had no trouble with the rest of the aircraft. Though at first glance Larry's proposition seemed to make sense, a little bit of analysis and experience proved the opposite. At the center of gravity it is far better to have the disposable load—the fuel, oil, and ammunition—not the engine or the pilot. In the case of the P-39, there was gasoline in front of the center of gravity, and all of the cannon ammunition was stored somewhat forward. This meant that firing of the cannon or using certain tanks of gas would lighten the forward load and make the airplane more and more tail heavy. The P-39 was famous for what pilots called "tumbling," a series of violent snap rolls or stalls, no doubt caused by depletion of ammunition up forward and too much fuel in the rear.

As Chief of Flight Test, I inherited the B-29 engines that overheated and sometimes caught fire. My coworkers were Col. Ozzie Ritland, Bob Ruegg, and Harney Estes. (Harney was later lost in the Far East while I was in Okinawa just after the war.) One of our tasks was to put time at high power on a B-29, testing the improved engine-cooling equipment being incorporated in the field. We flew the tail off that airplane at high power (highest authorized continuous) and never had a failure. We flew it all day long for several months with no more problems.

When there was a slack hour or so, just for relaxation we flew the old XB-19, then recently equipped with four 2,400 hp, 24-cylinder Allison engines. It was relatively slow and had a built-in delay in the elevators. That is, when one moved the wheel back in order to climb, nothing would happen for perhaps 5 to 6 seconds, then the nose would start up. Test pilot Maj. Stanley Umstead discovered this peculiarity the hard way when he took the plane up for its first flight several years earlier at Santa Monica. It was natural to keep pulling farther and farther back to get some reaction. When he finally got it, the nose went up—way, way up, and rapidly. He damned near lost the airplane. But Stanley was a great pilot and managed to get it under control. Later he was able to tell the rest of us about the lag so that we could act accordingly. But enough of these bomber stories. I'm really a fighter man at heart.

In late 1944 I received orders to France to join the 1st Tactical Air Force (Provisional). I never found out why it was provisional; it certainly didn't sound very permanent. But permanent or not, it put out a tremendous war effort. The war in Europe was rapidly folding as the Germans retreated on all fronts. The Battle of the Bulge was just winding down as I got to Vittel, headquarters for the 1st TAC at the time. That fine fighting unit had come all the way from North Africa via Marseilles, supporting General Patch's 7th Army. Gen. Ralph Royce was commanding when I arrived. Here I was—a fighter pilot, a test pilot, a project engineer—arriving very late in a war where the things I had been producing, testing, and flying were being used in battle. The crews and pilots were old hands; I was a newcomer. It wasn't easy!

My first assignment was to help the French Air Force Service Command, then at Besancon, with the support of their aircraft. While there I was able to go over to Dijon where Brig. Gen. John Doyle had a B-26 bomber wing. I got out on a couple of B-26 missions, including a big one in February on which the entire enemy front was saturated with Allied airplanes. No German fighters were seen, only scattered antiaircraft. Victory was close.

One day while working with the French Air Force, I had reason to fly into Nancy where an American P-47 wing was operating. Soon after I arrived in early January, I landed a C-45 on the snow-covered Nancy runway, and while taxiing down toward the far end between the walls of piled-up snow at the runway edges, we saw a P-47 coming in on his downwind leg for an emergency landing, engine on fire, smoke and flames engulfing the entire plane. He was deadstick and had only one place to land—right where we were. No more taxiing to the runway end, we had to clear! So we headed at full speed for a wall of snow. Just as our tail cleared the right half of the runway, the Jug slid past down safely. It was my first contact with my old friend P-47 for some time.

As the war continued to wind down, I was called back to Vittel and assigned to set up support for the 358th Fighter Wing at a sand strip on an old GAF base called Sandhofen, near Mannheim on the Rhine. The 358th Group, equipped with P-47Ds, was commanded by Col. Jim Tipton, an outstanding fighter commander. After working for a few days at getting bombs and ammunition stores in proper shape, I managed a couple of P-47 missions with the wing, Tipton leading. The strafing mission was interesting. We had about 14 or 16 aircraft and we swept the countryside for about 150 miles toward Berlin. I had known that the technique, particularly when flying at low altitude, was to weave and turn continually. Well, that we did, and violently, too. There was little movement on the ground. No enemy aircraft, some ground antiaircraft, but mostly weak, no losses. We shot up a bunch of railroad cars and locomotives, mostly stopped before we arrived. We saw one soldier on a motorcycle scooting down a narrow street through a small village. A couple of P-47s went after him, but I felt relieved when I saw bullets hitting all around him and not getting him. When we passed, he was still riding like all hell. I was glad he got away. He was no challenge and he could do no harm to us or our armies. My P-47 flew like a dream. When we landed at Sandhofen the Crew Chief found what looked like a .45 caliber slug sticking in my tailpipe. I don't know when or where I got it.

The second mission was a bombing and escort trip to Friederichshaven on the Baden Sea. When we got there an overcast had moved over the target, and for some reason, we not only did not drop our 500-pound bombs but we took them back to Sandhofen. I am sure Jim Tipton felt it foolish to drop them indiscriminately as had often been done in the past when the target was denied. It was easy to see this war was won. Once more I had been able to see my P-47s in action, escorting the bombers, but there was little or no drama.

Recently I wrote to Jim, who is enjoying a leisurely retirement in Alabama, asking him to comment on the Jug. His answer: "It was the greatest ground attack aircraft in the war, without a doubt. It took punishment like no other and delivered firepower, guns, and bombs with authority and versatile attack techniques unlimited. Indeed, it is doubtful if we ever achieved its full potential in that respect. With most of our effort devoted to dogfighting ground units, we sighted our eight guns to converge at 1,000 yards, for example, and psychologically sledge-hammered army units and equipment."

In 1945 we moved to Okinawa, and after a short time the war ended. We moved into Japan right after General McArthur and set up headquarters at Johnson Field, then the Irrumigawa Air Base, an old primary flying school for the Japanese. I flew our headquarters P-51 up from Oki and was glad to get on the ground. There were no radio aids, and I had to do the last 200 miles over the clouds. I'm probably not the first pilot who was tickled pink to see Fuji rising above the clouds and to find a hole just beyond it over Tokyo Bay.

About this time General Ennis C. Whitehead was appointed Far East Air Force Commander, and I became 5th Air Force Chief of Staff, but not for long. I was just getting used to some fairly plush living in Tokyo when General Whitehead told me I was to go back to Okinawa (1 February 1946) to take over the 301st Fighter Wing under the overall command in Oki of Brig. Gen. Pat Timberlake. And guess what—the fighter wing was equipped with P-47Ns. The N was a P-47 which had been put into production after I left the production business. It had more fuel and more wing, and hence was a lot heavier than the predecessors. It was so heavy it could hardly be called a fighter, but it was all we had to protect Okinawa. It had about the same rate of climb as an empty C-47 Gooney Bird. If you're asking "Who needed to protect Okinawa with the war won?" the answer is that you obviously never worked for General Whitehead!

Along with the P-47Ns, I took on a wing that had no experienced airmen for mechanics. To a man, the mechanics who had been there all the way from Australia had been sent home. I had several hundred willing but inexperienced ex-machine-gunners released to the Air Force from Army ground units. In addition, I had about 70 young pilots who had just finished flying training. Most had never flown a P-47N prior to arrival in Okinawa. I did have some good senior lieutenant colonels and a couple of colonels, among them Stetson, Coleman, McCombre, Keeling, and Cory. Instead of fighting, they had spent the war in the training command. They were in Okinawa hoping at last to get into the war when it all ended. We had to improvise everything. There were no skilled mechanics, so we had the pilots crew their own airplanes. They did pretty well, except for two or three bad accidents, which I always felt might have been averted had we had more experienced maintenance.

I was happy to have command of a fighter wing, and a wing of P-47s at that; but living and working conditions there at that time were pretty rugged. What little had been built during the short period after Okinawa had been captured was wiped out by the September 1945 typhoon. My whole wing was in tents. We were based at Yontan Airstrip, which had no hangars and no buildings of any kind, just a coral strip 6,000 feet long. We started to build. First, we needed a water system with filtration. A team of lieutenants built one: welded sheet steel tanks, midnight-requisitioned from the Navy, pumps and all. It took water right out of the Bishagawa Creek and made it potable. The mess where we ate was ghastly. I fired the so-called mess officer and put a fighter pilot named Green in his place. The mess improved.

Later, the only ice the airmen's and officers' clubs could get was from two lieutenant fighter pilots who had managed to come by an ice machine, had set it up in an old bashed-in Okinawa house, and had gone into business. These two entrepreneurs I found to be furnishing a regular supply of ice to at least two clubs and receiving a regular payment of so many bottles of booze a week in return. This sort of operation is not routine in the Air Force. So when I heard about it, I called these two ice-maker pilots into my headquarters and said, "I understand you gentlemen have an ice machine with which you are supplying ice to the wing. Is this correct?"

"Yes, Sir."

"Well, great! I think you deserve commendation for your diligence, and further I'm going to appoint you Wing Ice Officers. Henceforth it will be your duty to furnish ice to the wing, in addition to your flying duties." It worked beautifully but the profit from their enterprise fell off dramatically.

During the next eight or nine months, we put up Quonset huts for mess halls, headquarters, clubs, living quarters, and latrines. And we set up a retractable flag pole that could be laid on the ground when typhoon danger approached. To accomplish all this, we used for some time about 100 Japanese POWs who were more than happy to be alive and put in a full day for a full belly. Obviously we had some time off, especially during the rather frequent passage of typhoons. During one of these I remember a day-and-night long-endurance game of bridge held in my shack. About midnight, the wind still screaming and the rain coming down by bucketfuls, we decided to call the game because of dealer incompetence. The long cocktail hour had resulted in one player's receiving 17 cards on the deal.

Although we worked hard, I am afraid we were not very combat ready. We tried though. Finally, after a year of effort, we managed to "intercept" a B-29 coming in at 30,000 feet over the island. The boys had been trying for a long time but couldn't get up there fast enough. Their technique had been to climb at maximum power toward the reported position of the incoming bomber, but it would always go over them before they reached 30,000 feet. I didn't tell my staff, but I figured if I climbed directly over the target instead of toward the incoming bomber, I'd have more time to get to 30,000 feet. Well, it worked. But with the B-29 speed at that height, it was still almost impossible. General Whitehead, who had been less than understanding about our inability to intercept, was pleased, and I made a little hay in the eyes of my 301st wing pilots, too. I think that was the very last time I flew a P-47.

I was ordered home in November 1946, and so ended my association with the Jug. I respected it and I loved it!

GEN. MARK E. BRADLEY retired from active duty with the Air Force in 1965 after more than 35 years of service. He joined the Garrett Corporation of Los Angeles in 1965 and rose to become Senior Executive Vice-President in 1969. He retired from the corporation in 1972.

(Right) P-51 Mustang in flight. (Below) Armorer standing on the wing of a Mustang fighter in China scans the sky for aircraft returning from a mission.

P-51 Mustang

JOHN A. DE VRIES

THERE were one-cushion pilots and two-cushion pilots, and, if you didn't use a dinghy buckled to the D-rings of your back parachute, there were three-cushion pilots. Early in 1944, the Air Corps decided that a man 5 feet 8 inches or shorter was a hot fighter pilot. If he was taller, he was destined for multiengine flying. Thus, if a fighter pilot was fortunate enough to be selected to fly the P-51 Mustang, the multiplicity of cushions was necessary to boost him high enough to see out of the massive bubble canopy.

In 1946 the monsoon rains came early. Japan, and more specifically, Johnson Army Air Base, was socked-in for the last half of September. Assigned to the 40th Fighter Squadron, 35th Fighter Group, I had plenty of time to study the lean and wiry Mustang before I flew it the first time. The Squadron owned 25 of the bubble-canopied beauties, but only 14 pilots were assigned, and there were plenty of "ponies" to choose from. My choice was number 56—a K-model. The P-51K differed from the D only in the particular that it had an Aero Products propeller instead of a Hamilton Standard.

While the relentless rains fell, I studied the one and only P-51 flight manual available in the Squadron. Not the usual "Dash One," the manual was a how-to-fly-it book, filled with cartoons and simple illustrations that emphasized the important factors for achieving maximum performance from the Mustang. Because the first flight would be solo, every word was important!

The rains continued well into October, providing opportunity for three activities prior to checkout. Many, many hours were spent just sitting in the snug cockpit of No. 56 while the monsoon beat against the hangar roof. Gear handle, flap handle, throttle, mixture control, and propeller knob all fell closely at hand. The instrument panel was memorized as well as the armament control panel (which held switches for the six .50 caliber Brownings, the gunsight aiming point 16 mm camera, the arming controls for the twin bomb or long-range tank wing pylons, and the rheostat that adjusted the intensity of the light in the reflector gunsight). The "triggers" for all of the armament were clustered on the control stick hand grip. Soon I was able to pass the required "blindfold cockpit check"—touch any instrument or control instantly, without any visual reference.

The Squadron was only at half-strength as far as pilots were concerned. The crew-chief situation was even more desperate. There weren't any! Two Master Sergeants made up the entire maintenance section. They, together with the North American Technical Representative for the Group, established a crew-chief school for pilots. For eight weeks, we new Mustang drivers attended classes every morning and worked on our own planes every afternoon. Changing the 24 spark plugs of the 1,400 hp, 12-cylinder V-1650-7 Packard Merlin engine is a darn good way of finding out what goes on inside the Mustang! When I was ready to make my first P-51 flight, I really knew its innards.

The weather began to clear enough for flying in the pattern. But before we new pilots were turned loose in our superbly maintained fighters (after all, we were our own maintenance crews), we had to go through the ordeal of rear-seat landings in the AT-6. The idea was that if you could land the skittery trainer from the back seat, you would do well "when it came time" in the Mustang. However, the "Powers-That-Be" failed to realize two important facts: the almost 1,000 hp difference in the engines of the two planes and that unless one were a giant the overturn structure of the AT-6 effectively blanked out any forward vision.

With six controlled crashes in the AT-6, I was really ready for my first Mustang ride. The walk-around inspection wasn't really necessary. I knew every rivet and Dzus-fastener on No. 56. To please the check pilot, I approached my mount from the left. No bird's nests in the left wheel well; the sole landing light was firmly bolted inside. No oil dripping from the underside of the Merlin, and all of the cowl sections were firmly attached. The big, four-bladed Aero Products propeller was nick-free, and the carburetor intake under the nose was clear. No drips or loose Dzus-fasteners on the right side of the nose, and the right tire (like the left) was brand-new and properly inflated. The oleo strut spaced out to the proper hand-span, and the leading edge of the right wing was smooth. Aileron and the dropped flap looked "right," and the fuselage-mounted alternate static air source was clear of any foreign substances. The tail assembly looked OK—the fabric-covered movable surfaces were taut (later, the elevators would be replaced with metal-sheathed surfaces). A quick glance at the left aileron and flap, and then it was time!

The hangar hours had proven to me that I was two-cushion pilot. Two cushions and a dinghy (the CO_2 cylinder of which my gluteus maximus would soon learn to hate) propped me to the proper eye level—the center of my vision coincided with the pipper in the center of the gunsight ring, when it was projected on the sight-glass of the N-9 100-mil gunsight (the P-51 Ds in the Squadron had gyro-stabilized K-14 sights). With a casual familiarity born of many hours of cockpit time, I buckled myself in and began the round-the-cockpit check: ignition off, mixture-in-idle cutoff. Capt. Bill Hook, the check pilot, pulled the prop through four blades to clear oil from the cylinders. The fuselage fuel tank (over the left shoulder) was filled to 85 gallons (each gallon was good for one minute's flight). Flap handle up, carburetor air in the "ram" position, trim set—5° of right rudder, ailerons at 0, and elevator at 2° nose down. The gear handle was checked down, and the propeller control was to be "full forward" (full increase rpms). The throttle was opened to the "start" position (about three-quarters of an inch forward). The altimeter was set to field elevation, and gyro instuments were uncaged. Control locks were released (a pin was pulled from the bracket that held the stick and rudder pedals, the bracket springing flat against the cockpit floorboards) and the rudder pedals adjusted (full back for us shorter pilots).

With parking brakes set, both wing fuel tank levels were checked through their indicators in the floor (92 gallons each), the supercharger switch was put in "auto," and the fuel selector handle was set to "fuselage" and I was ready to start.

With booster pumps on (to provide fuel pressure), magneto switch to "both," and battery and generator switches on, I had to pause for a moment and run the coolant doors open. Liquid-cooled, the Mustang had to have its radiator uncovered for starting. Although the doors in the rear belly of the P-51 were thermostatically controlled and operated automatically depending on the temperature of the 30% glycol–70% water coolant mixture, their functioning had to be checked manually on the ground before starting.

A couple of tweaks of the primer switch and I raised the cover of the starter switch. Held in the "start" position, the lean Mustang shuddered violently as the big prop turned over. After a few rumbles, the Merlin caught. I advanced the mixture to "run" and the oil pressure rose to the proper 50 psi almost at once. The manual said to idle the engine at 1,200–1,300 rpm. All gauges "in the green" or coming up, the suction at 4.75 psi, and I was ready to taxi. Captain Hook, who had been kibitzing over my left shoulder during the starting sequence, gave me a pat on the back and leaped to the ground. Thumbs-up—and he pulled the wheel chocks.

Suddenly, I was alone in a rip-snorting bucking bronco. Easing the Mustang's throttle open slightly, stick forward to unlock the tail wheel, I was on my own. Out of the parking area, I eased the stick back to lock the tail wheel in its 12° taxi arc (6° right and left). Lordy, that nose was l-o-n-g! Unless I S'd the bird, I couldn't see anything in front of me. The positive action of the disc brakes helped me taxi.

By the time I reached the run-up pad at the end of the runway, Hook had climbed the control tower and it was he who "talked" me through the engine checks. Rpm to 2,300, check each magneto for not more than a 100 rpm drop (but no longer than 15 seconds operation on a single magneto). Advance the throttle to 30 inches of mercury for one minute and exercise the propeller pitch-changing mechanism. A rapid glance around the cockpit—prop forward, supercharger auto, coolant auto, fuel booster on, hydraulic and suction pressures, oil pressure and temperature in the green, and I was ready to take the runway. Hook checked the pattern from his tower vantage point and gave the go-ahead.

Gently, ever so gently, I advanced the big spade-grip throttle ("liberated" from a K-14-equipped D-model Mustang—a "sexy" touch in my N-9-equipped K). The Merlin wound up. At 30 inches, the bird was as docile as an AT-6; at 40 inches it was like riding a tornado; at the full 61 inches of takeoff manifold pressure I was caught up in a hurricane! The tail came up voluntarily as I pumped rudders to keep up with the enormous torque of the mighty engine. I could see over the nose, and the far end of the runway was approaching at an alarming rate. Somewhere along the route I'd attained flying speed, so a tug on the stick and No. 56 was blasting heavenward. Behind my left hip was the gear handle and I clutched at it before I exceeded the 225 mph gear-door critical speed. The Mustang did an involuntary dip as I raised the handle. Before I knew it, I had reached 500 feet where the manual said I should throttle back to 46 inches and pull the propeller control to 2,700 rpm for the climb.

For the next hour and a half, I attempted to get ahead of my mount. The Mustang was a thinking pilot's airplane: think about it, and the airplane did it. There was enough pressure in thought alone to make

30° banked turns; rolls took only a wee bit of fingertip pressure. There was no combination of throttle, propeller, and trim tabs that would permit the Mustang to fly straight and level by itself. Oh, maybe its altitude would hold for five seconds before a bump would disturb its equilibrium, but hands-off, and the fighter would establish a climbing or diving spiral. You had to fly the P-51 every second you sat in the cockpit!

A series of stalls—power on and power off, flaps and gear up and down—were part of the first ride. At 10,000 feet the book said, throttle back, dump gear and flaps, and slow the P-51 down to 125 mph. Simulate a final landing approach, and at the "landing point," jam on full throttle. It made me a believer: with a full 61 inches, old No. 56 turned every way but loose! I think I definitely did an inverted snap roll. I know the sturdy wings flapped! The point of the self-demonstration was to convince the neophyte pilot that the go-handle on the left side of the cockpit was to be moved deliberately but, oh so gently, particularly when the bird was near the ground.

Over Atsugi-Wan (Bay), over Mt. Fujiyama, with rolls and loops, my first two Mustang hours were over. Landing time was fast approaching, so I headed east, toward Johnson. I dove down into the Tokyo Plain at an easy-to-obtain 450 mph. With all of that Plexiglas around my head, the visibility from the cockpit was superb. No worry about running into another airplane.

I saw a field and let down to 400 feet—tactical traffic pattern altitude. The Mustang was difficult to slow, but by pulling back on the big spade-grip throttle we got down to the 240 mph indicated as required for pattern entry. Turning north, I stabilized speed and altitude and lined up with the strip. As the end of the runway passed under the Mustang's nose I pushed the propeller control to 2,700 rpm and honked the throttle back to idle. A sharp rightward and rearward tug on the stick, a boot of right rudder, and I was in a hairy chandelle. At its apex, I dumped gear and flaps (at about 180 mph) and continued around my 360-overhead pattern. Depressing the throttle-mounted microphone button, I called, "Base leg!"

"Don't see you," said Captain Hook, calmly.

I continued in my fighter pilot's pattern. "Turning final," I announced into the VHF radio.

"Still don't see ya'," Hook replied.

It was then that I looked up. I was perfectly lined-up and at the proper approach speed of 120 mph. But I was landing at Yokota—three miles south of Johnson! Coolly, I yanked the gear and flaps up and slowly fed the 100-octane to the Merlin.

"De Vries, where the hell are you?" Captain Hook blasted into the airwaves.

"I'm on one heck of a long final," I replied, trying to inject a note of confidence into my oxygen-mask microphone.

The abortive approach to Yokota had been good practice. The traffic pattern and landing at Johnson were good—for a beginner. I didn't notice, until I'd parked No. 56, the big prop grinding to a halt, that my flying suit was drenched and that there was a pool of sweat in my oxygen mask. The Mustang was a hot airplane in more ways than one! With only a couple of thin sheets of Dural between you and the Merlin, there was little protection from the engine's heat. But the heat was a small price to pay for the spectacular performance of the P-51— and it was very welcome on missions above 20,000 feet.

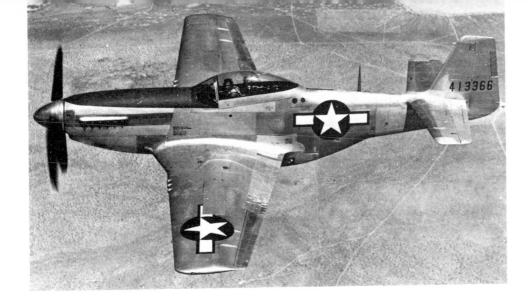

P-51 in flight.

The engine stopped; I dumped the flaps to relieve the pressure on the hydraulic system and proceeded, round-the-cockpit, to turn every switch off.

After 20 hours in No. 56, with the basics mastered, flying the P-51 became sheer joy. The 40th was a tactical fighter squadron so we were called on to perform every conceivable fighter mission. Today, it may be firing the six 50s at a towed sleeve over the Mito gunnery range or dive-bombing and strafing ground targets. When the machine guns let loose, the Mustang shuddered and bucked like its namesake and the flying speed dropped 10 miles an hour. With the 100-mil fixed gunsight, I qualified for aerial gunnery—put 40 bullets out of 200 into a banner target. Dive-bombing was easy: each diverging slash mark painted on the upper surface of the wings was associated with a specific bombing-run entry altitude. As the target disappeared under the appropriate slash mark, you'd begin a diving turn onto the bomb run. The "crack" on top of the forward fuselage, where the two removable cowling panels met, was the "sighting line." Point the crack at the target, roll to keep it lined up and kill the effect of the wind, and, at the proper release altitude, push the bomb-release button atop the stick. The 100-pound practice bombs would "pickle" right on the bull's-eye!

Another day we'd escort a Russian PBY or IL-12 from over Sado Shima island to Haneda airport, outside of Tokyo. With gear down and flaps half-extended (the flap-angle indicators were painted on the flap hinge line as black and white alternating strips, 5° per strip) we'd "formate" with the Russkys to keep them from wandering around the Japanese islands, photographing every military installation in sight.

On Thursday, we might be scheduled for a "surveillance mission." With only a few radar sites to protect Japan, Mustangs were sent on low-level sweeps up and down both coasts and through the inland valleys, for visual reconnaissance. We were charged with recording the numbers from the sides of any aircraft, sailboat, or railroad locomotive we'd run across. It was a sporty course, holding No. 56 steady while flying up a mountain valley, chasing an errant Japanese locomotive to get its number! Wartime cable barricades were still in place, from mountaintop to mountaintop, adding spice to the proceedings. Coastal surveillance missions were the most fun. There have been instances when exuberant young fighter pilots have been known to fly low over Japanese coastal waters with the intent of blowing over the sailboats manned by suffering fishermen.

Friday would see the Mustangers of the 40th practicing close-support with ground controllers and the infantry at Camp Crawford, or simulating interceptor missions with Hot Point Control, the Tokyo-area radar at Shiroi. On "special" days we'd sling 75- or 110-gallon drop tanks to our Mustang's wing shackles and fly 7- to 10-hour long-range missions. Often, our flights would be planned northward to the island of Hokkaido where dwelt the 4th Fighter Group. Arrival would be timed for about 5 A.M. so that our Merlins would act as alarm clocks for the sleepy pilots of Chitose Air Base. On one of these "alarm-clock raids" we dropped leaflets on the unsuspecting northerners. Shoved out the Very-pistol holes in the left flank of our Mustangs, they read, "Sleep soundly, 4th Fighter Group. The 35th is guarding your rest!".

Two and a half years saw 500 Mustang D and K hours in the log book. It was time to give up being a wingman and flight leader and move on. Later, much later, there would be 300 more P-51 hours, but this time it was in the H-model and the two-place TF-51D. The H was a lightened D with a towering rudder and a more potent engine. It cruised at 270-Indicated (compared to 240 mph in the D), and was even more responsive to the controls than its older brother, but the pilot was just a bit more mature, a bit more cautious (with a wife and three kids), and the missions were much less exciting. Flying as an interceptor and target while new radar controllers learned their business wasn't really fighter flying!

I loved the hairy Mustang. With a single exception, every pilot I know who flew the P-51 loved it. The one "sourpuss" was a B-24 driver who experienced two dead-stick landings and one bailout in his first three Mustang rides! But, this one individual notwithstanding, the pilots of the 15,000-odd 51s that rolled from the North American production lines at Inglewood and Tulsa thoroughly enjoyed the calm—and the panic—of their hours in the $50,000 "Pony."

After 30 years as an Air Force officer and pilot, COLONEL JOHN A. DE VRIES retired in Colorado Springs where he pursues a "second career" as an author of aviation history books and articles and as a designer of radio-controlled scale models for the model airplane press. His first book, *Taube—Dove of War,* was published in 1975, after 5½ years of research and writing.

His almost-5,000 Air Corps/Air Force flying hours were spread over more than 100 types and models of military aircraft, including 800 in the Mustang—after 1,200 in the AT-6, as an instrument instructor of French Cadets.

Author, age 22. Note the black stripes on the leading edge of the wing. They were painted on to provide a ready reference for dive bombing in the Mustang.